Between Dreams

Difficult Paths & Dangerous Places

Steve Harvey

Published by Fledgling Press 2016
www.fledglingpress.co.uk

ISBN 9781905916344
Printed by Bell & Bain Ltd, Glasgow

DEDICATION

I have written these memoirs for my grandchildren –
India and Sienna,
and any who follow . . .

I was in the same class at school as Sting in the sixties; at 'the Fringe' with Liam Neeson in the seventies; spent a day with Spike Milligan; spent several months travelling round India by steam train; went round the world; taught on Tyneside; joined the police; breathalysed Gazza; was on the front line at 'the Battle of Orgreave' during the Miners' Strike (although I loathed Thatcherism); was appointed to set up my force's Paedophile Unit in the nineties; ran creative writing courses in an old mill with outbuildings I'd bought in Normandy, with tutors including A L Kennedy; taught English as a volunteer in northern Iraq in 2004 (and visited Baghdad); ran the national Fatherhood Project in Scotland; was Safety & Security Officer for an international NGO in South Sudan; wrote a novel set in Africa; in 2010 travelled around New Zealand with my nineteen-year-old son for two months, working on farms and vineyards for our keep and then spent three months backpacking alone around South America . . .

I have asked difficult questions of two police officers who subsequently became Chief Constables of the Met; I've been inspected by HRH Princess Anne, the Princess Royal, and been presented to the Queen; I've been served food by the future President of Iraq at his country retreat and been greeted by the wife of the President of Georgia in the Caucasus Mountains; I've met lots of interesting people who have enriched my life; I married a beautiful woman and I have five wonderful children and – to date – two lovely grandchildren.

I begin writing these memoirs in my fifty-eighth year, not as a wrapping up of a life finished except for a few last scraps, but as a review of an ongoing journey.

I don't want them to be so much a list of things I've done – although this is to some extent unavoidable – as a chronicle of places I've been, adventures I've had, and people I've met along the way. Although there is a considerable amount of name-dropping in these pages, my defence is that I have met many interesting and talented people, and some of them have been – or have become – famous . . .

My motivation for writing these memoirs sprang from several sources. A publisher's reader had suggested my submitted novel *Malakal Academical* might work better as a factual account of my time in Sudan and, although I disagreed, it made me realise that I hadn't recorded all the real adventures and dramatic encounters I had experienced.

I am well aware that memoirs are normally the preserve of the famous, the infamous, or, currently, the instant and transient celebrity. I am none of these, and not likely to be. Not only have I not played a leading role on the world's stage, I have not even been in the supporting cast or one of the crew. It is quite clear to me, from my present perspective, that what I have been is an extra who, through good fortune, has happened to be on set with great talents or around when major events were taking place. My only leading role has been in my own life, a role I've really enjoyed, in a show I hope has many years yet to run . . .

I remember something I saw written on a wall in a community centre in Kirkuk, Iraq: words to the effect that a life well lived was a joy twice over – once in the living and then in the recollection. As one of my favourite writers, A.E. Coppard, says, in writing one's autobiography, "One lives again and has to grow up again." I have had a full and good life so far and I want those who follow after me – especially my grandchildren – to have some idea of the life and times of the frail and fading old man I might become. I hope it will give my children – and maybe me – a clearer idea of why my life was the way it was.

I have tried, as far as possible, to let the events speak for themselves. Nevertheless, they are events seen from my point of view.

Vitae summa brevis spem nos vetat incohare longam

They are not long, the weeping and the laughter,

Love and desire and hate:

I think they have no portion in us after

We pass the gate.

They are not long, the days of wine and roses:

Out of a misty dream

Our path emerges for a while, then closes

Within a dream.

Ernest Dowson

Chapter 1

I emerged on July 8th 1952 in a little pit village in County Durham in north-east England called Shiney Row, invariably pronounced 'Shiney Raa' by locals. I've always played this down because it makes me a 'Mackem' (from Wearside, Sunderland Football Club's catchment area) rather than a Geordie (from Tyneside, Newcastle United territory). My father was an ambitious Chartered Quantity Surveyor, (I was told always to give my father's profession in full to distinguish him from ordinary surveyors) who met his wife, my mother, while working in Norwich. They were called William and Audrey Harvey. He was generally known as Bill, although his mother used to call him Little Willie as his father was also William, which I always thought must have had a lasting, profoundly negative, psychological effect on him. I was called Stephen William Harvey.

My parents moved to North Gosforth, about five miles north of Newcastle, when I was three, by which time I had a younger brother, Peter. As boys, we spent much of our time in Gosforth Park, a large area of woodland and meadow which included within its extensive area Newcastle Racecourse and a golf course.

I was quite a studious young boy, rather geeky-looking around the age of nine and ten with my National Health specs, brace, and narrow, slightly hunched shoulders. My parents bought me *Look and Learn*, a weekly magazine containing information on all subjects. In a world before the Internet, this was my staple source of 'Knowledge', although there was another publication that went by that name. I was an avid collector of facts and figures, definitions and quotes. I would read the section called 'It Pays to Increase Your Word Power' in *The Reader's Digest*, trying to memorise all those little-used words and their meanings. Over the years I collected a whole range of things including bubble gum cards, postage stamps, coins and tokens, picture postcards and bottle tops.

I attended St Charles' R.C. Primary School in Gosforth. The headmistress was a fierce nun called Sister Albius. If she was an ambassador of any God, it was Mars. She displayed only one hint of human feeling, and that was an obvious favouritism towards John Maloney, presumably because he, too, was Irish. On my first day he pushed me off the rocking horse, initiating an infantile vendetta that continued throughout our time there. I recall one time he'd hit my brother (Peter has one of those faces that people seem to want to punch) and I hit him in the toilet while he was drinking from the water fountain, knocking a tooth out. I remember the shrill whistle from the school steps and my long walk from the far side of the playground like a condemned prisoner in short trousers. I was belted several times with a heavy leather strap. Years later, I returned to the school prior to attending teacher training college to see if I thought it was the right career choice for me. I remember standing beside her when she suddenly barked at some unfortunate child, and I was instantly a scared schoolboy again.

In 1963, having passed the old eleven-plus exam sufficiently convincingly to have also received a scholarship, I went to St Cuthbert's Grammar School in Newcastle. The original building was an imposing stone-built structure sitting on the brow of a hill and looking down on the Tyne valley. It was an institution which played a significant part in my life, and others who attended it included the musicians Ray Laidlaw (drummer with the Tyneside band Lindisfarne), Gordon Sumner (Sting), Neil Tennant (half of the Pet Shop Boys), the late Brendan Healy and the entertainer who is the Dec half of Ant and Dec.

Sting was in my class, and Neil Tennant was in the same year as my brother from primary school onwards. When a friend told me, over thirty years later, that I featured in a book about Sting – scoring a goal in a match against his team – I thought it was a wind-up. I had no recollection of this. Although I scored a few goals in my time at St Cuthbert's, I was kept out of the school first team, which shared the national school championship one year with St Michael's of Leeds, by slim Jim Berryman, who, it turned out, was the author of this biography.

Sometime after that conversation I was in a music shop in Edinburgh with my eldest son, Matthew, who was buying a new guitar string. I remembered the title of the book, *A Sting in the Tale* (re-published in 2005 under the title *Sting and I* by John Blake), and was surprised to find a single copy on the shelf. I flicked through the pages and saw my name – as head boy – and a black-and-white picture of our class. I was gratified to find, a few pages later, my name in a goal-scoring context:

"I latched onto the pass, slipped the ball to Steve Harvey and he rattled it into the back of the net."

The book wasn't primarily about Sting; it was really 'Jim Berryman's Schooldays' – and they were my schooldays too. I felt like a former pupil of Hogwarts who'd attended the school at the same time as Harry Potter suddenly discovering that all those fantastic childhood and adolescent adventures had appeared in print. Thirty of the forty-one chapters cover the years we were at St Cuthbert's together, and I knew virtually every pupil and teacher mentioned in them and recognised many of the incidents.

Gordon Sumner, as Sting was in those days, wasn't known for his musical talent so much as his athletic prowess, representing the county as a sprinter. I only recall hearing him play once – The Kinks' *'Lazing on a Sunny Afternoon'* on the bus on a school trip to Bamburgh Castle one summer. The best musicians in the class were the diminutive, bespectacled, self-assured Barr twins, Callum and Gary – school day precursors of the Proclaimers, only cool. I remember an impromptu, spellbinding rendition of John Fahey's *'The Death of Clayton Peacock'* on bottleneck guitar as we waited on the platform of Sunderland station for a train back to Newcastle after a few days on religious retreat one Easter Sunday morning.

In his autobiography, *Broken Music*, Sting paints a wonderfully accurate portrait of our English teacher, Mr McGough, and I share the same sense of recollected respect and ongoing gratitude. He seemed to us a giant of a man, physically and intellectually. His nickname was 'Tiny', with schoolboy irony, and he struck fear into the heart of anyone he focussed on. I once saw him lean forward over his desk and pull an errant, chubby new boy towards him, combined desk and seat and all. His customary curse was, 'Damn your eyes!' Tiny's reactions to my contributions in English lessons ranged from 'Thank God we've got you in the class' to 'Master Bloody Harvey'.

As for Gordon Sumner, I only met him once after leaving school, outside what was the Gulbenkian – later the University Theatre – in

Newcastle. We were both teaching in those days and he'd just been playing with his band, Last Exit. The next time I heard of him we were both in 'The Police' – he was on his way to his first million and I was listening to him on the car radio while on my way to begin night shift.

As Jimmy Berryman said, I was head boy, although this was as much to my surprise as everyone else's: I wasn't exactly a model pupil in terms of behaviour or academic performance. I had made quite a hash of my exams – first at 'O' Level and then at 'A' Level (except English in both cases). I loved learning but disliked written tests, at which I was slow and generally underachieved. I had stayed on for a third year in the sixth form to do resits and was scurrying past the school tuck shop one lunchtime to clip Peter's ear for some cheek, when Fr Walsh, the Master of Discipline, called me over. I thought I was in for another rollicking, but he said some of the staff had suggested me for Head Boy and asked me how I felt about it. I was so flabbergasted and relieved not to be getting a telling off that I agreed.

◊

After the exams, I went off to work at Butlin's holiday camp in Pwllheli for the summer with three school friends – Steve Ashton, Mike Knox and Jim Mullaney. Jim and I hitchhiked down, getting a lift on the M6 near Carlisle from a lorry driver who had stopped for a girl in hot pants. She'd inclined her pretty head slightly towards us and said, "I don't take lifts in lorries," so we'd clambered aboard instead.

"Whit aboot the lassie?" he asked in a gruff Glaswegian accent. We shook our heads and muttered something about her waiting for someone else. He didn't speak for the next twenty or thirty miles. Seeing the footballer tattooed on his burly arms, I tried to break the silence and distract my senses from the stench of whatever the wagon was carrying by asking, "Who do you support?" The way he said 'Rangers!' implied that even to mention the name of their arch rivals was to risk being thrown out of a moving vehicle.

Newcastle United had beaten Glasgow Rangers in a torrid two-legged semi-final just two years previously in the old Fairs Cup, before going on to win the trophy (1969 is still the last time we won any silverware of note). After the second game, which took place at St James' Park, the Rangers fans had gone on a rampage in Newcastle city centre. I had been walking Moira, my dancing partner, to her bus from the Newbegin Dance Studio, and had witnessed the Pilgrim Street police station under siege by drunken Scotsmen. Although I'd attended the home matches in the earlier rounds (I'd gone straight to the stadium from school and been first into the ground for the Real Zaragoza game), I'd not been able to get a ticket for the semi-final and there had been warnings of potential crowd trouble . . .

"Were you at the Newcastle game?" I ventured.

"Aye, an' ah spent three days in the polis cells after."

"Why was that?" I enquired with affected nonchalance.

"This Geordie was laughin' when he looked at me, so ah smacked his heid intae a wall."

Silence settled back over the cab like the overpowering odour from the back. We were carrying a load of bone meal to Warrington.

It was a wonderful summer on the Lleyn Peninsula. I remember it as hot, hard work, and much fun. We stayed in chalets and made £8 a week working in the kitchens, putting two sausages on passing breakfast plates until our fingers were as burnt and bloated as the links themselves. Sweat would drip off our brows and mingle with the mixed grill, giving an extra sprinkling of salt. We'd get short breaks between the meals but you couldn't do much with them apart from taking a stroll around the camp or down by the sea.

This Butlin's was an old P.O.W. camp from World War II. Now, instead of interned or captured Germans or Italians, it held British holidaymakers and staff, many of whom returned every year like gulls to their coastal colony. This year there was also a group of thirty or so Finnish students. To me they were like exotic birds and I ended up going out with Tuula, a slim, smiling girl with small, pointed breasts with whom I had a very innocent romance. She taught me a few simple words in Finnish and I composed small, pointed poems for her while preparing the salads.

We supplemented our basic wage by working as waiters in the bars at night, where we could make more in tips than our weekly pay. I learnt a lot here about human nature, power and money. The person who allocated this bar work wielded a great deal of control over us all. And then there was the waiter who, when one of us was signalled over by a thirsty reveller, would dart in first. After this had happened a couple of times, I got the other three waiters together and said that I would tail him and beat him to every call, or block him, and the four of us would pool our tips. This soon solved the problem.

We worked incredibly long days: up early to prepare breakfasts, up late clearing up after nights working in the bars. I have two stand-out memories. One is of Steve and I sweeping the floor in the deserted building and somebody's last selection suddenly coming on the jukebox – Judy Collins' 'Amazing Grace' drifting through the air with the dust. The other is a rare night off when we all walked up Snowdon at night, following the rail lines up the mountain.

At some point during our time there, we received our 'A' Level results – I'd done even worse than I had the first time around. I had set my heart on studying English at Lampeter and decided to make my way there anyway to plead my case. It was difficult to justify, given that I'd failed to make the quite modest grades they'd asked of me. Nevertheless, I took to the road with my rucksack to hitchhike there. It was likely to take me several days, if I got there at all. How long my money would last and where I would stay on the way, I had no idea.

The weather was conspiring against me. Towards evening on the first day, the sky was growing ever darker and clouds were glowering ominously like an angry examiner. On my way through a tiny village in mid-Wales I called into the post office in search of some sweetener such as a Mars Bar and then continued along the road leading through a forest. I hadn't gone far when a battered old Land Rover, driven by a guy with a battered old face, pulled up alongside and he offered me a lift. Heavy drops of rain began splattering off the windscreen as I clambered in. He had seen me in the shop and taken pity on me. His name was Douglas Hague and he worked for the Royal Commission on Ancient and Historical Monuments in Wales. He told me his special interest was lighthouses and, then as now, I could listen for hours to an expert talk about their subject. My interest was intensified by the increasingly inclement weather and the rough comfort of the front seat of the vehicle. Douglas said he would have offered to put me up overnight but they were having guests come to stay and his cottage was small. A neighbour ran a B&B and he was happy to take me there if I had the price of an overnight stay, but he wasn't sure if she was away at present. Given that I had no other options, I was only too pleased to take the chance. As it turned out, she was away.

Douglas told me I was welcome to dine with them if I didn't mind sleeping in the back of the Land Rover. Rosemary, Douglas's tiny partner, had a kindly, lined face and made me very welcome although some of the conversation with their friends about family and the past, naturally, I couldn't share in. It was a different eating experience from what I was used to and I remember it was the first time I had even heard of elderflower wine, never mind drunk it. Just before retiring for the night to my 4x4 chamber, I noticed a photo in the dining room of Rosemary with her arm around the hottest British actress of the time.

"How did you come to have your picture taken with Julie Christie?" I asked.

"She's my daughter," she replied, a gentle smile on her wrinkled face.

When I left the next morning, I asked them if there was anything I could do towards repaying them for their kindness. As a result, for years afterwards, whenever I saw a postcard of a lighthouse – especially an old or unusual one – I sent it to their cottage so that they could track the changes in the structures over time. *Lighthouses: their Architecture, History and Archaeology* by Douglas B. Hague and Rosemary Christie was published in 1975.

The university authorities at Lampeter were very accommodating, but still required more evidence of academic ability than I had been able to provide. I can only remember two things about the journey back: one was walking along a country road on a lovely warm day and seeing an old man and a young boy by a farm gate. The man asked me if I played snooker and when I said yes, wondered if I would be so good as to give the boy a game as he wasn't up to it. I followed the boy to an old barn and up a ladder to a full size snooker table. The second was getting a lift from a young lad in a Jackson's bread van one evening and him stopping later that night to pick up two girls who squeezed into the cab with us. They must have been high on drugs because every time we stopped at traffic lights they raved about the fantastic colours.

Chapter 2

On returning to Newcastle, I decided to go to St Mary's, Fenham, the teacher training college that my mother had attended as a mature student. My plan was, while doing the course, to resit my 'A' Levels to get the minimal requirements Lampeter had asked of me. Mike Knox happened to be with me when I went in to get the application form and, when the Registrar asked him what he was going to do and he said he didn't know, she gave him a form as well – an act that was to shape both our lives . . .

But there were still a few weeks left of the summer and Steve Ashton and I decided to go into the Students' Travel office in Newcastle and book a flight to wherever took our fancy, was within our budget, and available for the date we had in mind. We ended up booking flights to Athens and back from Rome, allowing about three weeks to make our way from one classical capital to the other.

◊

Athens was hot, dusty and polluted even then, in the late summer of 1971. I remember, when leaving, it took us nearly a whole day to walk across the city, carrying our heavy rucksacks. We made our way to Thessaloniki, passing through Thermopylae where the 300 Spartans under Leonidas had stoutly defended the pass against the might of the Persian army. The pass had been eroded over the centuries but 300 trees had been planted to commemorate the act of heroism, the driver told us, as he drove his wagon through the rain.

Our plans to get as far as Turkey were scuppered by a dramatic absence of lifts. Apart from a ride in the back of a cart, allowing me the opportunity to do Ben Hur poses, free transport disappeared, apparently due to a local man having been murdered by a hitchhiker a few years back. So we headed in the opposite direction, across Greece towards Corfu, to catch a ferry to Brindisi on the east coast of Italy.

The route, which we travelled by a series of short bus journeys, happened to take us through Meteora, famous (though not to us) for its majestic scenery, with monasteries perched precariously on pinnacles of rock. We slept at the foot of some of these inland cliffs, waking in the early morning sun to see eagles circling in the thermals far above us. We made our way on foot in the heat up to one of the monasteries, only to have the door closed in our faces as we approached.

All our money earmarked for food was being spent on transport and we were foraging for whatever we could, mainly apples from the early autumn bumper crop, offered to us in great quantities by locals. I've always had an over-acidic stomach from boyhood and by the time we reached Corfu – or Kerkyra as the Greeks called it – I was in a lot of pain with stomach cramps and diarrhoea. Steve ate squid on the pier while I tried to get some sleep. We managed to get a lift in a lorry heading from Brindisi to the UK – I would have been tempted to stay on it the whole way, but we were travelling in the back on the rough boards, between which anything shaken out of your pockets could disappear forever. There were about 500 miles of noise and fumes, spelks and dust and discomfort before we reached Tuscany. We visited Arezzo and then travelled to Florence. I love sculptures but after several days I was ready to leave.

◊

It took us three days to get away from the city. Each morning dozens of young girls in hot pants or short skirts were decanted by buses on the outskirts of the town. We knew that they would all have to get lifts before we stood any chance. It was early September now and the nights were getting cold under the clear skies. We slept by a pylon, far enough from the road to minimise the sound of traffic, our sleeping bags under a plastic cover that produced a lot of condensation.

One night we went for something to eat at a little local café. All we could afford was a bowl of pasta each with a little tomato sauce and some bread. At another table, an Italian family was eating well, laughing loudly, and enjoying themselves. As they got up to leave, the waiters moved in to collect the tip and clear the leftovers, but not before the head of the family, in one movement, lifted the hardly-started bottle of red wine between two fingers and deposited it on our table. A simple thing, but it was one of the most graceful and gracious acts that I have ever witnessed and we were very grateful beneficiaries. We took our vino rosso back to the pylon and every time the cold awoke us in the night, took a swig.

I didn't enjoy Rome at all: by the time we reached it, I'd lost a lot of weight and was feeling pretty ill. Steve was his usual chipper self and went to look at some monument or other while I gave up my pretence of looking at postcards in the gift shop and sat on my rucksack in a corner. An animated little Italian man came over and started tugging at my sleeve, telling me the shop was closed. This was clearly not the case as customers were still entering and I resisted his attempts to remove me from the premises with increasingly angry responses. A man who claimed to be an off-duty police officer told me in broken English that the police had been called and I had better leave before they arrived. I was hot, dehydrated and had a headache, and all I wanted was to be left alone. I was also, no doubt, very smelly, and, looking back, can understand why the shopkeeper would have wanted me removed. At this juncture, luckily, Steve returned and persuaded me we could find somewhere better to rest.

◊

When I got home, my mother took me to our GP, Dr De Peiris. He was an archetypal tweed-wearing English squire, whose surgery walls were lined with photos of him with hunting dogs and caught trout and salmon. He was rotund, Sinhalese, and very dark-skinned. He had large mournful eyes, like his spaniels', a wonderful, low, soothing voice, gentle hands and a benign manner in the way he dispensed wisdom and prescriptions. In my case, he recommended a mixture of cold tea and St Julien red wine – this seemed to do the trick, but I can't imagine this cure being on the NHS.

I was late starting college. I remember the black-and-white photograph of me holding my name in front of myself, taken for my student ID. It is one of the few pictures of me as an adult without a beard. My face is gaunt and very white and my thick lips stand out, unsheltered by any moustache. I look like an anaemic Puck. I'm wearing a long cardigan – a blue one I affected at that time, a parody of middle class conventionality which I often wore over purple cords. The trousers nearly got me into trouble when I went on the history department's field trip to Russia the following Easter – I wasn't studying history, but only one male student, Dave Collins, had signed up for the trip to Moscow and Leningrad (as it then was) and the rooms were all on a twin bed basis. I'd responded to a college advertisement and raised the money to go. On arrival, I was approached by various people offering to change pounds to roubles at black market rates or offering to buy items from me, especially the purple flares. How they expected me to complete this transaction, I never discovered. I was also aware that lots of those approaching me would be plain clothes police officers, as Meggan, our lecturer and guide – a large, fierce Welsh woman – had warned us.

Although the Cold War was very much the focus of the prevailing political climate at the time (1972), the authorities seemed keen for their brightest young students to mix with us in order to improve their English. Some even invited us back to their family homes, but Meggan had told us that it was illegal for foreigners to visit Russian residences. One day, while looking for souvenirs in one of the state gift shops (a Beriozka or Silver Birch), I was flicking through the LPs and my young Russian companion pointed to a picture of a man in tails on the back, saying it was his father: he was the conductor of the USSR State Orchestra and his name was Yevgeny Svetlanov.

On the eve of Easter Sunday we gathered at night outside a locked Orthodox church to attend midnight mass. Suddenly, lorries drew up and dozens of uniformed Komsomol – members of the youth wing of the Soviet Union Communist Party – jumped out and started jostling the throng which was mainly composed of older women. Never one to accept this kind of treatment, I reacted angrily and it looked like a flashpoint would occur before Meggan intervened. She told me later that they were going to arrest me and claimed they thought I was Jewish because of my beard.

The positives from the trip were the friendliness of our young student guides; the magnificence of the metro underground stations and the Kremlin (we queued to see the embalmed Lenin); the overnight trip on the Red Arrow express (with its silver samovars of black tea); Leningrad (with its bridges over the Neva and majestic Hermitage); the Bolshoi's version of *Swan Lake* (although it was the reserves, the primary troupe being on tour earning foreign currency, and I confess to closing my eyes and listening to the music). But there were many negatives. This was the Soviet Union of five-year-plans, Aeroflot's monopoly of flights, 'matrons' stationed at the end of each floor of tourist hotels (not that there were many tourists), baths without plugs, and bakeries without bread. The bread, when you could get it, was black and tough. I can still taste the buttered toast that Meggan bought for us in the Savoy on our return.

◊

St Mary's College was run by Roman Catholic nuns of the Sacred Heart order; they had also established the Girls' Grammar school in their convent grounds which my sister attended. The college itself had been exclusively for females until a few years before and I remembered visiting my mother there once on my way from school and a young student had asked how old I was. When I said "Sixteen," she'd said, "Come back in a couple of years," to the group's amusement – and my embarrassment – and now here I was. Even then, males were outnumbered 8-1 which meant, if you were sporty like me, you got to play for the football, rugby, and badminton teams and even the gawkiest youth thought he was Jack the Lad. My idea of this being only a temporary stay while I resat exams, faded imperceptibly away.

Although one visiting lecturer described St Mary's as being like trying to commit suicide by throwing yourself into cotton wool, it suited me perfectly. The pupil, whom some staff at St Cuthbert's had tipped to read English at Cambridge, was now happily studying for a Bachelor of Education degree, specialising in English & Divinity (later renamed Religious Studies).

I joined SMADS, St Mary's Amateur Dramatic Society, which, under the guidance of lecturer Richard Cooper, ambitiously put on productions at the Edinburgh Fringe, and I was there two years running. Shows included *Death of a Salesman* and *The Lion in Winter* plus a couple of Richard's own plays – *The Mandala* (a passion play) and *Torres* (about the Colombian revolutionary priest, Camillo Torres). The actor who played Christ was Steve Cahill, one of the most charismatic guys I have ever met: he was one of those people who has everything – looks, athleticism, talent – but is talented in too many areas for their own good. The members of the cast I remember getting mentioned in the *Scotsman's* review were Steve Ashton and Dave McEwan. The one who went on to make his name as an actor was Liam Neeson. Liam was going out with a girl called Monica at that time, but she ended up marrying her childhood sweetheart, Jim, who was a local butcher. Liam was a good guy, but then, so was Jim.

I was very much a bit part player, my main role being minibus driver, ferrying cast and props from Newcastle to Edinburgh and around the capital. I remember pulling into a petrol station in Dalkeith and getting wedged under the solid awning, having forgotten that I had Pilate's 'throne' on the roof rack.

I loved Edinburgh and the thrill of the Fringe, and recall those times as among my happiest – I was involved, valued, surrounded by good and talented people, and having lots of new experiences and fun. The Scottish licensing hours for drinking back then were ridiculous. 'Last orders' was at 10 p.m. so we would often flee Lauriston Hall still wearing large amounts of make-up to buy a couple of pints which we then had ten minutes to down.

I wasn't much of a drinker in my early twenties, not particularly liking the taste of beer or the effect I saw it have on others. I didn't see anything attractive in drinking so much that you lost all control and couldn't remember the next morning what you'd done the night before. Also, I was one of the few drivers around and got to borrow one of my parents' cars or the college minibus to take groups out for drinks in country pubs or village dances in Northumberland, which I loved – places such as Simonburn, Great Whittington and Middleton (The Ox).

I'd started a Poetry Society at college and contacted the Scottish poet Norman MacCaig to ask him to be a guest reader. I booked a back room in a country pub called The Dyke Neuk, which is now open plan and very different, and he travelled down by train from Edinburgh for £20 and a bottle of whisky. I transported some students out there by college minibus and others travelled by car. I'd prepared little blue booklets of copies of what I considered some of his best poems. It was a magical evening and years later when his voice was used on TV adverts promoting Scottish tourism it took me back there every time it was shown.

◊

Direct experience of teaching began with short, weekly visits to local schools. I went to George Stephenson Middle School in Howdon, near Wallsend, where the teacher, on hearing I was interested in creative writing, insisted on calling those children out to the front who'd scored highest in English, despite me saying I wanted to work with a small, mixed group. One poor, summoned girl got halfway up the aisle before the teacher said, "But no, you didn't do well, did you, Jenny?" and she shook her head and was sent back to her desk. I learnt a lot about how not to teach and wrote a scathing, sarcastic piece about it. The experience reinforced the precept of James Mill (1773-1836), father of the more famous philosopher John Stuart Mill, which I'd read in a slim, sample edition of *Encyclopaedia Britannica* a salesman had left at our house, and which I've not been able to trace since:

'The purpose of Education should be first to render the individual a source of happiness to himself, and secondly to others.'

I've never read or heard anything to better that definition.

Because at that time there were half a dozen institutions in Newcastle training teachers, students were often sent up to a hundred miles away on teaching practice. I spent an idyllic week at St Bees Primary on the Cumbrian coast one summer, staying with a friendly couple, Peter and Margaret, sleeping in a rooftop room with a skylight through which I could see the stars. I spent another six weeks in January and February 1973, 'snowed in' some of the time, in the village school in Caldbeck on the tip of the Northern Fells, which I fell in love with the first time I saw them.

I did my final teaching practice at Whitehaven Grammar, staying in (Brylcreamed) Jim and (shuffling) Elsie's hillside, terraced council house in Bransty, overlooking the quirky port. Here, one class had been quite difficult to control at first and the ringleader was a big lad who'd told me they were playing rugby the next day and asked me if I'd like to play. It was a clear challenge which I had to accept even though I'd never played rugby league before and had just had a front crown replaced, having had it knocked out playing rugby union for the college the weekend before. Once I'd taken the obligatory tackle and demonstrated that I could play and was not afraid, I had no more problems with that class.

My one major faux pas on my final teaching practice involved a creative writing class, as ever. I wanted to do something dramatic to fire the pupils' imaginations and took myself too literally. I decided to inspire the class to write about fire by setting alight a piece of newspaper and then depositing it in the metal litter bin I'd placed nearby. I'd already tackled the issue of arson and how dangerous irresponsible lighting of fires could be. The session went as planned, except that the paper refused to extinguish and set fire to the paint on the bin. All the classroom windows were locked and, trying to appear calm, I sent a couple of boys to run and get some water. They returned a few – long – seconds later empty-handed and then ran up to the bin and squirted the water stored in their chipmunk-like cheeks into the bucket. The sides of the bin sizzled and smoke filled the room. Of course, I got no grief whatsoever in the staffroom about the incident . . .

Caldbeck, however, was the placement that made the biggest impression on me. I'd passed through the village on our way back from St Bee's when the college coach had collected another student from there. She'd told me the digs were great and so was the whole place. I approached the woman at college who organised placements and ended up with Caldbeck Village School against my name when the list went up. The digs, however, were entirely different and I found myself being greeted on my initial, preparatory visit by a high-pitched, Scottish voice screeching, "I suppose you're the student? Well, don't think I'm going to run after you. Help yourself to something from the fridge and make yourself a cup of tea . . ." I carried out the instructions given by that disembodied voice.

Of course, Eva's manner belied her kindness and George was an amiable Brummie. I ended up visiting them for years afterwards, staying in their little caravan out the back if there was no room available.

There were three rooms in the old, village school up the hill, but only two teachers, so it was ideal for a student. The headmaster, Fleck Stangar, was, I believe – incredible though it sounds – only the second Head there since the end of World War One, both taking positions there on being demobbed. There were around thirty pupils on the school roll and I had the eleven eldest in my class, although the average attendance during my time there was nine. It was a severe winter and many children lived on the outlying farms. Boys would take a detour on their way into school to help a sheep stuck in a drift or were kept off to do some job or other. The Oddfellows Arms was the village pub and I became scorer for the darts team led by Tommy Hadwin, father of one of my pupils, Hilary. He took his darts – and, in summer, his bowls – very seriously, and he wasn't best pleased when I told him the wrong double on one occasion, but he did eventually forgive me. Another local resident with whom I became very friendly was Ted Pickering, Head of English at the local secondary school, Dalston Comprehensive. He wrote poetry and had a bushy black-and-grey beard to rival those of Dickens and Tolstoy. In his little upstairs study, we'd discuss literature and he'd read his poems to me.

◊

In my last year at college a trip to India was mooted. The nuns had a sister college in what was then called Bombay, and the British Council had been persuaded to part with £100 per student towards the cost of the trip, promoting awareness among these future teachers of the mixed ethnic backgrounds of immigrants from the subcontinent. Of course, I wanted to go . . .

We were due to travel to India in July, in the middle of the monsoon season and were looking to raise more money for the trip and to give to good causes out there. I saw that Spike Milligan was coming to give a performance entitled *For One Night Only* at Newcastle's Theatre Royal in May. I remembered that he'd spent his childhood there, discovered his agent's address from a writers' guide and wrote asking him to be a guest reader for the college Poetry Society.

I remember opening the envelope in the college library and I must have shouted something such as 'Yes!' because I got a mixture of disapproving looks and enquiries as to whether I'd got a teaching post. I replied that it was better than that – Spike Milligan was going to read some of his poetry at our college.

When the day came, I went down to Newcastle city centre in the students' minibus. My pal, Steve Ashton, was driving. I went into The Turk's Head in Grey Street, where Spike was staying. I met up with him and, as we were leaving the hotel, a flurry of middle-aged women approached. He muttered something like, "Fucking blue-rinsers – they never buy any of my books but they'll be after my fucking autograph." I managed to get him out and into the back of the minibus without too much fuss.

He was not in the best of moods: apparently some new stuff he'd asked his PA to send up on the train hadn't arrived. I told him that his audience would be only too pleased to hear whatever he had with him and marvelled at my audacity as a young student, reassuring a comic legend. I was also surprised by how professionally he approached an unpaid reading. On reaching the college, he asked for a quiet place to prepare for his performance and I found one of the little study rooms upstairs that was empty and left him there while I went down to the hall to check everything was OK. The hall was packed. My friend and flatmate, Mary B Kelly, was on the desk, selling tickets, and she reckoned there were three hundred people there.

I hurried back upstairs in time to see a tearful female student with an armful of books coming away from the study room.

"What's the matter?" I asked.

"I just asked him for a few autographs and he told me to fuck off!"

"Couldn't you have asked me after the performance and I'd have tried to get you them then?"

She sniffled off. Great – it would be all round college in minutes and yet he wasn't the one at fault. Anyway, I'd have to worry about that later . . .

I led him down to the hall where he asked Mary B how much it was to get in and gave her his 20p. He then went up to the lectern and asked me what the open bottle of red wine was doing there beside the water. I told him it was for him. He asked me if I thought he was a 'plonkie' and said the water would do fine.

I don't remember much about his performance, except that it was very well received. Afterwards, he asked if I knew where there was a squash court and I told him there was one near where I lived. He asked me if I played and I said yes, although in truth I'd played just two or three times. When he asked if I wanted a game, of course I said, "Sure," but told him I'd no kit with me. In a short time we were driving in the minibus to Gosforth Park where I was supplied with some hired gear. We knocked up for quite a while. He said he was playing on his doctor's advice and wasn't bothered about keeping score. During a break, sitting with his back against the wall, he invited me out for dinner. He said his illustrator would be there and asked if I had a girlfriend to bring along. I gauchely said I hadn't at that time, but could I bring my pal Steve along? He suggested that it would be better if there was another woman to balance the company and I said I'd ask Mary B.

After I'd dropped him back at his hotel and the minibus at college, I hurried home to get ready. When my mother heard where I was going – or rather, with whom – she insisted I get smartened up and wear a jacket and tie. I agreed reluctantly, on the grounds that I might not get into wherever we were going if dressed inappropriately.

Of course, when I collected Spike he looked disapproving and wondered what had happened to the student look. I said it was alright for him because he would get in anywhere, whatever his appearance, but I soon realised that the mantle of celebrity privilege covers those in their entourage as well. He told me he'd said he'd put in an appearance at the People's Theatre where they were rehearsing a stage version of his book *Puckoon*. When we got to the venue in the suburb of Jesmond, I was mortified to see that the cast were, in my opinion, murdering one of the funniest things I'd ever read, in front of its creator – and, to compound matters, I recognised some of the perpetrators, including Mrs McDonald who'd babysat me as a child. I prepared myself psychologically for a verbal blitzkrieg from Spike, but, unpredictable as ever, he could not have been more charming to everyone.

While there, I was approached by a woman who can best be described by the cliché, 'mutton dressed as lamb'. She sidled up to me and asked who I was. I said, "I'm nobody, really."

"Oh, but you must be somebody if you're with Spike – some up-and-coming actor or writer . . ."

"No – I'm just a student . . . his driver . . ."

Realising that I really wasn't anyone important, she turned her attention elsewhere.

Spike had made a reservation at an Italian restaurant in the city centre, just off Grey Street. The table was in a little alcove which we had to ourselves. His companion, his 'illustrator' – even at the time this struck me as a bit of a euphemism – was Margaret, an attractive redhead with a pleasant manner who had an arts 'n' crafts shop in Alnwick, Northumberland's county town, thirty miles to the north. The conversation was lively, with Milligan in a fairly serious mood, any attempts at humour coming from me. When he ordered – I think it was a fish dish – I said I thought he was a vegetarian. He went off on a bit of a rant about how when you try to do something, other people are never satisfied and always try to push you further. I said that wasn't the case here – I merely thought he was a vegetarian . . .

His intensity subsided again until we got into conversation about religion, when he disputed something I'd said and we got into a theological disagreement which he suggested we should get a priest to settle. At his insistence I went to phone the college chaplain, Leo Pyle, but was unable to contact him. The evening ended amicably, though, with sambucas and smiles and 'thank you's' all round.

When I subsequently wrote to him, thanking him and asking if there were any particular causes in India he'd like to receive the money when I went out there, I got the following reply:

Spike Milligan
9 Orme Court, London, W.2.
7th July 1975.

Dear Stephen,
Ta for the letter. Going to India, good. My particular cause is tying
French letters on to Indians pricks and nailing them there. That's
about the best thing you could do, to feed them seems very human

*and charitable, but logically you are just stoking up the next
generation to starvation. It is a terrible truth to have to accept,
but there has to be a new brutal Christianity which is interlocked
with nature and understands that both go hand in hand.*

*Congrats on passing the exams. Go forth and teach. I see you are
headed for Sikkim, isn't that what you say to a dog when you
want him to bite someone? If you ever get to Poona where I was
born and lived, could you get a photograph of No. 5 Old Sappers
Lines, Climo Road.*

Write to me from time to time.

Love to Margaret. Keep taking the tablets.

Spike

I tried to catch his brilliance and volatility in a poem:

FALLING STAR
(For Spike Milligan)

Thrown out of orbit, falling in
Imaginary flames, the intense heat
Inside his head has caused him
To run wildly from his house, his face
And forehead dabbed at with a cloth
Clenched in his hand. He burns away
Towards the east, fleeing the sunset
And the constellations waiting
In the wings to take their places
For his final 'One Night Only'.

Chapter 3

As the departure date approached, I found myself faced with a dilemma: I didn't just want to go to India for the three weeks planned. Steve and I talked about travelling around the world but the decision was complicated by the fact that we'd both been offered teaching posts. I'd been offered a job in a lovely little school at Blucher, a village on the West Road out of Newcastle, towards Carlisle. I stood at the window of my parents' home and weighed the options. I made the choice in a matter of seconds – there would be other jobs; there would not be many other chances of untrammelled travel across the globe, free from mortgages or other commitments. Steve and I agreed we'd fly out with the other students (one of whom, Mary Thomas, was later to become his wife) but not use the return part of the ticket.

People were a lot less used to visiting distant countries in those days, as a look at the origin of the term 'Gap Year' on the internet will reveal. About three of our group were ready to get on the next flight back to Heathrow after our bus journey through Bombay to the college. I found the experience exciting and things only improved when we arrived, where we were greeted by a throng of beautiful young girls. It was the rainy season and everywhere was damp and smelled of rotting vegetation. I soon found that anything leather, such as a belt, quickly gathered green mould. From my room window, I looked down on little shacks from which immaculately-dressed women and children emerged each morning after nights punctuated by downpours and the squealing of rats.

We visited various educational establishments and rural communities in the state of Gujarat, riding on tractor trailers. In the time allocated for personal travel, Steve and I were part of a group who made our way by train to the hill station of Simla (now Shimla), the former summer capital of the British Raj in India, situated in the northwest Himalayas. It was a fascinating and beautiful place.

We returned with the others to Bombay, and when the time came for them to fly back to the UK, Steve and I began the next stage of our adventure. We said goodbye to the Sophia College staff and girls (one of whom, Marina, had invited us to stay with her family in Calcutta) and took the train to Poona, where we stayed in an ashram for several days. We lived on lentils and I remember feeling listless and wistful and writing several poems which formed the bulk of the short report written for the British Council. I'm sure they were not quite the return they had expected on their £100 investment.

This was one of them:

> ALBINO IN BOMBAY
> Here, where beggars are black and numerous,
> Malformed, maimed, or incapacitated
> In the usual ways, or simply poor,
> Where white people are wealthy and well-fed,
> Well-dressed, and conspicuously healthy,
> Her misfortune is to be poor and white,
> But weirdly so, unnaturally,
> Like a small rodent in its winter coat
> Blinking in the fierce glare of summer.
>
> I say 'her', but it is arbitrary:
> A grubby, layered frock over a pair
> Of rolled-up trousers; close-cropped hair; no shoes;
> 'She' shakes her reassuring hoard of coins,
> One hand before her weak, pink, rabbit's eyes
> To hide them from a winged and taloned sun.

Our other reason for being in Poona, was to attempt to get a photo of Spike Milligan's childhood home, as he'd requested in his letter, so one morning we presented ourselves at the army base, which had belonged to the Indian Army since Independence nearly thirty years before. We had been tempted to go wearing our pith helmets and long white naval shorts, but I think we realised a bit more deference might be in order. It took us some time to talk our way up the hierarchical ladder from sentry to Deputy Commandant and by then it was lunchtime, and we were served a very good meal by a resplendent, turbanned attendant. Our cause was not advanced by the fact that none of these soldiers had heard of Spike Milligan, who they consistently referred to as 'Mike Spilligan'. They were, however, unremittingly gracious and accommodating, and after lunch we were taken to The Old Sappers Lines, Climo Road. Number 5 was pointed out to us, but, as Steve got out his camera, heads began shaking and fingers wagging. "Not possible, Sahib . . ."

"But that's why we've come here," I said in disbelief, sweat trickling down my brow and neck and making me feel like the Alec Guinness character at the end of *The Bridge on the River Kwai*.

"Not possible. The taking of photographs not allowed. Military establishment . . ."

"It's a . . . bungalow," I responded, managing to drop the adjective from the uttered version.

The officer remained courteous but intractable. At this point, one of the bungalow's occupants came out and asked what was going on.

"I might be able to help," the young man replied on hearing our predicament and returning inside. A short time later he re-emerged and produced a negative of the building. The impasse was resolved to everyone's satisfaction and we gave our thanks and made our way back to the ashram and out of the sun.

I mailed the negative off to Spike's office, together with a covering letter and a photocopied poem by Janet Frame called 'Rain on the Roof' which was – and still is – my favourite. On the bottom of the page was another poem of hers called 'The Whelk'.

We met a Thai student in Poona who invited us to stay with his family in Bangkok. After leaving the ashram we travelled down through India using, as our only guide, a battered map of the Indian railway system some clerk had given us. We visited Bangalore, Kerala and Goa, where fishermen invited us to join them in their little canoe to go fishing through the night. I was quite keen but conscious that if we got robbed and tipped over the side, no one would ever know. Anyway, they didn't wait for us to make a decision, pushing their slender boats into the ocean and towards the darkening sky.

We bought knives (although I was already carrying two large ones

– different times) made from a bicycle axle. One side was beaten flat, probably by a man with a hammer and a lot of time. Boys came onto our train offering to repair our boots, belts or anything else made of leather. I hit on the idea of asking one to make us sheaths for the knives and he did.

We travelled by ferry over to Sri Lanka and stayed at a wonderful place in Kandy owned by the Worthington brewing family. It was an empty bungalow which we had to ourselves for pennies and we were served elk for dinner by a tall, elegant waiter who seemed to be the houseboy.

◊

Back in India, we called in at the British Council office in Madras. I wanted to try and get out to the Andaman Islands but the Indian authorities were not so keen for me, or any other foreigners, to visit. It had been – and may still have been – a penal colony, and there were also reports of cannibals still indulging their special dietary requirements there, although this might well have been a rumour put about to discourage overweight Westerners from attempting an expedition. We did, however, get on very well with Geoff Court, the British Council official who explained all these difficulties to us. He invited us to his house on the Friday night and so we tried to find our cleanest/least crumpled shirts in our rented room, in which I'd seen a rat run across the floor, and presented ourselves for drinks. Geoff asked me what I'd like to drink and I naively said, "I know what I'd like but I doubt if you've got it."

"Try me," he smiled.

"I'd love a Drambuie."

I'd reckoned without all the privileges they enjoyed and was served a large glass of the whisky liqueur.

When we caught the train to Calcutta early the following morning, I had an awful hangover which had pretty well cleared up by the time we arrived, forty-eight hours later. The distance was about a thousand miles but we stopped at every station, where vendors tried to sell you a range of things from platform stalls or baskets. I drank lots of tea, the small clay cups being the only thing I ever saw thrown away in India. There was all sorts of food, including barbecued starling-like birds on sticks, but we tended to take the safest option and ordered omelettes on the train, our requests then being telegraphed ahead and collected in tiered metal serving dishes. I spent the nights standing or sitting on the carriage steps, staring out of the open door as the steam train headed north.

TRAIN OF THOUGHT
For Steve Ashton, fellow traveller

"Life, you know, is very like a train journey..."
And so it is, it strikes me now
As never quite before,
Not just a cliché from a padre parody,
As I stand at the open door,
The engine steaming
Through the night
And India...

It seems to me as if the stars
Hang ripe and gleaming
Just in reach...
I'm dreaming.
I know that, and that many more
Have had this dream.
Did Eve dream this?
The prospect and the impact of the fall,
Were these as nothing to the thought
Of holding in one's hand the shining fruit?

When we crossed the Howrah Bridge over the Hooghly River, we knew we were nearly there, because it staples Howrah and Calcutta (now Kolkata) together. We were made very welcome when we reached Marina's house. There were several letters waiting for us, including one dated 4th September 1975 from 'Mike Spilligan':

Dear Stephen,
Thank you very much for the negative, but alas, that is not my
  childhood home; its [sic] the one that flanks it. I am drawing a
  little picture of it, in case you ever get a second chance.
Anyhow,
Thank you for your most interesting letter. What a strange land
  you are in now, I wish you very well in your travels, and I enjoyed
  the little poem about the whelks very much.
Love, light and peace

                              Spike (signature)

There was a drawing in red felt tip of the respective bungalows. I could only assume that, as part of establishing their new identity, the Indian Army had re-numbered them.

During our stay in Calcutta, we visited the British Council (we visited their offices in very much the same way that the two protagonists in *Motorcycle Diaries* visited local hospitals and civil guard stations, shamelessly playing on our novelty value as a pair of enigmatic travellers). Tony Cassidy was the member of staff who befriended us there. I like to think we were good value for whatever hospitality we received on our travels, telling stories, cracking jokes, singing songs and generally being good company. We also visited Mother Teresa's but she wasn't there at the time – not that we were seeking hospitality from her.

After resting at Marina's for a while, we set off to make our way by train to Kathmandu. We arrived a few days after the mountaineer Chris Bonnington had left, which was disappointing because I knew he lived just outside Caldbeck at the time and I wanted to get word back to the Hadwins, who babysat for his children, that we were OK. The only other Westerners in the city seemed to be stranded hippies, left on the high tide line when the sixties receded.

We were keen to head off, if not into the mountains, then at least into the valleys. It took us a while to get our trekking permits, but at last we received them and made our way east along the Sun Kosi River. We walked for several hours to leave the capital well behind us, carrying on long after nightfall by the light of a full moon, before camping just off the track, high above the snaking, sparkling river. I remember the sense of freedom and vitality I experienced when I emerged from our tent the next morning to survey the surrounding scenery – although you wouldn't think so from the picture Steve took of me in my pyjamas, rubbing my eyes. Luckily, it was a hazy photograph due to him dropping the camera in the river later on.

For six days we headed east, using the map from a tiny booklet we'd got with our trekking permit in Kathmandu, with its broken lines indicating footpaths and solid lines depicting rivers. There were no roads or railways in this area of the Himalayas. We were walking through the most spectacular surroundings, sometimes turning a corner leading into or out of a village and seeing the most magnificent mountains with snow-capped peaks like white islands in the sky. In these villages, and every so often along the trails, there were chai shops serving sweet, milky tea. Often these were strategically sited halfway up steep climbs where you were keen to stop for a cup or sometimes even two. At night, they often doubled as free hostels, the owners content to make their money from the goods they sold you. It was hard going, for although not a very high altitude, we were going up and down a few thousand feet several times a day, sometimes finding ourselves in impassable canyons and having to work our way back and around. We were carrying large, heavy rucksacks and keeping up with the Nepalese porters carrying goods to and from market in large baskets, the handles of which went round their foreheads. Once we saw a porter carrying a (presumably wealthy) woman in one of them and realised that the only way out of the place – say, if you broke an ankle – would be to pay one of these porters to carry you down to the nearest large town, however far away that might be.

We also realised we had another potential problem: Steve had miscalculated the amount of money he had changed into Nepalese rupees and had only half the amount he thought he had. No other currency would be acceptable in that remote place. We knew we had to take some fairly drastic measures as, generous as the Nepalese villagers were, we couldn't and wouldn't want to rely on their charity. We met a schoolteacher who taught at a school funded by a trust set up by Edmund Hillary, conqueror of Everest, with Tenzing Norgay, his Sherpa guide. He spoke good English and we told him we had decided to head due south until we reached the road shown running east-west on our minuscule map. He was the only person we'd met in a position to give us any money for our equipment. We sold him our tent, trench spade, etc., for a modest but valued sum. He gave us directions to a chai shop en route, owned by a former pupil of his, and wrote a note for us to give to him, asking him to put us up for the night.

We headed off, lighter and buoyed by the prospect of somewhere to sleep that night. The teacher had given us directions but by nightfall we still hadn't reached the river we needed to cross. It was pitch dark by the time we heard, then saw, the wide river but we couldn't find the bridge. I had already fallen once – traversing the paddy fields on one of the narrow little ridges, I slipped and fell backwards, my rucksack becoming wedged between two of these ridges, my arms and legs in the air, giving an impression of an overturned turtle. I was lucky that there was no one there to witness it except Steve who pulled me out. We then did as he suggested – what Englishmen always do in a crisis – we brewed a pot of tea. Steve got the primus going and we were just savouring a hot cuppa when I saw a string of stars descending slowly and diagonally to the south. It took a few moments to realise that this was a line of lights moving down the opposite hillside, that someone must be carrying them, and that the only place they were likely to be heading was the bridge . . .

We threw away the dregs of the tea and packed away the stove as quickly as we could before mirroring their progress along our side of the riverside trail, trying not to repeat my upturned turtle impression. We knew this was probably our only chance to find the bridge that night. It was only when we were a few feet from the bridge that we could see it, as a few dozen Nepalis crossed from the other side carrying burning torches just like those seen in films set in medieval times.

We acknowledged our unwitting saviours, literally in passing, as we hurried off along the trail on the other side, over the river into the darkness. Our relief gradually evaporated, however, as we walked on without reaching the chai shop. It was one of the few occasions on the whole trip where we had a disagreement. Steve gets tetchy when he's hungry and he was starving. He wanted to stop and eat, and sleep in the open. I was all for pushing on, as I'm inclined to – often pushing others too hard. We continued on our way, me marching on ahead, and a short time later came upon the chai shop and handed the owner the note that the teacher had written.

There was one other incident on the trek when we might have fallen out: we'd been down to our last ration of soup, which we were heating on the primus by the side of a river. The handle had broken off the pan and we were using a fork, the tines of which we'd bent to slip under the bracket to be able to lift it off the stove. On this occasion, my hunger made me a little too anxious and as I went to lift it, the pan slipped and its precious contents disappeared into the sand. To his credit, Steve didn't give me a hard time, knowing that I was just as hungry and disappointed as he was.

◊

Over the next few days, after leaving the chai shop, we ate only every other day, mainly cabbage and rice, and yogurt out of a bucket with mucus and cow hair in it. We needed the toilet even less. We had originally washed with naked abandon in rivers, until we had to remove leeches from our white bodies. I pulled one off an area where I was shocked to find an extra – black – appendage.

At one point we stumbled across a group of women and children gathered round a campfire, eating, in the middle of a wooded area. They ran off as soon as they saw us: I don't think they'd ever seen Westerners before.

It took us several days from the time we left the track to head south to reach the road. Often, we travelled in line with others who seemed to be making for the same destination. Some were men carrying briefcases, dressed like western businessmen from the waist up, but like local peasants from the waist down, wearing *dhotis*.

When we eventually reached the road, it stretched left and right into the heat haze without a vehicle in sight. Within a minute or so, a shimmering shape started to form to our right. It slowly assumed the form of a bus.

It stopped for us and we got on board. For half an hour, neither of us spoke. We hadn't seen a machine for ten days, although we once thought we'd heard an aircraft. We were in culture shock. After several hours, the bus came to a stop and the conductor told us we must all get off.

"But we've paid to Darjeeling," I said.

"Bus at other side," he replied.

"Other side of what?" I asked.

"River."

"But where's the bridge?"

"No bridge. Bridge not built."

Our little map had clearly anticipated the Russian-funded road being completed. Everybody got off the bus with their various items of luggage. Some of them were paying local boatmen to ferry them across the wide, fast-flowing river. Others were wading over. Steve and I had virtually no money left and to the surprise of our fellow travellers, we stripped to our underwear and set off determinedly into the water, holding our rucksacks over our heads and taking great care placing our feet. We both managed to negotiate the crossing and after drying off the best we could, boarded the bus which had appeared to take us to Darjeeling.

◊

I loved Darjeeling. I loved the cultural mix, with Anglican churches and cinemas and horse chestnuts roasted over burning braziers, overlaid onto the local characteristics. It was autumnal and magical.

We returned to Calcutta and Royd Street. I looked like a mountain man and had a shave at a local barber's in that pre-AIDS age. We bought green coconuts from street vendors who scalped them with machetes, enabling us to drink their sweet, cool milk. After a few days, we said our goodbyes to our hosts, the Lobo family, and those who did their cooking and washing. We began the next stage of our adventure. We flew to Burma.

We were told by fellow travellers to use our duty-free allowance to buy a bottle of Johnnie Walker 'Black Label' and 200 '555' cigarettes, and that we could live for a week on what we got selling them on the black market. You were only allowed to stay a week anyway, and penalties for visa infringement were severe. Burma (Myanmar) was a repressive state then, as it is now. You had to change money at their extortionate rate: if you didn't, they would want to know how you were able to live in their country for a week without breaking currency or customs laws.

We arrived in Rangoon (Yangon) on an aeroplane that looked like it had been abandoned at the end of the war. True to the backpackers' grapevine, we were approached by a number of suitors with covetous eyes on our purchases. We were taken on sightseeing trips to view lakeside buildings of great beauty and offered ever-increasing sums to part with our duty-free booty. Eventually, when all the others had sold theirs, we agreed a price for ours. Rangoon itself was dirty and impoverished. We purchased drinks from street vendors who crushed sugar cane to make a sweet beverage.

Inspired by poems of Kipling, we took the train north, following the Irrawaddy valley north to Mandalay, where we saw saffron-clad monks playing *chungi* – or what we would call keepy-uppy – with small, soft, footballs.

When our week was up we left Burma without regrets, except that of seeing people repressed by a corrupt government. From the huge Buddhas to the waterside buildings there was a pervading smell of damp and sense of decay.

◊

Our next stop was Bangkok. We made our way to the address Peerasak had given us back in Poona and found a house built on stilts on the river. His mother and sisters made us very welcome in their simple but elegant home with its beautiful, polished wooden floors. I am told none of these houses survive now, swept away in a concrete tsunami . . .

The food was similarly simple but superb and we were waited on by his sisters, who gave the impression that this was their only wish and purpose in life. At the end of each meal, they would ask us if there was anything else we wanted. We didn't pay for our stay; as I recall, we had virtually no money left by this stage – only enough for our onward flights, wherever they were to be to. To save money, Steve suggested we took turns going out to the port to see if we could sweet talk some sea captain into taking us on board to New Zealand. One day, when it was my turn to travel to the docks, I got on board a vessel bound for New Zealand and chatted to the captain. I could see he was tempted to take on two English speakers, but he had an all-Filipino crew and thought they might be put out by the arrival of two green deckhands. Besides, his wife was due to join him soon, so he would have less need of other company.

It was after this disappointment that Peerasak arrived unannounced from Poona, due to one of the frequent college strikes there. One night he invited me to join him and his pal. We went to a bar where they were knocking back the cheap, local whisky in a way that suggested they were fortifying their courage for some enterprise. My defence mechanisms were working overtime as I downed the spirit but focussed on staying sober. I found myself wondering if they were going to mug me and then go back to the house and attack Steve. After stoking up their resolve, they got up and we headed off to another little bar that looked like a saloon in a Western. We were led up the rickety wooden stairs: first Peerasak, then his pal, then myself. There was a series of little, wooden, partitioned booths with red light bulbs outside, attended by a wrinkled and bent old man with a few thin strands of hair. The man looked like a tortoise that had crept out of its shell. He carried large bowls of hot water and grubby towels to various booths and made small pots of tea.

I was shown into an empty booth with a red leatherette couch. A group of seven or eight young, lightly-clad and very ugly girls were ushered into the cramped space. It was made clear to me that my companions had paid for the services of one of them and I was expected to make my choice. They were all wearing little plastic badges with numbers somewhere on their scanty clothing and the one who made advances was number 26, the only one I remotely fancied, as it happened. But, in the end, my choice was to forego the experience and sit and wait for the two others, whose endeavours in the flimsy booths were clearly audible. I passed the time doing an English language crossword, experiencing sexual frustration, moral self-satisfaction and intellectual stimulation all at the same time.

◊

Steve and I decided we needed to change our plans and make a move. If we couldn't get to New Zealand by ship, and it was too expensive to fly, then we'd head for the United States. We flew to Hong Kong where we spent a few days in that bustling colony, still almost a quarter of a century before it would be reabsorbed into China like some errant foetus.

30

We found a room near the top of a high-rise tower, having quickly realised that the higher the room, the cheaper the price. We ate well on the streets and took a little time to explore Kowloon and Victoria before flying on to Tokyo.

In Tokyo we could hardly afford to eat. It cost $10 a night to stay in the YMCA. We could have eaten well for a week for that in India. Everything was too expensive for us to sample or enjoy, except the sushi in the hostel.

We tried to book flights to the US, but it was soon after the end of the Vietnam War and it was proving difficult to enter the States from South-East Asia. We were advised to fly back to the UK and apply from there, but we didn't want to do this for a variety of reasons, not least because this would not constitute travelling around the world, and how could you go back to your home country and fly straight out again without upsetting the family you hadn't seen for several months? Eventually, we managed to book flights to LA, where my Great Aunt Anna (who had stayed with us in Newcastle about ten years previously) lived, but we still needed permission to enter the United States.

The US Embassy had told us we didn't have enough money with us to satisfy their entry requirements and the only way we could gain entry was on receipt of a telegram from someone in the States prepared to confirm that they would meet all our expenses during our stay in their country. We contacted Steve's sister, Bridget, who was married to Bill, a Chicagoan, in Downers Grove, Illinois. We waited all day for the telegram to arrive. Our flight was the next day but, to compound problems, that was Thanksgiving Day and the Embassy would be closed. The prayed-for missive arrived a few minutes before five p.m. and we managed to get cleared for entry. We were let out of the already locked building and were overwhelmed by a sense of relief.

The next day we boarded the plane, looking like the vagabonds we were. We planned to change into the only half-decent clothes we had left before we landed in LA, but, with all the cliff-hanger tension of the day before, had not appreciated that we would actually be going through US Immigration in Hawaii, where we had a stop. Before we landed there was a frantic searching through hand luggage and some attempts at taming hairstyles in the plane's toilet. We were worried that all our efforts would be thwarted by some crewcut official viewing us with suspicion and denying us entry for some spurious reason such as that we looked like drug-runners, fugitives or terrorists. Our fears proved unfounded and we gazed out over Honolulu from the airport with a sense of victory at having beaten the system by getting into the States virtually penniless.

◊

On arriving at LA International Airport we were met by more unanticipated situations. Firstly, when I tried to phone Great Aunt Anna from one of the airport phone booths, I couldn't get an answer at the number I had for her. Plans and circumstances had changed so quickly that there had been no opportunity to contact her in advance. Secondly, it was still Thanksgiving Day (we had crossed the International Date Line) so almost everything was closed for the national holiday, and the rapidly turning digits on the meter of the yellow cab taking us to my aunt's address in the suburb of Inglewood were worrying. I told the driver to wait while I went to the door. After a few unsuccessful attempts I got a response but the voice from inside wasn't Anna's and its owner refused to open the door. I ended up talking to her through the letterbox and she told me that she had bought the house from my relatives a while back and they had moved up the coast to Santa Barbara. Obviously the neighbourhood had gone downhill.

We went back to the airport in the taxi where we handed over most of our few dollars to the cabbie. I returned to the phone booths and looked up the surname Watkins, found an address in Santa Barbara and dialled the phone number. Thankfully, I recognised my great aunt's voice and, after explaining who and where I was, I phoned them back, having allowed them time to find the number of another relative living in Los Angeles. I contacted Peggy who came out to collect this British relative she'd never met before. And so it was that, about an hour later, Steve and I were decanted into a house full of my unknown relations with a table laden with turkey, cranberry sauce and all . . .

Chapter 4

We stayed in LA for a week – sleeping, eating and seeing some of the sights. Then we took a Greyhound bus to Chicago which went via Las Vegas and Salt Lake City and took 56 hours. From Chicago we made our way by train to Downers Grove and the home of Steve's sister, Bridget, whom I'd known from the time Steve and I had visited them when they lived in Alston in Cumbria. Although they were in the process of putting their house up for sale, we were able to sleep in a basement room. It was basic but it was beautiful in our eyes. It was December and the weather was getting extremely cold as the United States of America prepared to enter its Bicentennial Year. Even the fire hydrants were suitably painted in celebratory patriotic colours. But Steve and I needed to find some form of employment: Bill and Bridget weren't really in a position to support us and nor would we have expected them to do so indefinitely.

Downers Grove felt like some place in a Thornton Wilder play. We soon found our way around the town in our search for work. As the winter deepened, we made some money clearing snow from drives and paths, but we continued looking for something more regular. We walked the streets, keeping an eye on the signs showing the temperature and the wind chill factor as the freezing wind blew down from the north over Lake Michigan. Every few hundred yards I had to enter a store to ensure my nose and ears didn't suffer from frostbite. Steve got a job at the

Big Boy hamburger store which had outside, by way of advertisement, a huge statue of a red-and-white-checked aproned boy, with a quiff on which you could have ridden a surfboard, serving an obscenely large burger. I subsequently got a job as a bus boy there too, clearing cups and plates and washing them. I remember having to shave off my beard at the manager's insistence for hygienic reasons – which struck me as odd because I didn't deal directly with food except with its disposal as waste and he had the hairiest arms I've ever seen: a hair was as likely to fall from them as from my beard.

Patrick, Bill and Bridget's eldest child, watched me enter the bathroom. They all called me Uncle Harvey to distinguish me from their real Uncle Steve. After a while, I emerged, having completely shaved off all my facial hair. Patrick was still standing there, waiting for me.

"Where's Uncle Harvey?" he asked, perplexed and concerned, peering past me into the empty bathroom.

I pestered the manager of Dunkin' Donuts into taking me on as 'trainee baker'. This involved my baking trays of doughnuts at temperatures of 370 degrees Fahrenheit. These trays were lifted with the use of two metal grips inserted into slots at either side. Occasionally, these would slip as you were removing a tray from the burning fat and your natural reaction was to nip the tray with your elbows to stop its precious cargo falling onto the floor. For years afterwards I had lines on the inside of both elbows – pale badges of courage of the baker's trade.

We made an enormous range of flavoured doughnuts and you could eat them free at work. This, together with the double cream coffee, contributed to me putting on two stone, transforming me from the Himalayan mountain goat into a quiffless Big Boy. I would take discounted boxes of doughnuts back home to share while watching old episodes of *Upstairs, Downstairs* and *Monty Python's Flying Circus* (neither of which were favourites of mine back in the UK) on public subscription TV.

Sometimes I'd work with other bakers. I remember one of them making a phallic pastry and squirting cream out of the end to the outrage of the waitress. He asked me to help him start his car, the engine of which had frozen up (customers often locked their cars with the engines on to prevent this happening, sometimes leaving them running for over an hour). My colleague borrowed a friend's car and he drove up behind his vehicle while I put a tyre between them as he edged forward to keep it in place. I then got in next to him and he drove at speed while his buddy in the car in front tried to get the engine bump-started. Why I needed to risk my skin in this way, I wasn't sure . . .

The girls who worked as waitresses there were young, well-rounded, pink-skinned and heavily made-up. They would ask me questions just to hear my English accent which tickled them. I used to work nightshift sometimes and I'd be baking away, listening to Paul Simon singing 'Fifty Ways to Leave Your Lover' on the radio and watching the girls serving customers on the other side of the huge internal window. This allowed customers to see that their doughnuts were being properly prepared in a hygienic setting and meant the baker could keep an occasional eye on the dining area which was a little additional security for the girls. One night, the manager was in when a black truck driver came in and sat at a bar chair. I saw the manager, who I had always thought of as a bit of a redneck, stroll over and give him a smile and some extra coffee, before walking back through to where I was rolling the pastry.

"Gotta keep those bastards happy or they complain against ya . . ."

This taught me that you can change behaviour by legislation, but you can't remove prejudice. When I left, the manager gave me a signed certificate, attesting to my developing skills as a trainee baker at Dunkin' Donuts, Downers Grove.

Because we were saving up for our flights home, we saw little of Illinois except the inside of our workplaces and the house. I remember going into Chicago one day and not going up the Sears Tower, then the tallest building in the world, because it cost a dollar (I spent the money instead on two second-hand volumes of *New Poets of England and America* at the thrift store in Downers Grove). Other than that, my only memories are helping one of Bill's family move (followed by a visit to a pizzeria) and seeing in the Bicentennial with him at an Irish bar in 'the Windy City'.

◊

I flew home alone. My Nan, who I was very close to, was ill in hospital and weakening, and my dad told me that it looked like she would die in the next few weeks. I said my farewells to our hosts and to Steve who was bound for Canada, and flew from O'Hare International Airport to Keflavik, Iceland, where I was transported the 50km by coach to spend my three-day stopover in Reykjavik. I stayed at the Loftleidir Hotel in a deal which cost me only $30.

It was the end of January and daylight lasted from around 11 a.m. until about 1 p.m. I was taken by coach on guided tours of the local sights. We visited a geyser, where we had to wait for the group in front of us to leave. We then approached and the guide produced a plastic bottle of washing-up liquid which he squirted onto the geyser: this apparently caused a seal which sped up the heating process so that we did not need to wait too long to see the little plume appear. There were several such bottles discarded around the place. From the bus, we viewed geyser-heated greenhouses full of tomatoes and the venue for the World Chess Championship between Bobby Fischer and Boris Spassky in 1972 – it was a very unprepossessing building and looked like a large Nissen hut. Fischer was to die in Reykjavik, scene of his Cold War triumph, in January 2008.

After three days in which I had never eaten herring in so many forms, I was driven back to the airport for my flight to Glasgow. I recall the former Scottish international footballer, Ian Ure, was on the plane, drinking Glayva. My memories of this time are unusually negative, no doubt due to being in Iceland at the darkest time of the year as well as the fact that I was returning to a place I hadn't really missed, possibly to a family funeral, and certainly an uncertain future . . .

Chapter 5

It was January 29th 1976 and it was raining as I looked out of the train travelling from Glasgow to Newcastle. We passed through Edinburgh, a city I had loved since a boy, and down the magnificent Northumbrian coast.

Nan didn't die, bless her, and by March I was going for an interview for a temporary teaching position at St John Fisher Secondary School at Lobley Hill, Gateshead. As I entered through the front doors, a member of staff asked me if I was the new teacher. I told her I was there for interview for the post. I appeared to be the only one, and I got the job. When I was shown round the school and introduced to my new colleagues by Harry Watson, the Deputy Head, my having been Head Boy of St Cuthbert's was mentioned several times. 'Ex Head Boy of local Catholic Grammar gets job at Catholic school' was not the stuff newspaper headlines were made of, but the explicit connection in the introductions made me feel uncomfortable. It reminded me why I had not been looking to work in a Catholic school, but this had been the only vacancy to teach English.

I got the impression that several of the staff treated me with suspicion. The school was run by a small junta of senior staff surrounding Jack Doherty, the ageing, occasionally apoplectic Head. His favourite expression was, "Two heads are better than one – even if they're sheep's heads . . ." The huge, angry-looking lump on the back of his neck made the saying even more grotesque.

◊

My main responsibility was to teach English as cover for Pat Ross, who was on maternity leave. On my first day I went into a senior class that was studying *Macbeth*. I started off the reading with a pupil at the front. He stuttered and struggled his way through several lines. How unfortunate, I thought, to have begun with him and after long enough to spare his feelings, I asked someone else to take over. He was no better and the next boy was worse. The girls were only a slight improvement, mainly because they were trying to impress the new teacher. I was trying to teach Shakespeare to a class of fifteen-year-olds who could barely read.

In another class, at the end of term when exams were being set, I had an altercation with a pupil. The class had had to write an essay for me to assess their ability. When I returned the marked essays a day or two later, a couple of them were missing, although they had been nowhere else but in the class and the staffroom. I apologised to the two boys for asking them to write another essay with the same title, allowing them the same time as previously to complete them while I did something else with the rest of the class. One of the boys buckled down to it straight away, but the other's body language made clear that he was struggling with both the task and the injustice of having to write it. I had an occasional quiet word with him as I moved around the room, but eventually he stood up and said, "Ah'm not deein' it."

"You have to do it, Stephen," I said. "How else can I give you a mark?"

"Ah divvent care. Ah'm not deein' it." He was standing by his desk.

I walked towards him. "If you don't do it now, you'll have to stay behind and do it after school," I said, continuing to walk towards him.

"That's not fair. Ah've already done it once. Ah nivvor lost it. Ah've done nowt wrong," he said, accompanying each sentence with a step backward down the aisle.

"I'm not saying you've done anything wrong, but I need something from you to mark."

By this time his back was almost against the classroom wall and I was just a few feet from. "Fuck off . . . I'm not fuckin' deein it . . ."

It was at this point that I belatedly realised I'd literally and metaphorically pushed him into a corner. I walked back to the front of the room and away from the door. "Leave the room, Stephen. I'll speak to you later when you've settled down."

He hurried out, his face flushed.

I finished the lesson, casting an occasional eye towards the door, hoping to catch a glimpse of him through the glass panels to reassure me that he had not run off. I had already decided I would not be taking the matter further for a few reasons: lack of faith in the school's hierarchy among them, but mainly because I knew I had intimidated him with my physical presence. The school buses were lining up outside and I was sure he would be gone when I opened the door to let the class out, but there he was. I asked him into the empty room and said, "Stephen, I know it seems unfair. I know it's not your fault the essay's missing. Now John's done his and I want yours from you tomorrow so you're not the only one without a mark. And you never, ever speak like that to me again. Now bring it in tomorrow and that'll be the end of it . . . OK?"

He nodded, turned and then hurried out for the second time that afternoon. He brought his essay in next day. It wasn't great, but it would do.

◊

The post was only for a few months but I was kept on. I also helped with P.E. and one day had come into the class on a hot day still sweating from my exertions. I didn't have my tie on and someone spotted me. I was told I must wear a tie at all times. The next day I came to school wearing one of my psychedelic ties from the sixties.

As my stock with the junta waned, I became more popular with my other colleagues. I was still a probationary teacher, though, and as such, very vulnerable. If a teacher didn't successfully complete his probationary year, he could not continue to teach. I was informed that my probationary year was to be extended and I took the matter to my union representative, Vin McGuinness, who taught P.E. and Art at the school. A meeting was arranged at Gateshead Local Authority's Education Office. My teaching career hung in the balance.

In the course of the proceedings, Vin, who I'd labelled 'an affable bastard' from our earliest encounters, surprised me by saying that he'd taught with me more than anyone else and yet no one had sought his opinion of my teaching ability. That in itself, he stated, appeared to him to be a serious omission, casting doubt on the integrity of the process. Furthermore, although I had only been teaching less than a year, he would already rate me as one of the seven or eight best teachers in the school. How much of this he meant and how much was to discomfort those present and procure a satisfactory conclusion for a member of his union I'm still not sure, but my authority to teach was eventually ratified.

I enjoyed teaching, and felt I had a pretty good relationship with most of the pupils. One group in particular responded to my style of teaching. The girls in general were eager to please and I can remember the names of some them – Diana Bamborough, Diane Cushley, Joan Caisley . . .

I booked the St Mary's College Outdoor Education Centre at Walkerwalls, Wooler, to take some of the schoolchildren into the Cheviot Hills for the weekend. Marie, my girlfriend, who was a student teacher, would be coming along to look after the girls. Just after lunch on the Friday afternoon I was told that there was a problem with the transport and the trip would have to be cancelled. Several of my friends on the staff said that they would drive children up there if I could get permission for other teachers to cover their classes, making a return trip of well over a hundred miles in their own vehicles, at their own expense, to help us out. The Head refused. I was furious, but managed to get them all up there eventually.

◊

By this time I was living in a flat a few doors up from Nan in Haydn Street, Gateshead. (It was invariably pronounced 'Hayden', as I think my grandfather would have been the only resident familiar with the works of the composer). When Steve had returned from abroad, a few months after me, we'd decided to buy a property on the street that I'd heard was available from the Warner sisters for £1,500 – and that was for a pair of Tyneside flats: the lower one, which still had the original range in the living room, was let to two elderly sisters who seemed to keep a cat menagerie. Since making that decision we'd gone on an archaeological dig in Norfolk we'd heard about from our old school pal Jim Mullaney. The dig was at Castle Rising and the accommodation was at the pilgrims' hostel in Walsingham. It was the first of several wonderful summers spent excavating under the supervision of Beric Morley. I have great memories of fancy dress parties, music nights and storytelling sessions at the Oxford Stores pub.

One day, in the back of the bus on our way back to the hostel, two newspaper advertisements attracted our attention: one was a concert at Wembley featuring Joni Mitchell and Crosby, Stills, Nash & Young which appealed to me, and the other was a job advertisement for Science Editor for Oxford University Press which caught Steve's eye.

"What do you think?" he asked.

"I think you should go for it."

"What about the flat?"

"Don't worry about that. Go for it."

He did and he got it. We went to the concert, which was brilliant. I bought the flats for the reduced price of £1,400, borrowing the balance from my parents. At that time I considered myself a free spirit and hated the idea of being tied down by a mortgage.

Vin had asked me to take a football team in my first full academic year at the school and I enjoyed the experience, although the Wednesday nights and early Saturday mornings – together with all the marking generated by teaching English to children whose work used up a lot of my time and red ink – did impinge on my social life. The team included several pupils who had been taught by my old pal from college, Ossie Postle, at St Joseph's Primary – Jimmy Bagnall, John Robinson, the Gallagher twins (not to become famous musicians, as far as I'm aware). We did pretty well and reached the semi-final of the Gateshead Cup, something our small school's teams did not often achieve. The match was one of the best games of football I have ever seen. The advantage passed between the two teams throughout. There were difficult positional and substitution decisions and we had a very small squad, both physically and numerically. At the final whistle we were 4-3 winners and I was delighted, drained and hoarse. The final, however, was a dour affair. Neil Fannan scored a great goal from a distance but it was disallowed because someone else was standing offside – this being long before the 'not interfering with play' element was introduced to the rulebook. Eventually we scraped it 1-0, but we had won the cup.

◊

September and the new school year had come around again and Marie was now teaching at St Mary's Primary School in nearby Whickham. When the position of Head of St John Fisher was advertised, Jack Doughty finally having decided to retire, it caused considerable excitement in the staffroom: the ruling faction wanted Harry Watson, the deputy head, to get the job and preserve the status quo while the rest of us wanted a new broom to clean out the Augean Stables . . .

On the day of the interviews, Harry Watson showed the other candidates around, which seemed entirely inappropriate. One of his fellow applicants was married to Marie's eldest sister and Deputy Head of a large comprehensive in nearby Washington. To everyone's surprise, he was appointed.

One day, a short while after he'd taken up his new position, I got a message asking me to go down to the Head's office.

'Just like old times,' I thought to myself, having been summoned often in the past.

"Come on in, Steve," Pete said, smiling a wide smile, his tall angular body coming towards me and steering me towards a chair.

"How's Marie?" he asked, angling his head.

"Fine, thanks."

"Got over that cold of hers?"

"Yes, she's fine, thanks. Back to her usual rude health."

"Well, Steve, I was wondering . . . Who's causing the trouble in the staffroom?"

There was a momentary pause. I'd hoped, forlornly, that I'd misheard him.

"Sorry?" I said, now angling *my* head slightly to make sure I heard his words clearly.

"Who's causing the trouble in the staffroom? Who's against my new initiatives?"

I stood up. "Sorry," I said, "You've got the wrong guy . . ."

From that moment I knew I would have to leave the school, and I was always addressed as 'Mr Harvey' by the Headmaster thereafter. As might be imagined, this caused my always volatile relationship with Marie considerable difficulty: they were a very tight-knit family.

I applied for other teaching jobs and although I was shortlisted for one at the King Edward VI School, Morpeth, there was already a shoo-in for that one. It was obviously going to be very difficult getting another job teaching in the area, but Marie and I were now engaged and I didn't want to move away. And so it was that I turned to a boyhood aspiration of mine and applied to join the police forces of Northumbria and Cumbria. The police service in the late seventies was very keen to recruit graduates and Superintendent Whitehouse, Northumbria Police's Graduate Liaison Officer, came out to my humble flat in Haydn Street – twice – to try to persuade me and Mike Malone, a colleague who was also interested, to join up. Paul Whitehouse was a very likeable guy who would clearly go on to become a chief constable, which he did, in Sussex. In 2001 he was removed from office by the new Home Secretary, David Blunkett, in controversial circumstances. In 2005 he was appointed Head of the Gangmaster Licensing Authority, set up to control those managing teams of foreign workers after the Morecambe Bay cockling disaster of 2004 in which 23 Chinese cockle pickers were killed on the treacherous sands by the incoming tide.

Chapter 6

In the summer of 1979 I wrote to the governors of St John Fisher asking to be released from my contract in order to join Northumbria Police. They agreed and on September 3rd I became PC 3685.

As I turned into the car park at Dishforth to begin my initial training, I was conscious that my vehicle was not in the best condition and I was worried I might be pulled up for some minor breach of regulations. Sure enough, the officer on duty for our arrival asked me to reactivate my indicators. He informed me that, as he suspected from his initial observation, they were not flashing at the mandatory rate of between 60 and 120 times per minute. As a police officer, I was expected to ensure that every vehicle I drove complied with the legal requirements.

I was in a dormitory with twenty or so other new recruits. These were to be my classmates for the next ten weeks, together with a smaller number of female recruits. Next morning, when we made our way to our classroom there was a series of instructions written in large chalk letters on the board:

Sit down
Do not talk
Etc.

I smiled to myself – this reminded me of the way some teachers treated new secondary school pupils on their first day. Our instructors were Sgt.

Morgan from Humberside and Sgt. Tain from West Yorkshire. They entered, rather dramatically I thought – clearly everything was designed to make an impression.

Virtually the first question was, "Anyone here got a degree?" I was the only one to put my hand up. Everyone else looked round to where I sat in the back row. I had almost immediately alienated the rest of my class, through no fault of my own. They continued down through 'A' Levels and then 'O' Levels. My mind went back to the teacher and the little girl humiliated halfway down the aisle on my half-day teaching experience at Howdon.

◊

I liked both my instructors – Sgt. Morgan, dark-haired and droll, and Sgt. Tain, fair-haired and savvy – but they were part of an archaic, insensitive system, designed to begin with discipline and then build up from there. Over the following days and weeks I got to know them better, having been elected Class Leader by my peers. The purple cloak and badge of Head Boy were now replaced by a light blue lanyard, indicating my new status. 'Boys love badges,' I thought. 'What is this universal urge to distinguish one from another, to establish a hierarchy?' I asked myself. It did seem to me to be a particularly male preoccupation, but then I was sure women, as ever, had subtler ways of marking superiority.

A forty-year-old ex-army guy called Dick, with Derbyshire, was appointed 'Right Marker' by the instructors, responsible for all drill issues, and for marching us from one location to another around the site, saluting officers as circumstances demanded. My particular pal in the class was Martin Crown, who sat in the desk immediately to my left. He was a former sales manager with Scholl who'd taken a substantial pay cut to join the Nottinghamshire Constabulary. I, on the other hand, thanks to the newly-elected Margaret Thatcher bringing forward the pay agreement awarded by the outgoing Labour Government, was a thousand pounds a year better off (about 30%) as a trainee police officer than a graduate teacher with over three years' experience. We sat exams at the start of each week. I was expected to come out on top but, competitive as I was, I wanted to enjoy my weekends back in Tyneside with Marie, and the recruit who regularly came first, to my second, was an ex-plumber who reputedly spent most of his time at home revising.

Most Sunday nights I travelled back down to Dishforth with Bill Forth (PC 3684), collecting him from his house on the way south. We'd met each other at the interviews in the summer. He was a likeable guy and made the journey down the A1 more fun than it would have been listening to the radio or thinking that I should have done more revision for the following morning's exam. I was still doing well enough to be in contention for the 'Baton of Honour' for the best all-round student of the intake. I think I came 15th out of about 140 in the cruel cross country, much to the delight and surprise of our instructors.

"Keep going, Mr Harvey," I remember Sgt. Tain shouting encouragingly, a cigarette in his hand, as I neared the finishing line among a group of younger runners. (It was one of the quirks of the establishment that although we were constantly told to think and act as police officers, we were invariably addressed as civilians). Our team was doing well at the football too, until I was paired with a small compact lad in the self-defence session. He was apparently a judo expert and we got each other in a hold – his probably had an exotic Japanese name, mine was entirely improvised. Neither of us would give way, and I felt something crack in my chest. I had difficulty breathing, which became painful and shallow and was later diagnosed as a cracked rib. I missed the remaining football games and with it the chance of 'the Baton'. To this day I still have a pain in my chest in frosty weather.

Socially, we spent our time in drink and horseplay in The Packhorse bar on site. In an arm wrestling competition I beat all-comers until a farmer's son from Yorkshire called Dave sat opposite me. There was no contest: this jovial, ruddy-faced youth had been shifting bales since he was a young boy.

Towards the end of our training, the rumblings in the class about the Right Marker, Dick, came to a head. I told those who brought their complaints to me that there were only two options – put up or shut up – and that if they made any official complaint about his behaviour to the instructors, they would back him, because that was the way the system worked. Nevertheless, they went ahead, with the predicted result. I, too, was given the cold shoulder by the instructors, who clearly blamed me for not giving strong enough leadership. It was only resolved when I had a straight-talking session with them in their office. A sense of harmony was restored and we had a good night out to mark the end of our training.

I remember Martin and I having far too much to drink after our final exams. We returned to the dorm but I couldn't get into my bed, nor understand why, until the others burst out laughing and I realised they'd made an 'apple pie bed' for me. But it was entirely down to my inebriated state that when I got up to go to the toilet as the Duty Sergeant called "Lights Out!" I opened the wardrobe and not the dormitory door . . .

◊

My mother brought Marie down for my passing out parade. I had a heavy cold – it must have been late November – and I grabbed some blue toilet paper from the toilet before dashing out to take my place on the drill square. Over the weeks, I had actually come to enjoy the discipline of drill, although learning sequential routines has never been one of my strengths. As I marched proudly round with my colleagues, unknown to me, a blue ribbon of tissue was streaming behind me from my trouser pocket . . .

The following week the Northumbria recruits were back at the Kylins, getting prepared for our first postings. I found out I was going to Whickham, where the police station was about fifty yards from the school where Marie worked. My first operational sergeant was Ray Gibbon, a former dog handler, who was a steady, sensible and genuine guy. He used to smoke a pipe and occasionally would take me to visit friends of his in neighbouring Sunniside or – on night shift – the pit ponies at Marley Hill colliery.

The inspector was a very different character. Tommy Soulsby had been brought up locally, in the Teams district of Gateshead, a notoriously tough area. He was quite tall, but looked taller because of his military bearing, and he was always immaculately turned out with sparkling shoes, slicked-back black hair and a trim moustache. He seemed to know all the criminals round about and had a better arrest rate than most PCs, which was unheard of for an inspector. His long-suffering wife was often left shopping alone as he recognised somebody who was wanted on warrant and made an off-duty arrest, escorting his prisoner to the nearest police station or asking a startled shop assistant to phone for a police vehicle.

◊

I had my own share of off-duty incidents in my first few weeks. One day I was waiting for a bus to work on the steep road beside St Mary's Roman Catholic Cathedral in Newcastle. I had my police shirt and trousers on under my coarse, grey civilian jacket (or 'horse blanket' as some work wit called it). I saw a driver park his small van on our side of the road and then walk away. Suddenly I noticed it was moving slowly backwards, gathering pace in an arc towards a restaurant where some diners were eating on the other side of a plate glass window. I ran over and grabbed the passenger side handle, but it was locked. I held on as tightly as I could and tried to dig my heels in to reduce its momentum and felt something give. I managed to bring it to a stop by the opposite kerb. The driver came back, got into his vehicle and drove off with barely a word. I went back to my place in the queue and, on checking to see what damage I'd done, found I'd pulled the sole off my shoe.

Another time I was on the bus on my way in for night shift when I saw a large amount of police activity near the Central Station and an officer chasing a man on foot. I went to the front of the bus and told the driver I was an off-duty police officer and that I wanted him to slow down and stop just after he'd passed the fugitive. This he did and I managed to apprehend the man and hand him over to the West End officer, giving his colleagues my name and number and station, in case they needed a statement from me. I was late into work, having had to wait for the next bus which I got to stop outside Whickham nick for me. Dave Hepple, who was in the front office at the time, made some comment about probationers getting soft these days. I told him it was the second time that night I'd got a bus to stop for me 'on demand'.

◊

The shift was a good bunch, full of characters – Peter Clark; John Walker; Gordon Dixon (quietly spoken and bespectacled, but watch out if he took off his glasses); John Brown, another probationer, high energy and intense; and the biggest of them all, 'Big Eric' Wilson who worked in the front office for reasons best left unsaid. In those days, police officers were still mainly directed by radio from their local stations, and this was one of Eric's roles. Eric reminded me of Landburgher 'Lamb-burger' Gessler from the ITV series in the fifties about William Tell: he was huge and ate with his hands. He would go to the local butchers in his break and ask for some belly pork, instructing them to 'leave the tits on . . .'

When we were on night shift he asked me to keep my eyes open for any chrome tubing to use for making tackle for our proposed fishing trip, off the coast on the Monday morning when we finished our last of seven shifts. I was patrolling around outside the scrapyards in Dunston because we'd had some thefts from those recently. I found some abandoned cycle handlebars and brought them back when I came in for my refreshments at

1 a.m. Eric had a big pot boiling in the kitchen, melting down lead for the weights. When the Super walked in, making an unheard-of, unannounced night shift visit, I was convinced we would all be disciplined for abuse of police property or some other breach of regulations.

"What's that smell, Eric?"

"Preparin' fer wor little fishin' expedition, sir . . . Would you like a nice cod bringin' back?"

Nothing further was said and I finished my 'bait' and went back out on patrol, pleased to be out and about. I walked along the railway lines leading down to Dunston Staithes. Sgt. Gibbon didn't like his probationer constables being given lifts down to – or back from – their beats. All this walking was going to keep me fit. The lines ran past the back of the scrapyard and, being on a high embankment, overlooked it. Besides, if I were a nocturnal predator, this was the route I would use.

Sure enough, there in the dark, I could just make out a figure clambering up the embankment, carrying something.

"I can see someone on the railway line at the back of the scrapyard by The Dun Cow," I whispered as quietly as I could into my radio's microphone. "I'm going to investigate."

The inevitable consequence was that I ended up in quite a tussle, rolling around on the lines with the thief in the night. I managed to hold onto him until the sergeant arrived, panting, several minutes later. The prisoner was still struggling and it was with some difficulty, the sergeant slipping once, that we managed to get him down the steep side of the embankment and into the back of the panda car. We transported him back to the station and put him before the station sergeant where I outlined the circumstances of the arrest, and he was processed and put in a cell.

Sgt Gibbon then realised he had lost his radio, presumably somewhere on the railway track, so we headed back down to Dunston. When we got there, I contacted Whickham Office on my radio. Eric was to keep talking to help us locate the missing piece of communication equipment – it was a big deal if a police radio 'fell into the wrong hands'.

"Once upon a time," the deep Geordie voice boomed out of my radio as I searched for the missing one, "there was a probationer and a sergeant . . . In the middle of the night, the probationer found a bad man stealing something and the sergeant went to help him catch him. In the struggle that followed, one of them lost his radio . . . Now who do you think it was? The 'proby'? No, it was the 'sargie' . . . Ho-ho-ho . . ."

I had to turn my radio down because I couldn't hear the missing one for the noise from mine. I was laughing so much I thought the sergeant might hear me . . . Eventually, we found it and headed back to the station to do the paperwork in relation to the arrest.

My first arrest had been when I was out on patrol with the inspector. It was after midnight one night shift and we'd been checking out The Poacher public house on Swalwell Bank because the alarm had gone off. I was at the other side of the building from the inspector when a guy opened the door and tried to get past me. It was a radio blackspot and I wanted to try and sound my whistle, which we still wore then, but he was a fit young man and determined to get away. I managed to detain him until the inspector came round looking for me. It was a rather bungled burglary in which he'd hidden in the toilets until the staff had locked up and left.

◊

On 'early days', we used to go to a greasy spoon café called Ma Brown's in Swalwell, just round the corner from the pub. She was an ancient, taciturn woman with elephantine ankles. On wintry mornings, especially if it was icy, one of the drivers would go and collect her shuffling frame from her house and bring her down the bank. She gave police officers a quarter bacon and tomato stottie (a large, flat, round local bread) and a mug of tea for 25p. One morning I went there after night shift for a breakfast before bed and was the first one in. The second person in was the burglar from The Poacher and I was surprised to see him out and about so early – until I realised he was due at court that morning to answer the charge. The next few people through the door joined him at his table, clearly friends of his. It looked like things could turn tricky as I was off-duty and therefore had no radio, truncheon or handcuffs with me. Luckily, the next customers were a pair of Traffic lads with their order for the rest of their team and I was able to head home untroubled.

It was always difficult dealing with other officers – or members of their families – who had committed offences. I once had to arrest the young son of a police officer for shoplifting. While processing the arrest, in the presence of the boy's mother who was separated from the detective sergeant father, he contacted me by phone at the station. I sympathised with his situation but drew the line when he began asking me if I'd cautioned his son properly and how much service I had in. After terminating the conversation, I went into the Inspector's office and informed him of the call. A few moments later his phone rang. He used the first name of the DS and I made to leave the room, but he indicated for me to stay.

"PC Harvey is young in service, but is a mature officer who has handled this matter absolutely correctly, and I suggest you discontinue this call as otherwise it could have an adverse effect upon your police career."

It was heartening to get such an unequivocal show of support from such a well-respected supervisor. He had a much more monochrome view of policing than I did and we had some interesting discussions when I was out on patrol with him, usually when we were doing licensing checks together – visiting licensed premises and noting who was there, numbers, and whether everything was in order. I claimed to be an 'idealistic realist' and he responded that, in time, I'd learn to be 'a devious idealistic realist . . .'

He had a natural air of authority – polished, like his shoes, by years of patient application. On the occasions when anyone challenged this, such as some youth in a bar making some rash comment, he'd approach them and, his moustache twitching slightly, very much like the prison warder, Mr Mackay, played by Fulton Mackay in the TV series *Porridge* – although somehow not comical – he would say out of the side of his mouth, "Don't spoil my night and I'll not spoil yours." I never saw this fail to work. He did have a very dry sense of humour to match his wry style of delivery. His speech at his retirement do, when he finally left his beloved police force years later, was one of the funniest performances I've ever witnessed, comparable with the best of stand-up comedians.

I was beginning to settle into the shift and was learning how to use the information in the collator's office, where all the intelligence on local criminals and their photographs were stored in those pre-computerised days. I knew my beat well and would call in to the old chandler's by the staithes or the paper shop by the Rocket tower block in Dunston and have a chat. My local knowledge was growing and this was reflected in the number of arrests I made.

◊

By this time Marie and I were engaged. We'd bought a semi-detached in Whickham, and were due to get married on August 2nd that year, 1980. Until then, as a good Catholic girl from a good Catholic family, she would still be living with her mother and younger sister in Heworth. Unfortunately, as we made final arrangements for the wedding, only seven weeks away, I felt an increasing sense of unease. I had to tell Marie I couldn't go through with it. We spent the next few days driving round to the woman making the dress, the firm from whom we were hiring the vehicles, the place we'd booked for the reception, cancelling them all. It was something we felt we should do personally, rather than by phone and it wasn't easy. Most people were incredibly understanding and some even gave us refunds, but Marie's family found it hard to take. My mother thought it was just last minute nerves, but I knew it wasn't: it was that gut feeling that I've learned to trust over the years, telling me that it wasn't right. It wasn't that I didn't care for Marie. She was a great girl and I still fancied her like mad, but I couldn't see us being happily together in a few years' time.

◊

On my appraisal it said I had "a good arrest rate for a quiet sub-division." These words consigned me to a move to the West End, one of the busiest – if not *the* busiest – sub-divisions in the Northumbria Police area. While I was still in my first year in the police, I'd been approached to apply for the Graduate Entry Scheme. This was intended to encourage young graduates to enter the police service from universities, the armed forces or elsewhere by offering the incentive of accelerated promotion and the lure of becoming an inspector in five years. Recent recruits were also eligible and Northumbria persuaded me to apply, but I did so rather reluctantly as I didn't want any preferential treatment because of my degree. The force was obviously short of people who met the criteria.

I went down to Sussex Police HQ in Lewes where I spent several days being interviewed, observed during exercises and tested in a variety of ways. We were divided into groups of six. I remember in my group there was a quietly confident guy, currently working for the Post Office, and a preening self-promoter on the point of leaving the Royal Navy. Each group had a panel of three interviewers. Ours included a Deputy Chief Constable and a retired member of MI5. Although I had less than a year's service, I was still the longest-serving officer of all the applicants attending. On the first evening, when introductions were taking place, I wore a Northumbria Police Athletic Association tie, the force not having one of its own at that time. We were standing in a line being introduced to the panel members as they walked along in front of us. The ex-MI5 man asked me what the tie was and I told him. The naval guy, who was next in line, piped up, "Actually, I think it's cheating – wearing a police tie."

"And what's yours?" asked the panellist, moving on to him.

"The old Harrovians' Rugby Club, of which I'm a drinking member . . ." he trotted out.

So wearing a police tie was cheating, but wearing a tie announcing you'd been to Harrow Public School was fair play. Old school tie stuff indeed . . .

We were clearly the two strongest characters in our group and tended to disagree with each other during discussions, unsurprisingly. When the subject was the NHS and whether it was a failing organisation that should be abandoned, he argued in favour of that proposition, whereas I maintained that on my travels I'd found our health service was the envy of virtually every country I'd visited.

Each group had an observer present, and in our case it was Sir Kenneth Newman, then Chief Constable of the Royal Ulster Constabulary, and subsequently Commissioner of the Metropolitan Police. He was a small, elfin figure with large pointed ears. At the end of my personal interview by the panel I was asked if I had any questions and I said I had one for Mr Newman. One panellist responded that Sir Kenneth was there as an observer and not to answer questions from interviewees. I responded that I was keen to learn and would probably never have the opportunity again. Sir Kenneth chipped in that he was more than happy to answer any question I had for him and I said that I'd recently read an article suggesting that the presence of international media in Belfast had an inflammatory effect on the situation, rioters performing for the cameras . . . He agreed with this argument and referred me to some other sources.

In the course of my interview I'd been asked which paper I read and I'd said, "The *Guardian* – the wrong one, I know."

"And why do you think that might be the wrong one in our eyes?"

"Because of its views, not all of which I share. But I've bought it in the past for its advertisements for teaching posts and summer jobs on archaeological sites and I like its style."

"So what do you think would be the 'right' newspaper, Mr Harvey?"

"The *Telegraph*, possibly the *Times*."

"Well, I assure you, there's no such thing as the 'right' paper as far as we're concerned."

Needless to say, I wasn't selected. The Post Office and the Navy representatives were, so I reckoned that constituted an honourable draw between the forces of Good and Evil. I read the results in the only newspaper which printed the names of the successful applicants – the *Telegraph*.

Chapter 7

I was not entirely happy about my move to the West End. The police station was much bigger and a lot less friendly than Whickham. Despite my best efforts, things did not go well. A few months after my transfer, on New Year's Eve, my relief was on night shift. I was double-crewed in a panda, driven by an experienced officer. We were out on patrol when, just after half-ten, a call came in about a fight at the Hawthorn Pub on Benwell Lane, right on the sub-division's western boundary. As we drove there the radio updates reported a large disturbance and officers requiring assistance. I was out of the vehicle almost before it had stopped moving. As I entered the premises the combatants seemed to stop for a second before resuming the several battles even more furiously. I separated two men who were fighting right in front of me, getting each of them in a headlock. The next moment I felt a third man behind me pulling me back and down. I fell on him and the two guys who I was still holding fell on top of me. I felt a tearing sensation inside my left knee and then a searing pain. My leg was now useless and I was defenceless on the floor. I managed to crawl through the gap in the counter and lay behind the bar as other police officers arrived and the fray continued.

I was taken to Newcastle General, opposite the West End Police Station. It is not the place you would choose to spend your New Year's Eve. The scene there was scarcely more orderly than in the pub, and the poor medical staff were struggling to cope. I was told to come back in the morning. My knee was locked and extremely painful. I gritted my teeth and managed to make my way across the road to the station where I had to complete an injury-on-duty statement. The Inspector told me it was too busy for him to spare anyone to drive me to my house across the river in Whickham and I was unable to contact any of my friends or family as they were all out partying and mobiles were yet to be invented. You couldn't get a taxi to save your life, so I had no choice but to try to drive myself home. I drove most of the way in third gear, barely able to press the clutch. When I parked up at home, I sat still for a couple of minutes, sweating with the strain and pain. It was New Year and I was on my own. It was one of several miserable New Year's Eves I've had. I spent an almost sleepless night, unable to escape the pain or find a comfortable position.

The next morning I was on the operating table. I'd asked the consultant, Mr Pinder, to save as much of my cartilage as he could because I was a keen footballer, but he told me later it was torn right across and he'd had to perform a full medial meniscectomy. The only person I'd managed to get in touch with was Ossie and I'd asked him to tell my parents. This was before the days of keyhole surgery and I was off work for three months, initially on crutches, and in the house by myself. I was concerned that the injury would finish my police career in its embryonic stage and played down the extent of my pain and discomfort to people such as the Criminal Injuries Compensation Board doctors. (I think I received a thousand pounds in the end).

I went to the Police Convalescent Home in Harrogate for intensive physiotherapy. One of the larger-than-life coppers I met there was 'Swazie' Turner, a moustachioed sergeant in the Merseyside dog-handling section who had lost a couple of fingers after being bitten by his Alsatian – think Scouser Jimmy Edwards with a special glove. He subsequently wrote his autobiography, *Off the Cuff*. After the loss of a leg following an attack, he undertook numerous challenging journeys in a standard NHS Lomax wheelchair, raising money for charities and wrote *Onto the Final Leg*. Others who were there included Steve Cram's father, Bill, from my own force, and an inspector from Strathclyde called Laurie Macintyre. He was an astute, ambitious guy with a wry sense of humour from a relatively humble background, who'd got himself selected for accelerated promotion. I visited him several times as he progressed through the ranks to Chief Superintendent. After retiring, he became Head of Security & Facilities for Glasgow Rangers.

◊

Time dragged while I was off work and recovering alone in my new house. On March 12th 1981 my sister took me for a trip up to Edinburgh. It was Mike Knox's birthday. On leaving St Mary's College he'd got a job at Holy Rood High School there. Helen and I went to the olde-worlde Sheep Heid pub nearby and met up with him when he'd finished work. It transpired that there was a surprise party for him and we were invited along by the friends who were hosting it. There were one or two people I'd met before. I said, 'Hello' to a tall, good-looking guy I thought I recognised as John Kinane, one of Mike's ex-pupils who'd visited me in Gateshead with him. It turned out to be his older brother, Michael. I met a couple of their five sisters, Ellen and Margaret, both stunning.

By April I was back at work and, as suspected, things were no easier for me at the West End. My supervisory sergeant gave me a scathing appraisal – I was totally incompetent at all aspects of police work and couldn't be trusted to function properly on the streets. I had my appraisal appointment with Paul Whitehouse and my defence was that a police officer who was seen as a good prospect, with a good arrest record and appraisals, doesn't suddenly become a useless one: appraisals say as much about the appraiser as the appraised. As subtly as I could, I was asking him to read between the lines. He talked of extending my probation, which in the police was two years. This recalled wry memories of my teaching days. I felt my only hope was a transfer to another station, although for an officer to have three different postings in his probation was extremely rare. He decided to send me to Gosforth, a generally middle-class area to the north of Newcastle, from which it is separated by the Town Moor. It was where I'd attended primary school and only three miles from where I'd grown up, so I knew it pretty well.

I was welcomed to the subdivision by Superintendent 'Jock' Telfer, a bluff but affable Scot. He was very direct and said he'd read my file and that anyone looking at my last appraisal would think I was a wanker. After I'd answered several questions, he said he didn't think I was a wanker, and that I would be given a fair chance to show that I had the makings of a good police officer.

◊

One morning, on 'early day' (6am – 2pm), I was given the task of covering the mobile police station at the Newcastle Hoppings. Every year, in the third week of June, the largest travelling fair in Europe is held on the Town Moor. A huge area of land was covered by scream-generating rides and penny-rolling amusement arcades, coconut shies and shooting galleries, candy floss and toffee apple stalls, walls of death and halls of mirrors, 'freak shows' and strippers' tents, boxing booths and fortune tellers' caravans. My task was simply to take over from the night shift officer until I was, in turn, relieved. Maybe that was the cause of the problem: it was too easy. The muddy landscape (it always seemed to rain that week) was empty except for crushed cans, plastic bottles and fast food wrappings, around which a few scabby dogs scavenged.

I locked up the cabin behind me, walked down the two temporary steps and watched my police boots sink into the squidgy surface. I took a lonely stroll around the deserted site under a grey sky. The contrast with the vitality and bright lights that I knew would have filled the scene the previous night was striking. A few early workers were starting to make their way along the footpaths crossing the Moor to the city. I made my way back to the mobile station, taking care to try and minimise the amount of mud I took with me on my boots. I felt in my pocket for the key. It wasn't there – must be the wrong pocket. It wasn't in any of my pockets. I had a sickening feeling in the pit of my stomach. I spent several minutes checking and rechecking every pocket in my uniform. On the opposite side of the cabin from The Great North Road, a few yards away, traffic was now beginning to build up as people travelled to work. I was going to be out of a job, the way things were going.

Reluctantly, I radioed my sergeant, Dave Hand, and asked for a conference point with him at the temporary station. He bounced up to the cabin in his boyish, chirpy way and I explained my dilemma, details of which I had not wanted to give over the radio where everyone would have been able to hear them. It was bad enough to have to tell him I couldn't find the key. His response sent my spirits down into the mire. The station had been transported up from Sheffield and there wasn't a spare key. I didn't want to believe this was true. I had a sharp image in my brain of a queue of officers turning up for their overtime shifts in the afternoon to be told that some wanker of a probationer had lost the key. Dave Hand drove off. I turned and walked disconsolately away. A woman approached me and I thought, 'Please God, don't let this be anything that requires access to the cabin'.

"Excuse me, officer. Can I hand something in?"

I took my notebook out. At least I could record the details there.

"Yes, what is it?" I asked wearily.

"A key."

"Where did you find it?"

"Just walking along through here just now."

I looked up from my writing and recognised it immediately. I wanted to pick her up and swing her around.

"Thank you," I said. "I'm sure whoever lost it will be very grateful."

As soon as she'd gone I opened the station door, radioed Dave Hand and told him the situation had been resolved and thanked God for the miraculous recovery of something so small that it could have been buried anywhere in the mud on a site stretching over several acres.

◊

The Toxteth riots broke out in the summer of 1981 and several riot-trained officers from our sub-division were sent to Liverpool. I was on twelve hour shifts, covering for the missing, more experienced officers. Starting foot patrol at 6 p.m. and finishing at 6 a.m. was exhausting and on occasion I found myself hallucinating due to fatigue. I was probably still not eating properly as I struggled to make my mortgage repayments.

One morning, just before I was due to finish, I was patrolling in the early morning light when I saw a young guy carrying a wicker shopping basket. It was covered so I couldn't see what was in it and it seemed an incongruous thing for him to be carrying. I greeted him but he didn't respond so I picked up my pace. He started running, dropped the basket as I chased after him, calling in on my radio. It was a long chase and I still wasn't at full fitness after my knee injury. As he turned a corner he took a look behind him to see how far ahead of me he was. When I got round the corner there was no sign of him so I made my way back to where the basket was and collected up all the coins that had come out of it. I put the basket and its contents through POFP (Property Other than Found Property). I was really frustrated at not having caught him. It felt like fielding on the boundary in a cricket match and having nothing to do all game until the last ball when the batsman skies it towards you and you drop the catch.

It transpired that the cash was from a one-armed bandit in a High Street café which had been broken into overnight. I discovered from the collator's records, when I went in early the next evening, that there had been another burglary at the café recently and the culprit had been arrested. I then went to the photo album of offenders to see if it was the same youth I had chased. It wasn't. I next looked up who his 'associates' were and went looking for their photos. Sure enough, there was my man. The crime had been passed over to CID for investigation by this time but I told my sergeant, an ex-RCS (Regional Crime Squad) guy called Dennis Forman, about the result of my enquiries. We arrested the suspect, who was so astounded at officers turning up at his door that he 'coughed' the offence. Apparently, he had hidden under a vehicle once he was out of my sight, something I always watched for subsequently in similar circumstances. Unfortunately, my sergeant didn't just use this incident to praise my persistence and police work but took the line, "If a probationer could do this, why couldn't detectives?" Naturally, this didn't endear me to CID.

◊

I continued to develop my reputation as a good thief-taker and my probation was successfully completed. I was sent on a police driving course, which qualified me to drive police vehicles. A couple of incidents come to my mind from this period of my service. Each caused me a different kind of guilt.

The first was one of my earliest attempts at stopping a vehicle and advising the driver. I had illuminated the POLICE STOP sign on top of the Panda and the car had pulled in behind me on Grandstand Road. I spoke to the driver about his minor offence and gave him appropriate advice before letting him go on his way. I then drove a short distance and pulled into a lay-by to write up my notebook. After a little while I looked up and saw a vehicle in my mirror. It was parked up behind me with the driver inside. I got out and as I did so, I noticed that the POLICE STOP sign was still lit up. My thoughts were racing as I strode slowly towards the car.

"Evening, officer," said the nervous driver through the open window.

"You know why I've stopped you, don't you?"

"Yes," he replied anxiously.

"Well, don't let it happen again. Now off you go . . ." I said, turning and walking back towards the police car.

The second incident took place on a night shift. It was about 2 a.m., cold and crisp. Again I was single-crewed while other members of the shift were on their refreshments. I was driving slowly around Broadway West, a local council estate. There was nobody on the streets except a man out walking his dog. I stopped to speak to him and noticed what looked like steam from a central heating boiler coming from the side of a house on the other side of the road, so went to investigate. As I walked down the side of the building, I realised it wasn't steam but smoke. The kitchen door was slightly ajar and I could see the room was well alight. I knew from my training not to enter through that door as I would give the blaze an oxygen boost. I radioed in that I had found a house fire and ran back to the car for my gloves.

I then knocked on the door of the adjoining house and a young man came out. I asked him if there was anyone in the house next door and he told me the whole family was in. As I shouldered and kicked the front door, the thought of not being able to get in while a family died in the fire gave me the adrenaline I needed and with the neighbour's help, I broke in. He searched the downstairs while I crept low up the stairs, under the smoke, but I couldn't find anyone in the bedrooms. I came back down and the neighbour said he'd not found anyone either. My relief was tempered when I realised there could still be someone in the kitchen. I was steeling myself to go in when I heard the fire engine's siren as it came up the street. I went outside and told the first fireman we had searched everywhere but the kitchen. Two men wearing breathing apparatus went straight in.

After they had put out the fire and searched the building thoroughly, I went back in.

"Who found the fire?" asked the lead fireman.

"I did," I said, rather too eagerly, stepping forward.

"Give the man a medal," said one of the firemen, damping down in more ways than one.

The Lead Fireman pointed at one wall where, written in blistered paint, were the words, 'I HATE YOU DAD'.

"Well, it should be detectable, anyway," I said.

The first police officer at the scene was the night shift CID.

He told me to go back to the station and write my statement regarding the incident.

It was only then that I realised none of the shift had turned up. When I got back to Gosforth I found out that my sergeant had continued playing cards with the station sergeant and the other members of the shift on their refreshments.

When I submitted my statement to the CID officer who went on to become a senior officer, he told me to 'write the neighbour out' of my statement. I got a commendation.

Chapter 8

Heading up to Edinburgh for Mike Knox's birthday party, I wondered if the girl I'd met the year before would be there. She was, and we got on really well. Although Maggie spoke with a Scottish accent, her parents were both Irish – her mother, Anne, was from near Limerick and her father, Jerry, was a Tipperary man. They had met and married in Edinburgh and had had eight children in nine years. The last time Anne was pregnant, Jerry had returned home from his job on the buses to find an ambulance outside the house and his wife in the back of it.

"What's the matter?" Jerry had asked breathlessly.

"I'm having a baby," she'd replied impatiently.

The crew had delivered a baby girl. To everyone's surprise, one of them then said, "I think there's another one."

"Turn the light off," Jerry had said. "I think it's attracting them." They delivered the other twin a few minutes later.

◊

The following June, Maggie and I got engaged with a view to getting married the next summer. She had another year to go at Edinburgh College of Art where she was doing a degree in Drawing & Sculpture.

We went on a trip to Ireland with my sister and her friend, Ian. I had been keen to meet Maggie's relatives and I wasn't disappointed. We stayed with members of Jerry's family in Tipperary, playing cards and being very well looked after on the farms. One day we went to see her Uncle John on his hill farm, up a narrow boreen (country lane), with another of Jerry's brothers, Michael, who was a bulky figure and formerly a good hurler with characteristically huge hands with notched fingers. He now suffered from depression and moved in a slow, bovine way. His face showed little expression and he spoke in a low, considered manner. As he sat, filling the front passenger seat, we made our way back down the boreen, having been plied with bacon, cabbage, spuds and poteen. The magnetic crucifix my Nan had given me fell off the dashboard of my Chrysler Alpine.

"That's the second time he's fallen off today," I commented.

"Sure," Michael said, dryly, "Didn't Jayzus fall a third time?"

I was very happy with this wider family I was marrying into.

◊

Maggie's last year at college was naturally a busy one. She was building up her pieces for the final show and I helped in the casting of a brilliant bronze head of her mother. Our wedding was arranged for July 28th, just a few days after her graduation. Towards the end of 1983 my father was diagnosed with cancer of the oesophagus: the prognosis was not good – they told him six months might be a possibility if he was lucky. He went onto a strict regime of nuts and pulses and lived to see his five grandchildren born.

As the Orwellian year, 1984, arrived there were increasing signs that there would be a miners' strike. By now I was riot-trained and likely to be deployed if required. I had mixed feelings, in that I had a lot of sympathy with the miners' cause: my 'A' level History dissertation was entitled, 'Thomas Hepburn and his Union: Being an Account of the Durham and Northumberland Miners and Their Leader, Especially during the Strike Years of 1831 and '32'. I deplored Thatcher, but nor did I like Scargill, or the way he conducted things. However, I was a young man who did not want to be left behind while his colleagues went off to take part in what would clearly be a historic dispute.

Just before I was about to be deployed – it might even have been the evening before – I was on duty in Kenton with a lad called Gordon Barrass. Two calls of public disorder came in at almost the same time, one to a location in Jesmond and one to the car park of the King's Court in

Kingston Park (now a Boots). They could hardly have been much further apart within the sub-division. Most resources were already travelling to Jesmond as we made our way to the King's Court.

We could hardly believe our eyes on our arrival. At least twenty young men were fighting outside the pub. We jumped out of the Panda and I tried to separate two youths, but one of them continued fighting. I immediately recognised him as a local youth who'd tried to wind me up before when I was not in a position to do anything about it. Well, he'd had his chance to stop fighting and rejected it. I arrested him for breach of the peace but he continued to struggle violently. Another youth came to try and prise him away from me and I saw that Gordon had drawn his truncheon in an effort to prevent any of the other youths attempting to help their friend escape. The youth I had in a head grip fought ferociously as his pal kicked at my legs and tried to trip me up. I was getting tired by this time and at one point went down onto one knee, still holding the combatant. As his pal swung back his foot, I had a momentary mental image of standing in St John's Church, Portobello, on my wedding day, with a broken nose. I turned my head away at the last instant before impact and the boot hit the left side of my chest.

I did not realise it at the time, but it jammed my police radio button on in my left pocket, so all the other officers in the sub-division could hear a stream of blows and expletives. I could have done with them being there, especially my sergeant, a big jovial bloke called Dave Peart whose hobbies included Cumberland wrestling. Eventually, he and the troops arrived, scattering or arresting the others. Little Jimmy Cockburn got hurt trying to prise the pal off me, but I was left kneeling astride my arrest. He spat in my face, so I twisted his neck, turning his head away from me so that he couldn't repeat it. At this point a bystander approached, identified himself as a local councillor, and told me he'd just seen me use unnecessary force on a detained person. I was tempted to say if he'd been there for any length of time I'd arrest him for the common law offence of failing to assist a police officer in the execution of his duty. I may have said something else.

As I travelled back to Gosforth with my prisoner – Kenton had no cells – I became conscious that the full-blooded kick to the chest had done some damage to my back. I had considerable discomfort to the lower right side, something I'm still experiencing even as I write this now, all these years later. I was examined by the police surgeon – as was Jimmy – but was worried it might prevent me from heading down south with my sergeant and other colleagues.

I was passed fit for duty and was part of the contingent from Northumbria Police sent to RAF Scampton, home of The Red Arrows aerial display team, near Lincoln. Most of that time is a blur of backache, boredom, shortage of sleep, and playing cards in the back of police vans. The plastic seat covers were used as card tables, making the wooden slatted seats even more uncomfortable, but I couldn't complain or people would question why I was there if I wasn't fit. I remember a little character called John 'Stumpy' Stevenson who would do things like pick up the ball in the middle of a game of football and kick it miles away, just for the hell of it – with his 'cheeky chappie' manner, he could get away with it. In between trips away on picket duty and normal patrol I was going for extensive physiotherapy with Eric, a local traffic warden who was highly rated for his restorative skills. The arrangement was that he would be paid by results but he could only lessen my pain briefly before it recurred with increasing ferocity.

◊

In June I was sent, with three colleagues from Kenton, to Yorkshire, and based at RAF Driffield. By this time I was having to wait until everyone else had got out of the van before discreetly lowering myself to the ground. On the morning of June 18th, we were woken around 3 a.m., provided with an airline meal, and driven to Orgreave coking plant. Northumbria Police officers were in the front line of what was to become known as the 'Battle of Orgreave'. We were in our ordinary police uniforms. As large numbers of striking miners approached us, a line of shield-bearing South Yorkshire officers was placed in front of us.

It was a beautiful summer's morning with the red sun of dawn becoming a golden disc above us. It was a strange stand-off with Arthur Scargill in his baseball cap walking among the strikers, rallying his troops, and the South Yorkshire Assistant Chief Constable, Tony Clement, riding up and down on horseback behind our lines. There was a lot of to-ing and fro-ing and insults being exchanged. We were called Thatcher's lackeys and 'beetle-brains'. After a while, some of the miners started throwing objects at us. There was one striker in particular who was lobbing rocks at us from behind a little knoll, a few yards behind the miners' front line. I was keen to get him. The South Yorkshire Chief Inspector in charge of that section gave the four of us from Kenton permission to go in and try to arrest him. We set off, but hadn't got far before our inspector called us back.

After a few hours, the miners went back over the hill and lines of officers were withdrawn from the back, together with the officers carrying long shields in front of us, leaving us unprotected, hot, hungry and thirsty. We'd been there the longest, standing in the heat for hours without a toilet break or refreshment. Suddenly a wave of miners came over the hill and we were subjected to a volley of missiles. It was like an industrial dispute version of the film, *Zulu*. A stone hit my helmet and ricocheted, injuring the officer to my left. I picked up the stone and put it in my pocket.

My recollection of what happened next is a little hazy, like the day itself. My perception of events is that, far away to our left, one of Northumbria's men (there were no women officers there, as far as I'm aware) broke ranks and was charging forward with his baton raised. I remember thinking, 'This is what really happens in a battle – not some general's brilliant tactics but some individual deciding, "stuff this for a game of soldiers", raising his weapon and charging, and those around him following suit.' Then the mounted section charged through and it really was like the set of a historical film. There was some hand-to-hand fighting as most of the strikers retreated towards the railway line, while other strikers sat in passive groups. I showed the piece of stone to the *Times* correspondent at the scene, explaining how we'd had missiles and abuse hurled at us for hours in the heat. "What other police force in the world would have tolerated that for so long?" I asked him, realising that we were likely to be portrayed in the media as having overreacted.

Afterwards, we were asked to provide statements in relation to the day's events. (In 2016, when searching online for details of my colleague Tommy Francis' funeral details, having been informed of his untimely death, I found our statements, counter-signed by each other, presumably released under the thirty-year rule).

◊

I returned to Tyneside safely. My wedding was only weeks away and preparations were well advanced. Anne had wanted the reception to be at The George Hotel in Edinburgh's George Street and so it was. I invited Mike Knox, Ossie and Michael Roche, as well as a number of villagers from Caldbeck. My brother was my best man and Steve Ashton my groomsman. I had about three stag dos in Newcastle, all involving 5-a-side games. There was a real danger I would be bundled onto some ship heading out of the Tyne into the North Sea the night I went out with my shift – it had been done before . . .

Our wedding day was the blur that you're told it will be. The only words I recall were from a tipsy passer-by calling out to Maggie, "Ah like yer hat, hen . . ."

The next day we drove down to Newcastle in our tin-can-towing car, removing them once outside Edinburgh. We flew from there to the Greek island of Santorini where we spent our honeymoon, staying in a little place run by locals, Joannis and Maria, and their daughter, Martha.

On our return, we headed back up to Edinburgh for the wedding of Maggie's 'big sister, Marian', as she always referred to her. Because the family home in Moira Terrace was full, we stayed overnight at a B&B in nearby Joppa, run by an old couple Jerry knew. Marian was marrying Miguel, a Spaniard from Gijon where she lived and worked, teaching English. It was just a family affair, with the reception held in a small function room at The George Hotel.

Nine months later our first son, Matthew, was born. The christening was a bittersweet occasion as a few weeks earlier Maggie's mother had died suddenly.

One weekend we took him down to Derby on a visit to see Maggie's brother John who was teaching there. He was a great all-round sportsman and played for a Sunday League team managed by the legendary Brian Clough. We went to a match and I was amazed to see Nigel Clough, then about nineteen but already in Nottingham Forest's first team, running the line. His brother, Simon, and one or two of his cousins were also in the team. Cloughie walked up to Maggie who was holding Matthew in her arms and chucked him under the chin, saying, "Fine boy you've got there . . ."

Thirteen months after Matthew, Martha Anne was born and we began looking for a bigger house to cope with our growing family. We found a buyer for ours but hadn't seen anything we liked. In the end we decided that rather than lose the purchaser of our property, we'd move into a police house until something suitable turned up. We spent a happy interlude living in 26 Brackenfield Road. Both Gosforth and Kenton police stations were within walking distance from there, which made life a good bit easier. I had lots of interesting little cases and decent arrests during the years I worked there. I remember taking a report from Brian Johnson of AC/DC at his house of the theft of his Blaupunkt car radio; I think it was worth £2000. I couldn't imagine owning a car worth that much, never mind a radio.

Another high-profile encounter I had there resulted from the report of an RTA in Broadway East. I was tutor constable for a young probationer from Sunderland. A pedestrian had been knocked over and the vehicle involved had been driven off. We cruised round looking for a vehicle fitting its description but without success. Some time later the city centre night shift inspector had radioed in to say he'd found a vehicle matching the one circulated, with damage that was consistent with having been involved in a collision with a pedestrian. The car was parked near St James' Park, Newcastle United's ground, and when we arrived, I was concerned to see the windscreen was badly smashed. The last time I'd seen a similar one had been a recent accident which had resulted in a fatality. Documents in the vehicle bore the name Paul Gascoigne – at that time he was an emerging talent at the football club. I asked the Acting Sergeant if we could go over to Dunston, where he lived, to pursue the matter. We took another officer with us, not because I was expecting trouble but I was never completely confident in following the breath test procedure, whereas he had aspirations to be a traffic cop.

Mr Gascoigne Senior was pleasant enough, considering he'd been woken up. He told us Paul wasn't there, but at his girlfriend's, and gave us the address. When we found Paul he started to flannel but eventually said that he and his pal, Jimmy Gardner, had had a couple of halves in the Three Mile Inn and then he'd gone to show him his clubmate Darren Jackson's house. He began to cry, believing his football career would now be over. (Billy Whitehurst, a big bustling bully of a centre-forward, had been recently dismissed by the club for driving offences). I tried to reassure him that was unlikely to be the case. It was interesting to read, years later, 'Gazza's (as he was by then universally known) version of events in his autobiography, written with the assistance of Hunter Davies, where he said he'd smashed the front windscreen to make it look as if the car had been stolen (pages 47-48 of *Gazza: My Story*).

Chapter 9

After seven years of shifts and foot patrol, much as I enjoyed old-style 'coppering', I was ready for a change. Although earlier I'd resisted the idea of being a teacher in the police service, I now saw training as the best option for promotion – more money and less anti-social hours. After discussing it with Maggie, I applied for a training course, and I was finally allocated one in early 1987. It meant being three months away from home, based at the CPU (Central Planning Unit) in Pannal Ash, Harrogate, an hour-and-a-half's drive away. It was far from ideal, leaving my wife with two toddlers, but we both agreed it was a necessary evil. I got home most weekends, but it still took its toll on both of us. Furthermore, we suspected that Maggie might be pregnant again. While I was away Maggie suffered terrible stomach pains and was rushed into the QE (Queen Elizabeth Hospital) in Gateshead. I dashed back. It turned out to be kidney stones and she subsequently miscarried.

After passing the course, I returned to the Kenton office briefly, before being posted to Probationer Training at Northumberland HQ. I enjoyed my time there but after several months I was next in line to go to the NEDPTC (North East District Police Training Centre) as a Temporary Sergeant for two years, becoming substantive sergeant after one. NEDPTC had moved from Dishforth to Durham since my days as a new recruit, and I could get to Aykeley Heads, the Durham Force HQ site where it was located, in less time than it took me to get to our HQ in those days, before the Western Bypass was built. Nevertheless, it still meant being away from home from Sunday evening to Friday afternoon each week.

I went to my Superintendent in the training department and said I would be happy to stay in Probationer Training if there was any possibility of being promoted in-house, as this was much more suitable for me, domestically. He stated it was not force policy to promote within the department in this way. I discussed this in depth with Maggie. As the alternative was to stay in the department and watch others leapfrog over me to promotion, we decided that the only option was go to Durham. The PC behind me in the queue (there were always two PCs in the department) was Kevin Bray, a married guy without kids who was keen to go to District Training. A couple of months later he phoned me at Durham to invite me to his promotion do. I was delighted for him.

"You've been made up to sergeant . . . That's brilliant, Kevin. Where are you going?"

"Er, nowhere," he replied awkwardly. "They've promoted me internally . . ."

◊

I hadn't been in my new role more than a week or two when Maggie gave birth to Joseph Jeremiah. He was christened Joseph for lots of reasons, including the fact that Joe Harvey had been captain of Newcastle United on two of the three occasions when we had lifted the FA Cup in the fifties and manager when we'd won our last decent piece of silverware – the old Fairs Cup in 1969. Jeremiah was my father-in-law, Jerry's, real name.

At the training centre, I was teamed up with a female officer from Durham Constabulary. Our class had some excellent students, several from my own force, including the best female five-a-side player I've ever seen. Five-a-side was one of about nine or ten activities for which there were prizes and they were all highly competitive. Our class won five or six of the trophies.

One day, during some free time, a trainer who I'd not really talked to before approached me and asked if I fancied a game of snooker.

"Sure," I replied.

As the game progressed, the trainer, chalking his cue as he eyed up a shot, said, "You know, Steve, this is the age of the mediocre man . . ."

I felt as if I was in a scene from *The Hustler*. I was being warned off.

My metaphorical thumbs were in danger of being broken. Kipling's line, "Nor look too good, nor talk too wise . . ." came to mind.

The culmination of the ten-week training period was the 'passing out' parade, and as chance would have it, this one was to be inspected by Princess Anne. Night after night we'd put in extra hours on the parade ground to ensure that all was perfect for the occasion. One day I had a narrow window of opportunity to pop back home to see Maggie and my three young children. I decided I should do it by the book and ask my Inspector's permission, which he somewhat grudgingly gave, but stated I must be back for the drill practice at 6 p.m. Unfortunately, I was delayed and as I took my place, a few minutes late on the drill square, I was bawled at by my Inspector in front of everyone and told to report to him after practice. When we'd finished, he put me straight up before the Deputy, telling him I'd gone home in the afternoon and tried to slip unnoticed onto the parade ground after drill practice had started. He omitted to mention he had given me permission to visit my family, but I knew any mention of this would seal my fate: he was covering his back and if I exposed him to any possibility of criticism he would 'get' me, one way or another.

My end of class appraisal was carefully penned by the Chief Inspector to minimise the considerable successes of our class and stress my difficulties in committing myself completely to my students due to my domestic circumstances. This was despite the fact that I'd never asked for any concessions except for that one afternoon and had spent extra hours coaching my students in law and at five-a-side. I had to attend a meeting at Northumbria Police HQ to discuss my situation with a senior officer who said I was to return as a PC. The only concession was that he would allow me to choose which station. I asked for Whickham. It was my nearest station and one where I had spent one of the happier times of my short service.

Back at Durham, the Inspector asked me how the meeting had gone. I said something to the effect of how did he expect it to go. He told me that there were two ways I could leave and it was up to me which one I chose. I managed to control my feelings and told him I was going back to Whickham.

"Well, that was the best I could do for you," he said, not realising I knew he'd had nothing to do with where I was to be stationed.

I left Durham with the chorus of the Roger Whittaker number, 'Durham Town', ringing in my brain and a pewter tankard from my second class which I'd had to leave halfway through their course, engraved:

'PRESENTED TO
SGT HARVEY
BEST WISHES FROM
CLASS 1 COURSE 2 / 88
N.E.D.P.T.C.'

I returned to Whickham. I was no longer a sergeant, having forfeited my temporary promotion by my enforced return to my parent force. All our sacrifices had been for nothing and I was right back where I'd started. I ended up on the same shift as one of my students from my first class who habitually called me 'Sarge' and asked me for advice. I had to refer him to the patrol sergeant because I didn't want to give any potentially conflicting opinion or appear to be undermining his position.

Graham Stafford, my previous inspector in the force's probationer training phoned me at work and said I could tell him where to go, but he would be delighted to have me back. I discussed it with Maggie and we decided it was a good option, domestically. This posting was a brief, but relatively happy interlude. Graham was an obliging boss, and he wrote me an appraisal that in other walks of life would have been well received, including as it did terms such as 'intuitive', 'innovative' and 'forward-thinking'. I told him it could not have been more damning in the bosses' eyes but we both knew I wasn't going to be promoted whatever he'd written.

My next move was due to two officers from my police past (I never really felt I had what I could call a career, as such, in the police). PC 3684 Bill Forth, from my probationer days when we'd travelled down to Dishforth together, was due to get promoted and wanted to move into training; Inspector Dave Hand, who had been my sergeant at Gosforth when I lost the key for the Hoppings mobile station, was his boss and wanted me to replace him. The post was PC in charge of the force's 'innovative' clerical Youth Training Scheme. Looking after half-a-dozen civilian trainers and 150 sixteen and seventeen-year-olds did not appeal at all, and I turned down the post at least once before eventually being persuaded to take it. As so often happened, it turned out to be one of the most rewarding roles in my police service.

I was based at Jarrow in an old brick building that used to be a police hostel. I relished the responsibility and introduced lots of new ideas, such as a magnetic board for moving around the names of the trainees for their different police and civilian placements rather than a messy board with marker pens. I travelled throughout the force area, from Berwick in the north to Birtley in the south, seeking out new and interesting placements for the trainees. I never took lunch but ate at my desk. I had rediscovered my motivation. The one day I did go out for a walk at lunchtime was remarkable for two reasons: the first was that the staff obviously thought something strange was going on and suspected me of meeting a woman, and the second was that on my stroll I looked through the glass door panels of a locked local church and saw a notice about a nun in Peru, supported by that parish – it was Maggie's Auntie Kitty.

Chapter 10

In time, the force decided to civilianise my post and I was subsequently promoted to patrol sergeant at Gateshead, which at that time was the joyriding capital of Europe. My inspector was Derrick Scougal who was several years younger than me and had been a probationer at Gosforth when I was there. For a second, I wondered how we'd get on and then I realised that there wouldn't be a problem. Although I didn't know him well, he was a Scottish graduate who was bright, confident and competent, and therefore wouldn't feel threatened by me – the usual cause of my difficulties with supervision.

Nevertheless, I was apprehensive as I drove the short distance from Whickham to Gateshead to begin my first night shift. I had done very little operational policing in the last few years, and now I was going in at the deep end as patrol sergeant at a very busy station. Would I be completely out of my depth? I managed to get through all the procedural stuff – reading out any information the shift needed to know before going out on patrol, pairing people up and allocating refreshment times – without any major gaffes. When the bait times came around at 1 and 2 a.m., Derrick did something I'd never experienced a shift inspector to do before. He contacted the control room and told them to use 'supervision' as a resource to respond to calls while the shift took their refreshments. That night was absolutely wild, with us chasing a succession of stolen vehicles and Derrick at one point driving blind at high speed over a crossroads in what was known as The Avenues area of Bensham. Towards the end of the shift, a traffic officer was chasing a vehicle north along Coatsworth Road in Bensham. Derrick drove flat out down Bensham Avenue, heading west towards Team Valley, the road forming the bar of the T-junction with Coatsworth Road, although it is an oblique rather than a right angle. As we approached at speed, the stolen vehicle came sharply out of Coatsworth Road and up towards us, with the traffic car in very, very close pursuit. We were in the middle of the road and the stolen car went to our right, passing between us and a wall, while the traffic car went to our left. The traffic officer was one of the few Asian officers we had in Northumbria at that time, but I swear he went white as he passed us by inches.

The stolen vehicle crashed and its driver was arrested. It was classed as a police RTA, but as I'd been involved in the pursuit, I was spared having to deal with it.

As I drove home a few hours later, in the early morning light, my sandwiches still untouched in their bag in the back, I saw the skid marks left from the near-collision. I don't think they were the only ones caused by that incident . . .

◊

Derrick and I were in lots of other close scrapes together, often while covering for the shift's refreshment breaks. I remember dropping him off one night at the bottom of Old Durham Road to check out an alarm and a report of someone acting suspiciously while I roared off up the hill towards another job. A few minutes later I heard Derrick calling over the radio for me to return to the scene. There was clearly a scuffle going on. As I drove down the steep hill at speed, I saw an object on the road beside some parked cars. Just then, two figures locked in combat rolled out from behind a parked vehicle in front of me. I swerved to avoid them but heard and felt a bump: luckily it wasn't them I'd gone over, but the object in the road. It was the only time I remember Derrick calling for assistance, an indication of the power of his assailant who we managed to handcuff and arrest.

One night there was information that a large rave was about to take place at the old Key Club, which had changed its name, having been the notorious location back in 1976 of the arrest of Liddle Towers, who subsequently died in police custody. I knew several of the officers who were involved in that case.

"Have you any scruffy clothes in your locker?" Derrick asked, before continuing as if it had been a rhetorical question, "Of course – all your clothes are scruffy – can you go and get changed and come back with the night shift CID?"

I was always selected for these roles due to my beard and informal apparel. I ended up queuing to go into the premises among youngsters passing 'E's to each other. I wasn't wearing a radio because it was bulky and I might have been searched on entry. As I got near the pay desk inside I could see through the doors into the club itself that it was already packed, but a guy on the door, who was a known violent criminal I had once wrestled with over the bonnet of a vehicle during a disturbance, recognised me. It was a scary situation, to say the least. This was a man who had been acquitted of at least one murder. I managed to talk my way out of the place.

Once outside, I found Derrick around the corner.

"Don't ever again ask me to get my civvy gear out of my locker on duty . . ."

He just grinned. We had no power to clear the place, but he knew someone who did. He called out the fire service and they closed the place for being in breach of the fire regulations by virtue of the numbers inside. Not a popular course of action with the party-goers, as you might imagine. I was detained much later than the rest of the shift, writing up my statement in relation to the incident. Later that morning my wife took a call requiring me to return to the station to see the Superintendent – it was not to compliment me on my actions but to ask me why I hadn't arrested the force criminal at the time for threats he'd made to me.

Another time, Derrick called me to attend the travellers' site in Gateshead. There was a gypsy in a caravan with a baby and a knife. I wasn't a trained negotiator, but he asked me to talk to the man. In its own way this was even scarier than the rave incident, since the consequences could have been fatal for the child. The guy was drunk and emotionally bruised and I just kept talking and talking until I found a point of contact. He was Irish and I talked about different parts of Ireland and horse fairs, enticing him to get involved in a conversation until I was able to persuade him to hand the baby over.

"I knew you'd find some common ground," Derrick said, smiling, after I'd emerged, drained, from the caravan.

Working with Derrick at Gateshead was one of the highlights of my professional life. What could have been a difficult experience for me was certainly challenging, but also extremely rewarding, often exhilarating, and generally great fun. When things went well for the shift – as they often did – then the credit was shared; when things went wrong, then it was about 'what can we learn from it?' not 'who can we blame for it?', the more common response in a punitive and scapegoating occupation. I used to tell younger members of the shift, "Don't think it's always like this. You've got an excellent inspector, but one thing you never do with a good boss is take a lend."

◊

1990 was the year the National Garden Festival came to Gateshead. It ran from May to October on a site to the west of the Team Valley Trading Estate and attracted over three million visitors. As a family, we went several times – and our family was due to increase in size again. It was a long, hot summer and by August Maggie was like a beached whale on the front lawn of our home in Cornmoor Road. I took Matthew with me to the Metrocentre, the largest retail outlet in Europe at the time, to get a sprinkler to cool her and the kids down. I couldn't believe it when I was stopped by a security guard from entering the shopping mall. The reason? Matthew, aged five, was not wearing a top due to the heat, and the Metrocentre was owned by the Church of England and the church commissioners had decided that no one without a top should be allowed in.

It was also the year of the World Cup Finals in Italy – Italia 90 with the BBC TV title sequence featuring the unforgettably moving rendition of *Nessun Dorma* by Pavarotti. I watched the West Germany v England game before going into night shift, but once it went to extra time, I had to drive to work, leaving Gazza's tears behind and the game in the balance. I was parked outside Gateshead Police Station listening to the car radio with my hands gripping the steering wheel as Chris Waddle blasted the ball over the bar.

It was also a bumper year for babies: five of Maggie's seven siblings were also pregnant, as was Derrick's wife, Susan, and their Callum and our Gabriel were born within a few days of each other. When I'd taken Maggie into the Princess Margaret late one evening, the nurse had taken us into a room saying she wouldn't be delivering the baby as she was about to go off duty and the night shift was due in. I had my doubts and sure enough Maggie's waters broke and she went very quickly into labour as I pulled the alarm cord. Gabriel was born in about twenty minutes, despite weighing in at a whisker under eleven pounds.

"Ah'll bet that's knackered the elastic," Bill, the front office man, later remarked delicately. My reaction was, "We're going to need a bigger car," and I went to an auction with John Hay, an ex-CID officer who was now a car dealer, and bought a Peugeot 505, one of those old family estates with three rows of seats.

The next year, 1991, my father for some reason gave me £25,000. Maggie and I discussed what to do with it. We didn't need a bigger or better house or car. Holidays were going to be more of a problem than before, now that there were six of us. We discussed a holiday home. I suggested Scotland or Ireland, but Maggie was in favour of France for the better weather and the chance for the children to learn a new language.

For our seventh anniversary, I organised a mini-cruise to Hamburg. The trip itself was easy to arrange; organising babysitters for four children under six was a lot more difficult. Eventually, I had a rota which allowed us to get away for the few days involved. There was a last minute snag with transport – the inevitable pre-holiday mechanical failure – so we borrowed my friend Sandra's car. It was so liberating to get away. We set off south, heading for Harwich and the ferry. We stopped for lunch at Cambridge, a place I'd never been, and I wondered how I would have fared if I had got in to the university – very badly, I suspected. It was such a beautiful day and such an attractive place, with buskers playing classical music in the sunshine, that I got a bit complacent and then realised time was getting on. As I tried, with thinly disguised anxiety, to find our way out of the city, I saw the dreaded radar gun in the hands of a police officer some distance in front of me, and braked. He signalled for me to stop.

I got out to speak to the two officers, conscious of the minutes slipping by as I stood there sweating in my shorts and T-shirt, desperate to get back on the road. The officer who was doing all the talking seemed to sense this and was milking it. His colleague had by this time walked over to the other side of the road in a move I recognised as the 'I'm not with this prick' syndrome.

"What time's your ferry?" he asked laconically. I told him.

"That check-in or sailing time?"

"Sailing."

"You're not going to make that then, are you? You in the army?" he asked, noting my short hair and khaki shorts.

"No," I answered, "the police." Might as well get it out in the open as soon as possible, I thought. If he was going to report me I just wanted him to get on with it and do it and I was getting very close to telling him so.

"What rank?" he asked.

Now I was really bristling. He was entitled to know my occupation but what did my rank have to do with it?

"Sergeant," I said between gritted teeth.

"Got a police sergeant over here, Pete," he yelled over the road. His colleague's body language said it all.

"So, what force you from then?"

"Northumbria."

"Northumbria . . . You've got enough problems already, haven't you?"

"How do you mean?"

"You've got our old Chief up there now, haven't you?"

"Yes, John Stevens." In different circumstances I might have been interested in what a Cambridgeshire officer had to say about our new Chief Constable, but not from him and certainly not at that particular moment.

"You'd best be getting on your way then," he said, folding up his notebook.

"Can you point me in the right direction?" I said.

"Couldn't really say from here, but mind you keep your speed down."

As soon as I was out of their sight I was sweating, swearing and apologising profusely to Maggie, and putting my foot to the floor. It was clear that we would be extremely lucky to make the ferry and, not for the first time, I was cursing my tendency to try to cram too much into one day. "If you can fill the unforgiving minute . . ." is all very well, but I always tried to get an extra second in, often to the chagrin of my companions. For one of the few times in my life, however, I was considering telling a lie. If we missed the ferry there was no second chance and Maggie and I would have to content ourselves with a few days at a B&B in East Anglia, but I couldn't bear the thought of having to tell the family and friends who had so generously given up their time to look after our children that we'd missed the ferry.

I noticed we were now facing another problem – the fuel gauge was tilting towards empty. Did I risk running out of petrol or did I risk missing the ferry by stopping to fill up with petrol? I saw an empty garage, gave Maggie some money and filled up to the exact amount. It might not have been Formula 1 territory, but we were back on track in under a minute.

As we approached the dock area, a policewoman or female security officer came out to stop us but I drove past and parked the car at a rakish angle by the ferry. I jumped out and told Maggie to hold the ship, grabbed our cases and sprinted after her. They pulled the gangplank up as my feet touched the deck.

"I'm going to bloody well enjoy this trip," I thought. "Everything is a bonus now."

The next thing I thought was, "Did I put the handbrake on and lock – or even close the driver's door?" There was no point in worrying about it . . .

The five days we spent in Hamburg were a brief respite from the demands of family life and shift work.

Back at work, things were a bit difficult. On the night of July 7th/8th 1991 I'd been doubled-crewed with Mick Dixon, the other patrol sergeant on our shift at Gateshead at that time. Mick, a bouncy little guy, was Acting Inspector, Derrick being on leave. He took an unmarked car out of the yard, a Ford Sapphire, and drove it around chasing stolen cars, following one of them over the river into Newcastle before losing it in the Jesmond area.

In the early hours of the morning we parked in a corner of the all-night garage on Bensham Road and went in to buy some snacks. It was a bit of a miserable night for July – damp and drizzling. We stopped and chatted with the night shift attendant and then heard a call reporting a ram-raid taking place – ram-raiding was when a stolen vehicle was used to crash through the windows, doors or shutters of closed commercial premises in order to steal things from within and drive off again in that or other vehicles. We said 'so long' and walked out and towards our car.

As we did so, Mick touched me lightly on my arm and whispered, "The car used in the ram-raid is down there," indicating a hard-standing over the wall and about ten feet below the forecourt. "They're out of the vehicle – I'll grab one of them. You drive round and block them in." He thrust the keys at me. It occurred to me it would have been better the other way round as I'd never driven this vehicle and was a bigger and more powerful bloke, but he was the more senior officer.

I got the car started and drove as quietly as I could in an arc, onto Bensham Road, before accelerating at the last moment as I drove down the lane running down the side of the petrol station. As I turned into the standing enclosed by brick walls on two sides, I saw that Mick had missed his target and all of them were in the Golf GTi and driving towards me. I had to make an instant decision – did I risk hitting the GTI and possibly knocking it into Mick, who was just getting to his feet? I braked and they sped past me and down the lane onto Bensham Road, then right towards the Team Valley.

Mick jumped in. I knew I wouldn't be able to catch them, but hoped to keep up with them long enough to get a traffic car involved in the pursuit. Mick was on the radio trying to get other resources there. As we approached the large roundabout at the north end of the Team Valley Trading Estate, they were still only a few hundred yards in front. They sped onto 'the Valley' without slowing noticeably, but a taxi was on the roundabout. I had to brake and then the Sapphire started slewing from left to right like a caravan being towed by a drunken driver. I lost it on the greasy road surface, got it back, lost it, got it back, then lost it again once and for all as we were on the grassy bank and sliding sideways to my left at speed. We were brought to a sudden stop by a lamppost and Mick took the brunt of the collision. I radioed in, reporting a Police RTA and that I required the attendance of an ambulance to deal with my colleague, and police supervision to deal with the accident. I was about three hours into my 39th birthday. When I eventually got back to the station, someone on the shift had left a Fry's chocolate 'Crunchie' Bar on my desk. That's police humour for you . . .

Mick had his shoulder in a sling for a while, but thankfully was not too badly hurt. The car was a write-off and I was grounded, as per procedure, pending the Newcastle City Centre Inspector's report being submitted and a decision taken. I was subsequently suspended from driving any police vehicle for three months.

◊

I was currently Patrol Sergeant at Birtley, a small satellite station. It was to Gateshead what Kenton was to Gosforth – a base from which to police the outlying area, but without any cells etc. It was a great place to be a sergeant: you were your own boss without any of the formality of the Divisional Headquarters. I had a really good shift with officers such as John Brougham, John Gardner, and Christina Recchia. We would do things like have an occasional French breakfast with brie, baguettes, olives and even snails, or go climbing together in the Lake District on a day off. Christina was a great girl – warm, funny, direct and brave as a lioness. Several times when I had called for assistance when struggling with one or more arrests, she'd been first to the scene and had dived straight in. She and John Gardner eventually got married.

Being grounded made carrying out this role really difficult. One day one of the shift was at a 'sudden death' and was asking for my attendance. I had to tell him over the radio that there was no one available to give me a lift up at that time.

"I'll come and collect you," he replied.

"That's right. Stay at that location until I can get someone to collect me . . ."

It was a cardinal sin to leave a suspicious death: protecting the scene was paramount.

One evening, not long afterwards, I was in the Patrol Inspectors' Office in Gateshead, having a discussion with Derrick, who was about to be transferred to Newcastle City Centre as part of his Special Course development programme. Suddenly a bevy of top brass entered the room – new Chief Constable John Stevens (nicknamed 'Psycho'), and an entourage of divisional senior officers. It was part of his whistle-stop tour of the force, one of the largest in the country. Apparently he had two civilian drivers working eight-hour shifts, allowing him to cover as much ground as possible.

After exchanging some questions with Derrick, he turned to me and said, "And have you got anything you'd like to ask, Sarge?"

I sat up in my chair and said, "Yes, sir. I've been grounded for three months and as a patrol sergeant that makes it very difficult to supervise the shift properly. I don't see what's being achieved by the ban. It's not punishing the ram-raiders we were pursuing."

He gave me the official line about the number and cost of police RTAs each year (Police Authorities were a special case, exempted from having to have insurance for their vehicles but required to put a substantial sum aside each year to cover claims).

When he'd finished, Barry Stewart, the Divisional Chief Superintendent and a senior officer for whom I had a lot of respect, said, "Sergeant Harvey's a married man with four children, sir. We took this action for his own protection."

I was taken aback by this comment, as I thought it was an uncharacteristically naff thing to say. It had the hallmark of a normally very rational man trying to explain an action, in keeping with force policy but fundamentally illogical, to his new boss.

"I am thirty-nine years of age, sir. I've been driving for over twenty years. This RTA happened in exceptional circumstances, driving a vehicle I'd only been given the keys to a minute before. If I were an officer with limited driving experience who'd had a couple of bumps in eighteen months, I could see the need for grounding and some element of retraining . . . And I'd like to thank the Chief Superintendent for arranging my appointment at the Family Planning Clinic."

I could sense the attendant officers shrinking back towards the walls. For a second it resembled one of those scenes in a film where someone says something out of line to the Godfather figure and everyone waits with baited breath for his reaction. The next second, 'Psycho' burst out laughing and those with him exhaled. The longer he laughed, the worse I thought it was likely to be for me later, and he laughed for a long time . . . Eventually, he gave me another defence of force policy in this regard and left with the local bosses in attendance.

Derrick gave me a 'you've really done it this time' smile and we continued discussing shift issues. I realised I'd probably talked myself into a station or court cells sergeant post, both roles I loathed.

About ten minutes later, the Chief put his smiling head round the door to say goodbye and, "Good for you, Sarge." I winced inwardly, as Chief Superintendent Stewart stood beside him.

About two minutes later the phone on Derrick's desk rang. "That'll be for you," said Derrick, inclining his grinning head towards the still-ringing telephone.

"Sergeant Harvey."

"Chief Superintendent Stewart here. I'm in the Chief Constable's car."

I breathed a silent sigh of relief, knowing that I was safe for a little while longer.

"The Chief Constable would like to thank everyone for their welcome and commend them for their candour."

"I'll pass that on, sir . . ."

It was a 'quick change', so I got away some time after 10 p.m. and was back in around 5.30 a.m. to prepare for the shift parade.

Barry Stewart was a boss who was always in long before the 9 a.m. of the proverbial 'nine o'clock shudders' – you shudder done this and you shudder done that. That morning was no exception. I left it a few minutes before going upstairs and knocking on his door.

"Can I have a word, sir?"

"What is it?"

"I'm organising Inspector Scougal's leaving do, sir, and I wondered if you would make the presentation?"

"Thank God for that," he said. "I thought I was going to get another bollocking." He was clearly under instructions from the Chief that there should be no repercussions because of my openness, otherwise word would have soon got round and no one would speak their minds when he visited other stations. Nonetheless, if I'd lost a little respect for him due to his statement the previous evening, he'd more than gained it back – not many senior officers would have dealt with it as well as that.

I had to serve my ban and take a one-day driver refresher course.

Chapter 11

I was involved in two serious incidents during my subsequent time at Birtley, both murders. The first occurred when I was out on patrol with the Task Force – this was overtime and normally consisted of a sergeant and two PCs working on after ten at weekends, driving around in a van and responding to any reports of disorder. The dispatcher in the control room wanted to send us to stand by some premises some distance away, where an alarm was sounding. He was short of resources and wanted us to await the keyholder's arrival. I was reluctant because this would take us away from the busy areas around the pubs and night clubs and our primary role. Besides, the reality was that the annual number of arrests due to officers attending alarm activations was always virtually nil – as soon as an alarm went off, the burglars generally scarpered.

The operator contested the point, understandably, as his mission was to allocate a resource to a job and he was not really interested in the bigger picture. My intransigence was vindicated a few minutes later when we received a call to a fight in the taxi queue outside the old Key Club. We were on the scene in a matter of seconds to find a man on the ground with his stomach slit open and his intestines on the ground. He was still alive when the ambulance arrived and rushed him away. I saw someone there who I knew from another incident and took them to one side. They told me the name of the man responsible. It didn't register at the time, but it was the guy I had nearly run over at the bottom of Old Durham Road a couple of night shifts back when he'd been grappling with Derrick. Night shift supervision attended the scene and I told them the name I'd been given and resumed patrol. About half an hour later I got a call to confer with them. When I arrived at the conference point, I thought they both looked rather sheepish – neither of them could remember the name I'd given them.

The other incident involved a man chasing after some youths who were interfering with his neighbour's car. There'd been a confrontation between him and the group. By the time I got there two brothers had been stabbed. One was several hundred yards from the other and I could see the life draining out of his face. The person responsible was already in the back of a police van. One of the arresting officers knew him – he was a joiner who'd done some double glazing work for him. He'd stabbed the boys with a screwdriver he'd grabbed as he ran out of his house after them. Now his life (and that of several others) was in tatters, and one was coming to an end. I had to go with a woman police officer and tell a mother that her two sons had been stabbed and one of them had died.

Derrick had given me an excellent appraisal and one senior officer had endorsed it in his own way, saying, "Sergeant Harvey's deceptively laidback manner belies the fact that he runs a tight ship." The implicit message was that as long as the shift delivered the goods then I was safe. For report writing, Derrick had given me an O+, O being Outstanding and the top grade.

One morning I got a call to attend the Chief Inspector's office. He pushed a bit of paper on his desk towards me, "Can you tell me what that word means, Sergeant Harvey?"

It was a word so obscure that I had no chance of knowing it. "No, sir."

"Huh, and you got an O+ for Report Writing . . ."

"Is that it, sir?"

"Yes."

I turned and walked out of the room.

It was, I realised, more of an oblique attack on Derrick than it was on me.

◊

Once Derrick had left for the next stepping stone in his career, my working life became more difficult. Those who resented his swift progress could now vent their frustration on me. Those who disliked me could more easily strike at my unshielded vulnerability. The fact that I now owned a holiday home in France did nothing to increase my popularity.

I had a fairly unpleasant time and decided to move on. I began looking for specialist posts within the force and I successfully applied for a position on the new Control Room Project Team. My main role was to bring a fresh pair of eyes to the project, looking at staff issues and assessing the appropriateness of systems from the perspective of an operational officer. I enjoyed the freedom to be creative, working out how to approach the problems that arose as I went along. One of the first things I did was to visit staff in the existing control rooms, and was amazed and annoyed that no one else had bothered to consult them. I'm a great believer in asking the opinions of the people who actually do the job.

I arranged a trip away with a couple of civilian staff to visit control rooms in other force areas that were using new touch-screen technology, as well as the AA centre in Cheadle. It was a one-off opportunity and I remember my frustration at getting a court warning to appear as a witness in one of my cases. It fell right in the middle of the information-gathering trip. I tried unsuccessfully to get it rearranged or to be excused. Predictably, I travelled all the way back up the country only to be told that as a result of plea bargaining I was not required. I got a train straight back down south to rejoin my civilian colleagues.

Derrick was working at HQ so we met up sometimes for a chat. I invited him to a party at ours, which was a joint celebration of Matthew's first communion and my 40th birthday. I also invited my new boss who was a chain-smoking workaholic. He always arrived at work early. If I arrived earlier than him, on the odd occasion, he would be earlier still the next day. One day, an inspector pal of his dropped in, wafting his way through the tobacco haze. When he queried whether I minded this fug, my boss retorted, "He's a sergeant – I'm a chief inspector." Although the force at that time had a no-smoking policy in relation to shared rooms, I could imagine the repercussions if I had sought to have it applied in my case. Each evening, before hugging my family when I got home, I stripped off my foul-smelling clothes and got into the shower.

Maggie had been feeling unwell for a couple of days with a sore throat when I got a mid-morning call at work: it was a doctor phoning from our house. He said she had quinsy and he had called an ambulance for her. My mother was going to look after the children. I got up from my desk and told the smoker the situation as I got my coat. As I was about to go out of the door he called out, "Steve – if it's serious and you need to stay with her . . ." I was surprised at this apparent show of concern from him,

". . . I think it's only right to dock you the whole day . . ." It was a good thing I did not have to pass him to leave the room.

I awoke one Sunday morning a short time later, March 21st 1993, to learn that a police sergeant had been stabbed to death in the early hours in Sunniside, about a mile away. Derrick and I took our boys to Gosforth Park to throw a rugby ball about and learned that it was Bill Forth, who'd joined with me – 3684 to my 3685. He was aged 34.

◊

I was posted to Newcastle City Centre. Coincidentally, Derrick was now there as Detective Chief Inspector to develop his investigative experience. Dave Peart, my former sergeant at Kenton was to be my Inspector. Derrick tried to persuade me to replace an injured member of his three-man team due to take part in Cheviot 2000, an annual ascent of the border hill by various services teams, organised by Dave Peart and other members of the Chaos Club. Because it was only a few weeks away and I'd been doing a sedentary job for a while, I didn't feel fit enough and suggested he recruit someone else. Just before the event, the replacement pulled out and Derrick approached me again. He was a guy I found it difficult to deny, and I reluctantly agreed.

We camped outside Wooler the night before, with many of the other competitors, and then set off very early in the morning. There had been a lot of rain in the preceding three weeks but on the day itself it was sunny and hot. Cheviot is notoriously boggy anyway and conditions underfoot were tricky, to say the least. At one point I sank almost up to my waist in the mud and Derrick's reaction was to struggle to get his camera out of his pocket before I got out of the bog – not that there was much chance of that, unaided. Eventually he helped haul me out as I hurled abuse at him. We were nearly disqualified, when we were deemed to have arrived at a station past the cut-off time, but we argued the point with the marshal and left others to be ferried back while we soldiered on. It was the closest Derrick and I had ever got to exchanging angry words. Neither of us was a quitter. We eventually completed the course in a time of around 12 hours and twenty minutes, just before the evening dinner and awards ceremony where I bumped into Alan Hinkes, a contemporary at St Mary's College who'd become a well known mountaineer. Derrick sent me up to collect the truncheon on a stand, presented to the team with the slowest time. In handing it over, Dave Peart announced it was the slowest time ever recorded in the history of the event. I subsequently presented it to the City Centre Superintendent who displayed it on his desk for the next twelve months.

There were lots of things I disliked about working in the city centre. Despite having a good inspector, there wasn't a good atmosphere on the shift. On the plus side, there was a lot of overtime available and much of it was at St James' Park – getting paid extra to watch Newcastle United play was a great bonus. I had arrived in time to police the promotion celebrations as the team returned to the top tier of English football as Champions, with Kevin Keegan as messianic manager in May 1993.

Although a very busy place, the city centre was a relatively small area and I enjoyed foot patrol there, especially on night shift, admiring the old maritime buildings on the Quayside, and chatting to the local characters. I later tried to recapture some of these experiences in a poem.

SOLITARY SCAVENGER

A solitary scavenger, you scour the early hours' streets,
Your eyes patrolling a few feet before your boots,
Scruffy, but not a 'down-and-out', more 'on the ropes',
A stubbly parody of a policeman on his beat,
You stop and look, bend down, recover property,
Take out an eyebrow pencil that you found last week,
And enter details in a small black book:
50p – dean street taxi rank. 3.30.
The official version, I stop and check you out –
Your previous entries read grey street, gallowgate, darn crook,
With times and findings on your route
All chronicled in stubby purple-black.
Deferential and unsure of my response,
You recount the things, spotted on your rounds,
You've told the police about…
And then, slowly, you relax
And tell me how your patch
Is not now what it was –
Takings are down, others have moved in…
How you're thinking of throwing in your lot with Maxi
Who collects the cans; since he got himself that trailer,
He's been cleaning up (Albert's not pleased)
Weighing all that aluminium in…
He wanders off along the redeveloped Quayside, quiet now,

Although, barely an hour ago, it echoed with the shouts and
drunken songs
Of disposable incomes, a disgorged throng
Who dropped coins coming out of clubs and bars,
Getting in or out of cars and taxis,
Pulling pens from handbags, pockets,
To write down numbers on the backs of hands…

The fingers of the false dawn clasp the night's
And arch above the dozing, dirty city
Which twitches while the seagulls and the rats
Are changing shifts with pigeons who've arrived
To clear more of the fast-food carrion –
Burgers and kebabs and fish-and-chips.

And all the while the Tyne flows, slow and deep,
Scarcely disturbing those few ships
Moored at its sides; it's known to keep
Its secrets and its bodies – when they're revealed
The crabs and eels have had their fill…

The morning has emerged. I climb the hill,
Hand daytime on to others and head home
With images I've taken from the night
Which, one day, I will turn into this poem…

I liked the vitality and variety of the city centre – sharing a cuppa with
the night porters in the hotels, going into the transvestite shop in Stowell
Street, and visiting the casino and listening to all the staff's stories about
their clients.

One night shift, I was walking along Westgate Road in the early hours
when I was sure I saw a light moving in a building that was otherwise
in darkness. It was the New Tyne Theatre which had been the old Stoll
Cinema when I was a boy. Sure enough, there was someone walking
around inside with a torch. He came over to the door and let me in. He
explained that he was one of the members and they were taking turns to
stay in the renovated old theatre overnight due to recent attempted break-
ins. I mentioned a former colleague at Kenton, Barry Wilmot, who was
a member. (I remembered being on duty with Barry one evening when
he called in at his house to collect his 'bait' and his daughter had picked

a piece of lint off his tunic saying, "Daddy, there's some fluff on your costume.")

The man offered me a cuppa, clearly glad of the company and the added security of a uniformed police presence. I told him that my great grandfather had been a music hall comedian and had quite possibly played in this very theatre. "He might even be on one of those posters," I said, leaning back in my chair as I nursed my cup of tea and inclined my head in their direction. I then did a double take: in that brief moment a billing had caught my eye. "You'll not believe this," I said, "but my surname's Harvey and the 'Harry Harvey, The Eccentric Tyneside Comedian' on that poster is my great grandfather . . ."

Chapter 12

I returned home one night from work to see Maggie sitting in a chair, white as a ghost.

"Who is it?" I asked.

"My dad," she replied. I knew he was fading but hadn't been prepared for this. "He was knocked down and killed by a motorbike." He'd been returning to his new flat from the allotment, crossing the busy Harry Lauder Road with his spuds.

In the morning, we got our four children into bed with us to tell them the sad news. Gabriel wondered if the potatoes had become mashed on the road. As we drove them to my parents we passed a house on Cornmoor Road where I used to take them to visit 'Little Bobby Foster', but he'd died and the place had been sold and demolished. A new house was being built on the site. "Will they knock Granddad's house down?" Gabriel asked.

LITTLE BOBBY FOSTER
(For Gabriel)
I was not surprised to learn he fell down often.
He'd fallen in the park. I turned round, walked him home
Along the narrow, leafy, suburban road, lined
With mainly thirties properties on spacious plots.

Diminutive size, a liking for alcohol,
Age, failing sight, were only some of the factors.
He spent weeks in hospital with broken bones when
A neighbour's dog jumped up against his brittle frame.
His house was much the same – a matchstick bungalow.
Burglars didn't break in; they walked in, looked around,
Then walked out with whatever they fancied. Sometimes
He'd gesture towards something to illustrate what
He was saying, not realising it was gone.
He sat for hours by the one-bar electric fire
Backed with baking foil to reflect the heat. He'd been
A mining engineer living with his parents.
Copies of *New Scientist* weighed down a table.
I took my children to visit him, reasoning
Mutual benefit was greater than the risk
Of them catching something. He gave them Kit Kat bars
(Which I let them eat back home, hands washed). The whole place
Was fumigated during his hospital stays
Two or three times a year. He'd a few tufts of hair,
Scattered stubs of teeth, and a squeaky, chuckling voice.
When he died, someone bought the place and knocked it down.
They built a modern bungalow with a plate glass
Sign above the door that said *Foster's Lodge* in case –
So local rumour ran – he came back to haunt it.
Bricks and double glazing and security gates
Aren't proof against the spirits of the dispossessed.

We spent almost a week in Portobello. I collected new arrivals at Edinburgh Airport each day. Each night was a new round of drinks and stories about Jerry. In the early hours of the day of the funeral I got up and wrote down this poem – I always imagined it being printed in the *Tipperary Star*, the paper sent over to Jerry from 'home' each week . . .

IN MY MIND'S EYE
(For Jeremiah Kinane)

In the kitchen, wireless blarin',
Tuned, for the hurlin' to *Radio Eirann*,

A hand of cards, some home-made wine,
"A piece of bread, some tea's just fine".

In the allotment with rotavator,
Preparin' soil for seed potatoes,
Cap on head and sweat on brow,
In my mind's eye, I see you now…

In the garden, cutting grass,
Tomatoes ripenin' behind glass,
And, as Autumn comes around,
Gatherin' windfalls off the ground.

In the street to do some shopping,
Laughing, joking, starting, stopping
Between the bacon and the butter,
In the bookie's for a flutter.

In the morning on the golf course,
Between the flags like an old war-horse,
Short of wind, but strong of frame,
Playing out the final game.

In the kitchen, in the garden,
When the ground begins to harden,
In the morning, everywhere,
In my mind's eye, I see you there.

It was a strange coincidence that Dave Peart was the supervisory officer granting me compassionate leave when both my in-laws died.

Dave Hand was now Chief Inspector at the City Centre. One day in the spring of 1994 he'd asked me to go out on foot patrol with him. We walked down to the Moot Hall, set back behind the Bridge Hotel by the High Level Bridge. Robert Black was on trial for the murders of three young girls and the abduction of another. Dressed in a suit and with his neatly trimmed, greying beard, he didn't look like the stereotypical paedophile. One of the girls, Caroline Hogg, he'd taken off the Prom at Portobello on my birthday in 1983 when I'd been in 'Porty' and the police had searched Jerry's allotment. My old pal from Whickham CID, Ron Finlay, had worked on the case of Susan Maxwell, abducted on the border between Cornhill and Coldstream. I had been driving on that road the same day, on my way up to Edinburgh, and I never cross that bridge without thinking of her and her family's loss.

I attended a course on Equality Awareness at the Training department. It struck me as the usual lip service that the police service paid to such issues. I gave examples of the racist culture which went unchecked. The next time I was back at the station, I was emptying my locker and being moved to Washington station, set in a 1960s 'new town' near Sunderland. Derrick was the Detective Chief Inspector.

There was a much better camaraderie on my shift there, with some great characters: Tommy, the station sergeant, was an old-time Sunderland police officer who was a natural comedian and the PCs were a great bunch. Andy was a modest, likeable young guy who'd been in the French Foreign Legion. Norman, an ex-plumber was one of the funniest people I've ever worked with. He went on a TV game show called *Supermarket Sweep* with another lad from the shift, an ex-squaddie whose grotesque party trick was to pull a condom over his head – not one for family TV.

One warm afternoon we got a call to an incident on Fatfield Bridge. It had been closed due to a well-built young man marching up and down its single track carriageway with what looked like a pit prop over his shoulder. There were crowds sitting drinking outside pubs on both banks of the River Wear. I was with another sergeant who was Acting Inspector and he sent a van back to the station for some shields. Our Horatius looked like he was high on drugs. A group of us were around him, but there was no talking to him. He was out of it. The number of onlookers was growing steadily and I thought, 'The TV crews will be here soon with their cameras . . .'

I tipped Andy the wink that I was going to jump the guy. As I looked back, I noticed his post was in one of the diamond-shaped gaps in the metal latticework running the length of the bridge, but it was too late as he then withdrew it. A little while later, I did make my move and Andy and the others piled in. It would have looked terrible on film, but it did take half a dozen of us to subdue him, so powerful and pumped up was he. We eventually got him into a van and back to the station. Although I was wearing a short sleeved-shirt, I was pouring with sweat.

"What have you done to your arm, Steve?" Tommy asked in the charge room. I looked down to see a huge purple bruise forming where the sleeve finished. He'd obviously got in a hit with the post, but I'd felt nothing due to the adrenaline. I was forty-three that year and clearly slowing down. The following week I was at HQ for some reason and met an inspector who'd been a PC with me at Kenton. He'd been hit on the head with a wooden post a few weeks earlier and suffered some brain damage.

◊

I decided to apply for an internal position running Washington's crime desk, but another sergeant got it. Soon after, however, he went off to become a trainer and the job was suddenly mine. I was by no means sure I would be any good at it. There was a bad vibe about the whole set up. I had the impression it was a workforce alienated by a succession of poor supervision, and the mistrust was palpable.

The rationale behind the establishment of crime desks was to deal with jobs over the phone that did not require (immediate or any) police attendance, allowing operational officers more time to discover, investigate and detect more urgent calls or more serious offences. Officers who work in this role tend not to be the best operational officers for a variety of reasons – they might be demotivated, cowards, or have a drink problem; they might be perceived as lame ducks by supervision or colleagues. At Washington, the crime desk was linked with the intelligence unit, whose role was to identify crime patterns and target particular offences, locations and criminals – information-led policing. When I held my first morning briefing I could sense them all thinking, "I wonder how long this one will stay?" I returned to my desk, conscious of the size of the task ahead of me.

The Local Intelligence Officers, carrying out the equivalent roles of the old-style collator with his boxes of card indexes, were George Thompson and an older colleague – a larger-than-life figure who wore loud civilian shirts and bling, before the term was coined. He resembled Bobby George, the dart player turned commentator, and had a similar gravelly voice. He was nearing the end of his police service and was obviously a fixture. His name was John Marlborough, but his nickname was 'Johnny Mars Bar', given to him by old George, the station driver/handyman with whom he had an ongoing verbal sparring session, with old George invariably coming off second best. Johnny was clearly the heartbeat of the team, so when he invited me to a quiz one night at a local pub, I turned up after work. John made a point of talking to me, but some of the others there – the civilians and the CID guys – were wary and seemed to resent their boss's presence during their leisure time. Having good general knowledge, being widely travelled and well read, I've always been good at quizzes, but my suggestions were not well received.

Although Washington was substantially a new town – and one whose numbered districts were a labyrinth, particularly frustrating to find your way through, particularly if answering an assistance call – it was built around the old original village which includes Washington Old Hall, the ancestral home of George Washington, and incorporates several other villages such as Blackfell, Oxclose and Usworth. John was a local, born and bred, and had always worked there so he knew almost everyone. As important to me as his local knowledge was his continued support. Never sycophantic, he would bring me a cup of tea from time to time and just have a word in my ear that such and such had a bit of a personal problem at the moment and might benefit from some encouragement or whatever. I always acted on his little hints.

Slowly I got to know the staff, what their strengths were and what they needed help with. Through studying the incident logs I got to know the area – there was an outlying station at Houghton-le-Spring which we covered as well – and the kind of crime that was current. Being a new town, Washington had a high turnover of population, absorbing a lot of individuals moving into the area from Northern Ireland and elsewhere. I began to formulate a plan as to how I could improve the way the combined unit operated. Bill Holmes was a local officer who carried out administrative duties at Washington, and when his post was due to be civilianised I wanted him to oversee the crime desk for me, freeing me to spend more time on developing the intelligence side of the operation. I was told I could create this extra post, but would have to advertise the position internally, which I did. Just before the closing date, I got a call from a policewoman living in Washington but based in Sunderland. She was returning to work after having a baby and was interested in the crime desk post as it would suit her domestically. I discussed it with Norman Gilberg, then Chief Inspector, and he said it had to be an internal appointment, but I had a good feeling about this WPC and persuaded him to let me see her anyway, as she might be suitable for some future vacancy.

When Wendy turned up to see me as arranged, I was taken aback by her appearance – she was a young black woman and she reminded me of someone – or had I met her before? After chatting to her for a short time, it transpired I had taught two of her sisters and a brother at St John Fisher. (I particularly remembered her sister, Andrea, a lovely girl). It was clear to me she would be a great addition to the team and help me re-energise the others with her enthusiasm.

I drew on all my experience and literary ability to draft a report, phrasing it in such a way that if I wasn't allowed this extra officer then I couldn't guarantee an acceptable level of performance. The Superintendent smiled and said to Norman Gilberg, "I think we've found our wordsmith." He authorised it then said to me, "But never submit another report like that to me." No boss likes to be put over a barrel by one of his staff, but he took it well.

I'd noticed in my analysis of the daily incident logs that there were lots of instances of indecent behaviour that were not classified as crimes and I became increasingly concerned about the threats posed to women and children. I remember having one of my spells of perception, standing at my office window and thinking, "If an SIO [Senior Investigating Officer] comes into the room and asks me, 'Who's done this Post Office job?', if I don't know one of my team will, but if an SIO comes in and asks me, 'Who's abducted this child?', we wouldn't have a fucking clue." It struck me as unacceptable that we invested a massive amount of time and energy protecting property, but virtually nothing to protect children.

I began researching paedophiles and how they operated, the most notorious group at that time being PIE (Paedophile Information Exchange). In order to assist in assessing the scale of the problem, I made contact with various other local agencies and found that they all had tales to tell about individuals whose behaviour gave them cause for concern. One of the crime desk staff was Malcolm, a thirtyish, intelligent officer whose body language displayed a deep sense of demotivation. I approached him one day and said, "Malcolm, I'm looking to use the Force Criminal Intelligence System for a specific purpose. I know what I want to do, but I don't have the technical skills to do it. I'd like you to have a go at it."

"What about taking reports of crimes?"

"The others can do that . . ."

I wanted to start keeping tabs on suspicious individuals. For example, we had one man whose van was often seen in the vicinity of courting couples in their vehicles at night. There were others who seemed to be displaying an unhealthy interest in children at the swimming baths or in parks. We had a high incidence of reports of indecent exposure. The problem of predicting when voyeurism or exhibitionism turned into something even more sinister was obvious from the beginning.

We had a young police officer at the station, PC Messenger, who had worked in I.T. before joining the police, and with his help and Malcolm's, I created M.I.S.F.I.T.S. – the Messenger Information System For the Identification and Tracking of Suspects. It wasn't very sophisticated, but it was a start. Addressing these issues was problematic for various reasons. One of them was convincing senior officers to invest resources in something that would not be likely to significantly improve their detection rates. Even Norman Gilberg, who was generally very supportive, stopped in his vehicle as he passed me walking out of the station and, in front of his high ranking passengers who'd obviously been his lunch companions, asked me, "How many burglaries today, Sergeant Harvey?"

"Seven," I answered. "Maybe eight."

"How many child abductions?"

His audience all laughed.

I just smiled. I told him, "One child abduction will cost you a million pounds."

I realised early on that there needed to be a multi-agency approach to this problem, with protocols covering the exchange of sensitive information. I persuaded the Superintendent to invite representatives from the Probation Service, the Health Service, Social Services and the local women's refuge to a meeting at Houghton Police Club, laying on sandwiches and refreshments. After he had welcomed everyone, I provided the details of our intentions and printed copies of protocols for discussion. Always one for a snappy acronym, I suggested we call this new initiative O.A.S.I.S. – Organisational Approach to persons Suspected of Indecency and Sexual offences.

One of the most sensitive aspects of all this was that many of the men (we didn't have any women in our M.I.S.F.I.T. system at that time) we were gathering information on had not actually been convicted of – or even arrested for – any offences. With no crimes known to have been committed, our 'Misfits' couldn't really be called 'suspects'.

I remember Wendy coming into my office one day and saying, "Can I have a word, sarge?"

"Of course, Wendy. What is it?"

"Well you've got this guy on your list and I don't understand why?"

I looked at the name and recognised it as that of a foreign national whose flat had been burgled recently.

"Well, I made a point of going to that burglary. There were pictures of women all around the walls – not pornographic, but panoramic. The way he talked about his ex was full of anger. Now look at the incidents which have brought him to our attention . . ."

"That's just it – there's nothing much . . . a bit of a dispute with a neighbour . . ."

"What was it about?"

"He passed a man and his daughter and made some comment about her . . ."

"What else?"

"An altercation in Tesco's."

"Involving inappropriate behaviour towards the checkout girl. He has a problem with women and there is a lot of anger there. I know I would have difficulties justifying his inclusion in the system to civil liberties organisations, but I also know I'm right . . ."

These last few words are very dangerous for a police officer to use and have sometimes led to instances of massive misdirecting of resources in major enquiries and, in several notorious cases, miscarriages of justice. I had nearly been guilty of apprehending the wrong man once, early on in my police service. There had been a burglary at a house by Kenton Bar and I'd detained three suspicious guys near a dodgy car nearby. I arrested them and had them taken back to Gosforth to process them before pursuing my enquiries. I then made a cardinal error. There had been some footprints on a broken pane of glass at the house and I took one of the trainers that seemed to match it to the scene. This was not done dishonestly but I'd broken one of the golden rules of evidence: my actions invalidated any evidential link between that individual and his presence there. It was an uncharacteristic procedural lapse in my eagerness to detect the crime. The householder happened to be someone who worked for the Forestry Commission, thirty or more miles further north at Kielder Forest. I showed him the shoe and said, "Look . . . it's exactly the same . . ."

He looked at the sole of the shoe and then the footprint like a native tracker and said, "It's the same pattern – but it's not the same trainer. See how this is more worn on this side and there's a slight crack here?"

I really couldn't see it and thought, 'Great . . . that's all I need – sodding Tonto. I've locked the offenders up and the victim's going to get them off . . .'

Neil Collin, a young officer doing his stint in CID arrived, and together we did some house-to-house enquiries. One neighbour thought she'd seen a black lad run away from the back of the house. There was only one black family living in that neighbourhood. We went to the door and a woman answered. Her brother was in bed. Neil asked to look at his shoes. She brought some Dr Marten style boots out.

"Has he any others?" asked Neil.

"Just his boxing ones . . ."

"Can we see them, please?"

She returned with trainers – they had the same pattern as the others. We arrested him and he admitted the offence. I never forgot the lessons I learnt from that case.

A few weeks later Wendy came back into my office.

"Yes, Wendy?"

"You know that guy I was asking you about the other week, sarge – the one you said had a bad attitude to women?"

"Yes."

"He was arrested for rape in South Shields last night."

Well, it was good to get one right, and I was glad of anything that would bolster the credibility of our work in this area. Nobody else in the Force area was doing anything like it, as far as I could tell.

◊

Every morning, I got a call from Alastair Leithead at BBC Radio Newcastle asking if I had any local news items for him. I never did. One day I thought I might have a story for him when we got a report of a woman having seen a man in the Galleries Shopping Centre she was sure was the handsome black man on the BBC Programme, *Crimewatch*, that week. The show had featured a reconstruction of the circumstances of a very nasty indecent assault by this man, on a young boy at the cliffs in Scarborough. Two officers attended and I was, naturally, very interested to discover if we'd arrested a suspect in such a high profile case. When the officers returned I asked, "So, was it our man?"

"Well, yes and no." Norman replied.

"How do you mean?" I asked, baffled.

"Well, the woman was right: it was the man she'd seen on *Crimewatch* ... only it was the actor – his other job is window dressing, which is what he was doing at the shop in the Galleries."

"That's a great story," I said, but realised as I said it that it was one we couldn't use – if we did, members of the public might be put off calling in on seeing someone featured on the programme, fearing it might be the actor and that they would be left feeling silly.

◊

One morning a call went out over the police radio reporting that a young girl – only about eleven – had just been raped on her way to school (although I almost never attended incidents, I always kept the radio on to monitor them). The first officer on the scene, a sergeant I didn't get on with particularly well, called in, "Ask Steve Harvey to look in his system." We could not have asked for a better validation of our efforts, although the offence was the very kind we were trying to reduce the chances of happening. Personally, I was desperately upset for this poor girl, but professionally I was driven by the determination to help identify and arrest her assailant. Although we only had about forty names in our system at that time, I found one local man who'd been convicted of an almost identical crime. I discovered he'd only recently been released from prison having served his sentence for this offence and from my contacts in the local probation service, learned that he was now working at a factory only half a mile from the scene of the crime. It had to be him . . .

Two CID officers were dispatched to speak to him. They returned without him – he had an alibi: his workmates were adamant he had not left the building at any time that morning. 'But it has to be him', I thought, and then remembered the case of the footprint.

This case was not solved by our system but the time-honoured combination of luck and good police work. A detective who'd been abroad on his annual leave when the crime had been committed returned to work and connected some details with an individual in Jarrow. After being under observation for some time, the man was arrested, charged and convicted of the offence. The message was one I already knew – our work had to be a patchwork quilt: we had started on one small square but it had to be joined up with all the surrounding squares which needed to be made, stretching not just across our force area, but nationally and internationally. The Durham Force area adjoined ours but their crime intelligence system was completely incompatible and we had no access to the information held on it, except by asking one of their crime intelligence staff to research some particular item at our specific request. Ultimately, an integrated system was essential.

◊

As usual in new areas of research and innovation, some individuals and organisations were doing good work on their own initiative, but it was isolated and piecemeal. I drew on my experience from my Control Project days, and contacted other forces in England (42), Scotland (9), the RUC and the Garda Siochana in Ireland. I persuaded my supervisors to let me travel down to London to liaise with NCIS (National Criminal Intelligence Service): it was salutary to discover that the national paedophile unit based there had one DC on loan from the Met, one Customs & Excise Officer (who was its OIC) and a civilian who did the admin part time. In the next room I could hear the squad that dealt with football hooliganism and they certainly sounded like a much bigger team.

The Met officer gave me a list of residents in our force area on whom they had intelligence in relation to child pornography. This information about individuals all over England and Wales was just sitting there – they had no one to whom they could send it. Taking possession of this information was a cause of concern as the problem then became mine. Of particular concern was the number of people now accessing material via the internet.

I'd talked myself onto a trip to a conference in Leicestershire on the subject, with some senior officers from my own force, by offering to pay my own accommodation expenses when they told me no further funds were available to cover my attendance. It was amusing to be in a room with two senior officers when this discussion was taking place, witnessing them both claiming credit for our initiative in this field.

I was co-opted onto the steering committee of a local group called 'The Derwent Initiative', an independent charity working 'to improve public protection by finding creative and practical multi-agency solutions to the problems of sexual offending' (as it says on its website. The fact that an Assistant Chief Constable is currently shown as an advisor, reflects the increased importance now placed on such initiatives). We were consulted in relation to the drafting of the Sex Offenders Act which became law in 1997. One of the most significant consequences of this legislation was that police forces could no longer ignore their responsibilities in this area: if certain classes of criminals had to notify their local force of their whereabouts, then somebody had to be appointed to deal with recording this information, at the very least.

◊

I realised I had been recognised by the force as their unofficial expert in this field when I was nominated to be their representative at a presentation given at the US Embassy in London by American Customs & Excise Officers on the subject of child exploitation. At that time, pornography in the USA was dealt with by them, including internet pornography. We were briefed by them on the practice of 'grooming' children by adults online, and we all came away with the realisation that we were taking a time bomb back to our forces. A representative attending invited me to address a class at the Scottish Police College at some point in the future. I was asked to brief senior officers at my force on the subject during one of their meetings. My message was clear – this was an area of criminal activity unlike any other: it was not confined to any age, class or gender, and we would encounter teachers, social workers, doctors, judges, and police and civilian staff among our own force involved in it. Furthermore, the demands on resources would be considerable. To have a known predatory paedophile actively searching for a victim in one's area without putting him under observation would be unthinkable – but who was going to take the responsibility for calling off the observations if he still hadn't committed any preparatory offence, but was continuing to act suspiciously after days or weeks?

I attended a conference at Southampton University dealing with sexual offences against children, primarily intended for social workers. I was one of only two police officers there – the other was from a local force so there was no expense for accommodation. One of the speakers, a US criminal psychologist, gave a chilling but fascinating insight into the minds of child murderers she'd interviewed.

◊

The revamped crime desk/intelligence unit became a model of its kind, attracting attention and visitors not only from our force but further afield. Late one afternoon, when many of the staff were away home, Trevor Martin, an ex-CID Sergeant who now shared responsibility with me for running the information-led policing of the area, had taken a phone call and then come to have word with me. It was John Marlborough's day off and he'd been out playing a game of golf. He'd got out of the car afterwards and dropped down dead. Trevor and I then had the task of telling the staff still on duty and phoning the others. The boss took the unusual step of giving them the following day off to come to terms with the news.

John had been a father figure to the whole office and I knew our civilians, Amanda and Angela, would take his sudden death particularly hard. On the day after he died, I saw a photograph of him on Amanda's desk – did I leave it there or remove it before they all returned to work the next day? Amanda had a very dominant and confrontational personality and could be difficult to manage. I remember her one day – during a private conversation in relation to some decree from above with which she disagreed – asking me if I never felt like telling them all to 'Fuck off!' I'd smiled and told her I had learned to choose my battles – and words – carefully. I picked up the picture and put it in my drawer.

A few minutes after the start of the shift next morning, she blew into my room.

"Where's my picture of John? Have you taken it?"

"I didn't want you to be upset as soon as you walked in . . ."

"Well, I am upset. It's like he never existed, removing traces of him! Where is it?"

I took it out of my drawer and handed it to her.

"I was acting from the best of motives, Amanda. I'm sorry if I made the wrong decision. I will miss him terribly too, you know," I confided.

Chapter 13

The force was advertising for a sergeant and PC to establish and run a Paedophile Unit. Everyone assumed I was a shoo-in for it, but I was not comfortable with this. For one thing, I thought it was a poisoned chalice and I wasn't sure that I would get the support I needed to run it the way I saw fit. Bizarrely, they interviewed for the PC's post first, which obviously meant that the sergeant in charge of the unit would have no say in who his colleague was, in a two-person team tasked with this most sensitive of roles. I got phone calls from officers asking me for information to help them prepare for interview, at least one of them from a DS who would be competing for the same job as me – that's why he was a detective. They appointed a woman DC and then I was up against six other sergeants, all trained detectives, for the senior role.

I was supposed to hear the result straight away, but I didn't. Then I got a call from Chief Inspector Chris Machell, a pal of Derrick's, and the man who would be my line manager if I got the post, telling me that it was probably mine – which is a bit like a woman going for a pregnancy test and being told that she's probably pregnant. I'd had to go for it and I'd had to get it, but everything about the process had been wrong from the start.

They had a little presentation for me in the crime desk office. I've still got the award certificate presented to me, as it records, by my then line manager, Chief Inspector Terry Atkinson, on the 11th July 1997 and endorsed with the handwritten best wishes of my colleagues. Throughout his short speech, he continually returned to the line, "Steve's . . . a character . . ." apparently at a loss to say much else of a positive nature, and, I felt, an implicit admission that I still didn't really fit in the organisation.

Chris Machell's replacement made it clear he had no interest in having the Paedophile Unit as part of his new empire, probably recognising it as the hot potato it was already proving to be. It was then absorbed into Crime Intelligence and I had my third boss in almost as many months. I felt as if I was being asked to paint a ship at sea – and it was a submarine. It was proving impossible to establish a solid foundation for the Unit with clear terms of reference and operating systems. I felt it was no good going after individual suspects until we'd established a structure. My new boss told me she wanted me to go and interview paedophiles in prison. I told her I couldn't do it. She told me I was a police officer and could and would interview them. I told her I wasn't a good enough actor: they tended to be extremely devious individuals who'd wrapped their desires and activities in a web of disguise over decades and were thus masters of dissimilation. I wouldn't be able to convince them I understood their sexual predilection. It became clear to me that the skills for which I'd presumably been appointed to the post and the experience that had led to me being the prime candidate were being ignored. Everyone else in the building was CID. I'd been on an Intelligence Officers' course for officers from several forces, but not even a CID course could have made me fit in there.

◊

As Christmas 1997 approached I went off sick with flu. I felt totally run down and spent several days in bed. When I tried to get up one day, my back had locked up. It eased up enough over the next few days for us to drive up to the cottages on Islay that my brother-in-law Mark had booked for us all for the New Year. Maggie and I walked to the local red telephone box to make a phone call to get the result of a test she'd had at the doctor's in Whickham. She was pregnant. I then spent Hogmanay at the little island hospital with Gabriel who'd nearly sliced off his ear on the banister while sliding down the stairs on a tray.

When we got back to Whickham, my back continued to play up. It was weeks before I could get an appointment for a physio after the holiday period. I was now on sick leave with my back problem, and my wife was pregnant – that wouldn't look good at work, would it? I found myself no longer caring, however. With a bad back and restricted mobility, I put on weight which caused me problems with the old injury to my left knee. In the course of the next few weeks and months I had physiotherapy at the force HQ's medical unit, including acupuncture and visits to the police convalescent home, but no amount of manipulation or number of needles could cure my malaise.

I had a slow procession of senior officers at intervals of several months trying to persuade me to come back to work. I told them I wasn't fit to return. I was told the Unit needed me. I was told how the work would suffer without me. I remained on sick leave. After six months I was put on half pay, a few weeks before our baby was due. As twelve months approached I was told I would receive no pay. You might imagine how my wife was taking all this. The Police Federation was of little use. They told me the force was looking to make an example of me. It was clear, just as I went on sick leave, that the Home Office had begun clamping down on medical pensions and the force's old medical officer had left his position. I went back to work and was assigned to the Training Department, under the supervision of one of the trainers from the YT Scheme at Jarrow, Amanda, who was now working on NVQs. She gave me something to do. My suspicions had proved correct: nobody now cared what I did as long as I was at work and not on the medical pensions statistics. I struggled through for a few days then went back on the sick and the whole twelve-month cycle was set in motion again.

Understandably all this was placing a strain on our marriage, although nobody else realised, and it was an additional pressure trying to disguise our difficulties. Maggie loved parties and dancing but it was difficult for me to socialise on long-term sick with a bad back. My consolations and diversions, apart from the children, were a weekly pub quiz, playing bridge, and writing poetry again. Maggie was becoming increasingly homesick and I promised her if I was medically pensioned we would move up to Edinburgh. During one of her visits to see her family, Maggie phoned me to say she'd seen the house she wanted – it was in an Edwardian terrace near Portobello Prom, between where the twins and her oldest brother lived. I explained that as long as I was an officer in Northumbria Police I had to live in the Force area – there was no way we could buy a house in Scotland, although we had accepted an offer from a couple who were keen to buy our bungalow and were prepared to wait.

An ACC (Assistant Chief Constable) had by this time attended our home to discuss my situation. I pointed out, politely but firmly, that my treatment by the force was having a detrimental effect on my wife. He assured me he would do something about it. We were a little encouraged by this, but nothing happened.

Nathaniel was now a year old and an absolute source of joy in this bleak period. I pushed him round in his buggy, taking Gabriel and Joseph to St Mary's Primary School and then collecting them in the afternoon. I've always used my sense of humour to address problems, but every witty thing I could think of to say about the situation had been used and I'd taken to avoiding friends and other parents as much to spare them the need to find something to say as myself.

Despite being told I would be informed personally as soon as there were any developments, a letter arrived one day announcing that I was to be medically pensioned as of 21st December 1999. I had been on the sick for almost two years, except for a few days. I pushed Nathaniel into Whickham and went to the library which had a computer in one corner which I'd previously used to look on the ESPC (Edinburgh Solicitors' Property Centre) website for suitable houses. They couldn't get the PC working (a bit like Northumbria Police, some might say) and I was on the point of leaving when they got it up and running. I found nothing new but then for some reason, I looked in a lower price range, although I knew it was extremely unlikely there would be a house large enough for our family in that bracket. There – at offers over £125,000 – was a house in the same terrace that Maggie was interested in. I took down the details and went to the Northern Rock Building Society a few doors away to see about a mortgage. I then went back and told Maggie, phoned my brother-in-law Mark, and got the name and number of his solicitor as I knew I would need a Scottish one. I picked the kids up from school and told Gabriel to get ready as he was coming with me.

"Where are we going?" he asked.

"Up to Edinburgh to buy a house," I replied.

It was a Thursday and as per the Scottish custom, viewing was on Thursday evenings and Sunday afternoons. We drove to Geraldine and Mark's and she came with us to see the house. It was a cold and damp November evening but there were a lot of people looking at the place. It was clear that setting a low 'up-set' price had been a shrewd move. The house was unoccupied and very basic. A tiny downstairs washroom had a huge Belfast sink with three brass taps labelled 'hot', 'cold' and 'mains'. At least one of the bedrooms had a meter for the gas fire. A dull board was lying in a corner with 'Bed & Breakfast' written on it, unconvincingly. The decor was outdated and dilapidated.

"It's terrible, isn't it, Dad?" whispered Gabriel.

"Yes," I whispered back.

"So you're not going to try and buy it?"

"So I'm definitely going to try and buy it."

I tried through my solicitor to put in an offer that would be accepted, rather than go to the sealed bid system, but with such a lot of interest the vendors were naturally resistant to this approach. House sales in Scotland are traditionally much more speedy transactions than in England and a closing date was set for about three weeks away. I knew that the property would go for a lot more than £125,000. The trick was to guess what the psychological cut-off point would be for the other bidders. It was a bit like a game of bridge.

I was desperate to get the house for Maggie. She'd always dreamed of a big house by the sea and I remembered her pointing out her Aunt Josie's house to me on the first night we had gone walking out together. With each day I was less confident of being able to save my marriage. In fact, I felt that we were more likely to break up if we did move to Edinburgh as Maggie would have a support system in terms of family and friends and she would have even less need of me. I have never been a quitter, however, and was prepared to do whatever it took to keep our family together.

I bid £183,003 for the property, and apparently beat the next highest bid by only a few thousand. But this was only the first step on the long and difficult road to move my family to Scotland. As speedy and easy as the process was to buy our new property, so protracted and problematic was the sale of our old one. Our prospective purchasers were still there, a year down the line, but they had not been completely open with us and their £150,000 cash purchase had acquired the element of the sale of a small property. This placed us at the end of a chain with four or five links and there was a snag over planning permission for a small extension to the property at the other end. I made numerous calls and visits to my solicitor and estate agents in an effort to get the problem resolved. The pressure on me built up as the solicitors acting for the vendors in Edinburgh were demanding I complete, but of course I couldn't without the sale of our bungalow. Matters came to a head when my Scottish solicitor informed me we had to complete by the next day or we would default on our agreement, lose the property, and be liable to pay the difference between our offer and the next highest prepared to complete. I didn't tell Maggie because I didn't want to put her under any more pressure but I was physically sick. I went to my English solicitor and decided to sit in his office until we got the issue resolved. Despite his obvious annoyance – he was the brother of an old teaching friend and the flat rate he was charging me was clearly not worth all this aggravation – he realised how desperate my situation was and our sale was completed with about an hour to spare.

Chapter 14

Maggie began packing and one day I came in and she said, "Look at this." It was an entry in her diary from August 1984 It said, "Returned to Newcastle from honeymoon. Met by Bill & Audrey. Drove up to Edinburgh for Marian's wedding. Stayed B&B . . ." – and what followed was the address of the property we'd bought. Her diary had fallen open at this page as she was packing to move into a house we'd stayed in for one night sixteen years earlier. Neither of us had remembered staying there.

Of course, the drama was not over yet. On the day of the move, our buyers' removal van sat on the road outside our bungalow, awaiting clearance to go ahead on confirmation of receipt of funds. Eventually, after several hours, we got the all clear and we were leaving Tyneside for Scotland. We weren't going to Edinburgh because the house needed a massive amount of work. I had travelled up on a reconnaissance mission with Dave, a retired police officer pal, and found the perfect interim place for us. It was a large farmhouse on top of a hill at Carberry, overlooking 'Auld Reekie' several miles to the north. You could see the Forth bridges from the picture windows downstairs. I later wrote a short story set there called 'The Big Windy'.

If the view and the space were the best things about the place, the cold was the worst. The house was exposed to the weather from every direction and, if the rent was relatively cheap, the outlay for fuel for the oil-fired central heating system wasn't. The location was excellent, however, as it was only a couple of miles from the A1. I drove the children into school every morning. We'd got Joseph and Gabriel into Maggie's old primary school, St John's, Portobello. Joe had opted to go there to be in the top year with his cousin Hannah rather than into the first year at Holy Rood High where Martha had started in third year. Gabriel's year group was full, so we'd agreed for him to go into the year below until a place became available with his own age group and his cousins Peter, Thomas, and Emma. We were quite happy with this, as Gabriel was dyslexic and we thought this would relieve him of being under pressure from immediate academic comparison with his contemporaries. We left Matthew behind with friends in Whickham, as he was going on a school skiing trip and for insurance reasons had to be a current pupil of St Thomas More Comprehensive, Blaydon, in order to take part.

I'd had three firms tender for the work on the house. The lowest by far was from a company I would not normally have used, run by a pair I'll call Suit and Overalls, but we would have to cut our cloth. They had six months to do all the work and used a series of guys who were clearly doing it as 'guvvy jobs'. Back on Tyneside I knew so many people who did so many things that I could have formed my own team, but here I had to rely on others. And these weren't the most reliable of guys. One day I went to the house on spec and found their squad literally sleeping on the job.

As the months moved on, the quality of workers and work noticeably deteriorated. I had a meeting with the two men running the operation, highlighting my concerns about delays and standards. They asked for more money. Our six months rental was coming to an end and couldn't be extended. There was little further activity and what was done was so poor it would need to be redone. I contacted them and told them I was not giving them any more money and did not want them on my property any longer. I received a call at Carberry from some men I'd got in to do some decorating, telling me that Overalls and a sidekick had come into the property, brushed past them and left with some items. Maggie and I drove down to the house. Overalls and his sheepish companion were sitting in a van on the opposite side of the road. Overalls told me he'd removed several key parts of the central heating system and cut pipes and disconnected wires. He warned me not to get anyone else in to restore them or they were in danger of being electrocuted, and he would only put it right if paid the outstanding couple of thousand pounds. I warned him that I knew how to deal with people who broke the law. My pulse was racing at the prospect of a physical fight with him I would be unlikely to win.

I contacted Suit and told him what had occurred. I was unsure of Scottish law so just said, "You know what laws he's broken entering my property and committing criminal damage, and that you're involved as his business partner . . ."

I withdrew £500 and Maggie drove me to their rented office with shared reception in town. Suit was apologetic and on the back foot. He said he would get Overalls to put things right and to forget about the money. I said I wanted a written statement acknowledging receipt of £500 as full and final settlement, signed by him. I'd decided to give the cash as a sop to Overalls's bruised ego, reducing the likelihood of our windows going in one night. I warned Suit that if my property or family suffered any repercussions I would report it to the police, together with the original offence which I had already spoken to them about, but not made an official complaint. The damage was repaired and I had no further dealings with them, except, incredibly, for a request to provide a reference.

Unfortunately, the property was still a long way from habitable and we had nowhere to stay and very little money left. All my lump sum from my police pension had gone into the house. Jamal, a native of Baghdad, married to Anne, a Scottish colleague of my sister-in-law, Anne-Marie, offered to let us have a one-bedroomed, third floor flat on the High Street, only asking that we paid the utility bills. We had Nathaniel with us, but our other children were staying with Maggie's siblings. One day Maggie and I were so exhausted we fell asleep on separate sofas. When we awoke we discovered that Gabriel was missing. Martha had put him on the bus to his cousin's, but it seemed she had put him on the wrong one. From my experience, I knew that the first hour was crucial in locating missing children and he had already been gone that long. He was beautiful, trusting and in unfamiliar territory. My professional training and parental anguish fought with each other as I set off looking for him. I stopped a bus and asked the driver to circulate a description of Gabriel, surprised at my calmness despite my thumping heart. Maggie's brother John came along just then, but he had no news. While I was still talking to the driver, I received a call on my mobile telling me Gabriel had turned up after completing a circular route on the wrong bus.

As well as the massive relief, I felt a terrible sense of desolation: we were living in straitened and strained circumstances, our children spread around the family. It seemed to me we were like refugees from a foreign country, dependent on the charity of others.

◊

It was at this time that I discovered the Edinburgh International Book Festival and I had been like the proverbial boy in a sweetie shop, deciding what to choose. On the day I was due to go and see an American undertaker author read there, however, I suddenly found I could not face leaving the flat. I felt that if I encountered the slightest mishap or wrong word or even look, I would not be able to deal with it. I was clearly running on empty, and it was all I could do to drag myself along to Charlotte Square. Inside the festival tent I saw one of my writer friends, but, totally out of character, I went and sat by myself. Thomas Lynch's reading – his soothing Michigan voice, his paternal manner and his wisdom acquired through experiencing the pain of others as well as his own – acted as a kind of balm. He read from *Bodies in Motion and at Rest* and the humanity in his gentle, measured, melodic prose warmed me. He was asked to read a notoriously vitriolic poem about his ex-wife, but said he no longer read it in public since the time when he was halfway through reciting it and looked up to see his daughter enter the hall. I felt there was a message here for me – one I already knew: not to vent my pain in writing things that would hurt my children, something I'm very conscious of while writing these memoirs.

◊

I knew it was important for me to make new friends and build my own social life as my chances of saving my marriage looked bleak. The house was still far from finished. We'd had another setback when the firm fitting the linoleum-style floor covering in the large kitchen, created from two dingy rooms, made a mess of it and I refused to pay. I opted for a different kind of material altogether from another company. I found a guy who agreed to fit a shower in the upstairs cupboard in exchange for a couple of weeks in our place in Normandy, although he never took us up on this, despite me contacting him several times afterwards. Even when everything was completed, we couldn't get the job signed off because the local inspector had a quibble over the bore of the pipes.

My mother gave me a couple of thousand pounds and I decided to use it for a family holiday to try and hold everything together and keep everyone's spirits up, particularly Maggie's. We booked a break in a villa in Puerto Pollensa in Majorca – not my kind of holiday but it was what she and the children wanted. The trip brought a brief respite. We returned to Edinburgh rested but with our relationship even more strained. Maggie was adamant she wanted to move into the house no matter what state it was in. It was great to have all the children back together, and I eventually got the shower technicalities sorted out and approval granted.

I arranged a fortieth birthday party for Maggie at a hotel overlooking the sea by Musselburgh Racecourse. Friends from our days in Newcastle travelled up and stayed overnight. At the end of the night, she made a short speech thanking everybody.

"And your husband . . ." shouted out Dave. Everyone laughed at her oversight.

I tried to give her as much space as possible. I threw my energies into planning to run creative writing courses at Le Vieux Chateau. After a parents' evening at Holy Rood High, Maggie and I went to the Sheep Heid pub in Duddingston Village for a drink – it was more a matter of doing something rather than going back to the house together. A woman Maggie knew from working at St John's nursery, Gina, came in with her husband, Harry. He asked me the standard male question, "What do you do?"

"Nothing," I replied, in keeping with my gloomy mood. I immediately felt ashamed of myself and apologised, saying, "I'm looking to run creative writing courses in France. I've got most of the planning done. I just need a logo now."

"That's what I do," he responded. "I'm in advertising."

Over the following weeks Harry and I met several times for a few pints and he designed a brilliant logo of an apple with a quill stuck in it, à la *Shakespeare in Love*, all in the red, white and blue of the Tricoleur.

◊

In May 2001 I ran my first course in France with the Scottish poet, Donny O'Rourke, as tutor and my new friend, Geoff, as one of those attending. On the way to my house from Dinard Airport I stopped to buy some cider from a farm near the Brittany/Normandy boundary. The name of the family was on the label: 'Ecrivain' – 'writer', as Donny pointed out. I took it as a good omen. The course went well, although would-be writers are not the easiest of people to cater for.

Chapter 15

Although Maggie and I hadn't separated, living together was becoming intolerable and she'd made it very clear she wanted me to leave. We still hadn't made others aware of the situation. As far as they knew, I was going over to France to do some work on the place. In my eyes, I was leaving for 'my French mistress', as I'd often referred to Le Vieux Chateau, because I had nowhere else to go. This is the first page of my journal:

Sept. 3rd 2001

Sixty-two years ago today, World War II started, or more accurately, we declared war on Germany. Twenty-two years ago today, I joined the Northumbria Police. Today I am driving alone from Edinburgh to France, to Le Vieux Chateau, our holiday home in Normandy. I left the house with a break in my voice and heart. Through tear-filled eyes I saw Margaret my wife and our five children by the gate of our terraced home. I'm leaving to write, perhaps set up a creative writing business, and to learn to live again. My life's been on hold for almost four years since I went sick . . .

I've been house husband, food shopper, family ferrier.
I've been childminder for Nathaniel, our youngest, for the three

years since his birth – and loved it. I've had time with him at
a stage I didn't with the others. His 'I loves you Dada' and his
chuckle are the two sweetest sounds on earth to me.
I've been there for them all. At home, part of the furniture.
And now I'm leaving and there's an end to it. Today everything
changes for ever. It is the end of my life. Tomorrow is not the first
day of the rest of my life; it is the first day of a new life, for better
or worse.
Arrive at my sister Helen's in Newcastle around 10 pm. My parents
live a hundred yards away, but they're too tired to see me, have a
game of cards.
Have a cuppa. Helen goes to bed. Open a tin of Ambrosia rice
pudding. An appropriately low-key welcome. A life-change in
progress and no-one else notices.

I was reminded of Auden's *Musee Des Beaux Arts*.

In Normandy, after lunch at friends, Ian and Alison's – Ian was a retired
BA pilot – I heard on the car radio a report of a plane having crashed into
one of the towers of the World Trade Centre. The surrealism I felt in my
own life was dwarfed by these events and was compounded by the fact
that I knew this was a world-changing day but couldn't get anyone to
appreciate what was happening. I felt like Cassandra. I returned to Ian
and Alison's and watched the horror unfold on their TV. The following
day I wrote this poem:

RECIPE FOR DISASTER

Take the required number of fanatics
Prepared, preferably eager,
To die for their cause;
Add minimum security
On internal American flights;
Stir in Middle Eastern conflict,
Mix emotions, flavour with
Hollywood disaster movies
And a pinch of evil genius,
Garnish with hate, then heat
Under a slow flame. When ready
Serve flambé…

116

The next day, Susan McLean and her friend Ashley were flying into Dinard to come and stay for a few days. I drove over to collect them. It is strange to explain, but I'd had a vision of a farmhouse and a courtyard near the airport where I could arrange to leave my car between trips. The flight was delayed so I drove to nearby Pleurtuit and found just what I'd imagined – a farmhouse with a covered open barn to leave my Peugeot 505 in when I flew back to Edinburgh. I knocked on the door and spoke to the farmer's wife who said that would not be a problem and she would happily do it as a '*cadeau*' – a gift.

It was a strange time, altogether. During Susan's stay, we went to various soirees and entertained visitors at LVC. There was a guy who showed a video of himself crashing at high speed at the Isle of Man TT Races two years earlier. He was still limping. There was an actor who had been the Robot of Death to Tom Baker's Doctor Who.

I organised a couple of courses to take place in May 2002. I was not feeling confident about them, which wasn't helped by the news that the local airport was going to be closed, due to the arrival of George W. Bush on the 27th – the day A L Kennedy was due to fly home.

My journal entry for 20th May:

> *Worked like a dervish until 5 pm, getting the place ready.*
> *Drove down to Dinard. Still lots of BH traffic, luckily most of it*
> *heading away from Brittany, but still enough to make me a few*
> *minutes late for Alison (A L Kennedy).*
> *She seemed unperturbed and we went off in search of somewhere*
> *to eat until the traffic had thinned out. Ended up in a creperie in a*
> *very dead, end of BH weekend, Dinard.*
> *Drove back to LVC, heartened by Alison's easygoing approach*
> *(esp. Re. Carpiquet closing on 27th).*

The course went well, but it was exhausting. At the end, I had to drive through the night to get Alison to Rouen Airport and then drive straight back, a round trip of several hundred kilometres. I then prepared breakfast for the guests, cleaned and closed up the place, and drove everyone to Caen for the Portsmouth ferry, which I also took. I didn't make any money out of it all, but I had never expected to. It was something to do, and I needed something to do.

I returned to the family home in Portobello. I used to love looking out of the Velux window, across the Forth towards Fife and at St Philip's

Church with birds of all kinds flying over the rooftops. When we'd moved in, the church, which was on the other side of the road leading down to the Prom, was a burnt-out shell, apparently due to one of the workmen leaving a blowtorch on overnight while carrying out some roofing repairs. It was a symbol for me. The burnt-out spire was my aspirations. I thought of a line from Edwin Muir's autobiography about a monument in Orkney being 'a sign of the fable of our lives'. I thought of *The Spire* by William Golding – I'd never read it, but remembered my adolescent writing being compared to his style by Mr Nichol at St Cuthbert's. I had treasured the praise like a piece of family lore or jewellery. I thought that when the church and its spire were rebuilt, my marriage would be restored. The church was to be rebuilt several years later and Maggie and her new partner were to get married in it . . .

Chapter 16

I had provisionally booked a place in Portobello for my 50th birthday party, but cancelled it in time to get my deposit back. Geoff organised a meal at a local Chinese restaurant, which was attended by a few of my friends.

Maggie's family was going on a summer holiday on the French coast near Biarritz. We'd eventually agreed we would go to Normandy with our children and then I would drive us all down to the south and go off on a solo walking trip in the Pyrenees, presented as a 50th birthday treat. We would then drive back up to Normandy and then on to Edinburgh where we would tell the children we were separating.

We reached the site where Maggie's family was staying. The kids jumped out and started playing with their cousins. I was driven by Michael to the local railway station, feeling like a criminal being deported, watching my children playing through the car window.

I arranged to be collected there at a time ten days away and waited for my train . . .

Although I can say I've never seriously contemplated suicide, that train journey up into the mountains, along the valley of the River Nive, was one of the few occasions when it crossed my mind. It was late and wet when I arrived at the station at the end of the line, outside the Basque town of Saint-Jean-Pied-de-Port. I had no plans, no accommodation booked. I followed the only other traveller who had not been collected, up the streets to the town centre.

A place of pilgrimage was appropriate for this journey as it is filled my memory with religious imagery – the outcast in the wilderness; the sense of penance for some unknown sin; a feeling of being in limbo.

It was, looking back, a return to the travels of my youth and the precursor of my subsequent foreign journeys as a single man. As always, it was brightened by people I met: the couple who included me on their trips; the kind, young farmer and his stunning wife who gave me the last raspberry of the season, lent me one of their sons' mopeds which I rode without a helmet down the steep hill to the village, the cooling airstream in my face and hair; the roadside pelota court with its bulging left-hand wall, part of the farm building where swallows were nesting, where I played games late into the evening against locals.

◊

When I arrived back in Bayonne, I spent a night on the site before driving back up to Normandy via Futuroscope in Poitiers which I wanted to be a treat for the children. Its escapism was a perfect finale. Back at LVC we told the children we were separating. I was still reluctant to make it public, hopelessly hoping Maggie would feel she'd made a mistake. When I eventually went down to Tyneside to tell my parents, my mother interrupted me, saying, "Can we just leave it till *Coronation Street's* finished?"

People's comments included:

'But you were like the Waltons . . .'

'I thought you were in it for the long haul . . .'

'I never saw you as a quitter . . .'

'Either you've done something really bad you haven't told us about . . .'

'Steve Harvey – reached for the stars and fell on his face . . .'

And these were things my *friends* said *to my face*.

Time for new friends, you might think, and it was new friends who helped me through this darkest part of my life. I spent the weeks after leaving the family home sleeping on Geoff's sofa bed in their living room or in Jamal's spare bedroom. Each weekday morning I would go with Jamal in his car to his office, dropping his children off on the way. Hamza was in the same year as Gabriel, and some days I would see my children walking along to the bus stop or heading into school. I felt like

Dr Zhivago seeing Lara through the bus window, his heart exploding inside him.

I would answer the phones for Jamal and take deliveries. When it was quiet, I created an anthology of my favourite poems, looked for jobs online, and drafted applications – anything to keep myself busy.

At night I would be the last to bed, flicking through the channels until I was exhausted enough to sleep. I remember Anne, Jamal's wife, saying to me one day, "I'm waiting for you to get angry." I knew what she meant: I was going through a process of bereavement and anger normally features in this. Yet I didn't feel any and didn't expect to.

"Who is there to get angry with? I could get angry with Maggie but she didn't want to have a broken marriage. I could get angry with God, but that seems a bit pointless. I could get angry with myself, but, although I could have been a better husband and done more to help Maggie, I did my best to hold things together."

My father made the surprisingly complimentary comment, "Well, I couldn't have shown the control you have." My view was simply that if you really love someone, then you don't want them to be unhappy. As in the words of Sting's song, "If you love somebody, set them free."

I spent my spare time – and there was a lot of it – visiting friends in Edinburgh or further afield. I felt like an outcast. As I knew would be the case, I stopped being invited to local social events, as Maggie's family would invariably be in attendance and people wanted to avoid any awkwardness. I understood.

I intensified my efforts to find work. Derrick Scougal was now Assistant Chief Constable in Fife and he was my main referee. I'd had no interviews at all but then got the opportunity to do an hour's session for a race equality awareness day for Children in Scotland, although I hadn't been shortlisted for the Arts Development Officer post I'd applied for there. I arranged to do some poetry work with children and got Donny O'Rourke involved. I then received an interview for the position of Emergency Planning Officer for the East Coast of Scotland with the British Red Cross – for the same morning. I had no commitments for weeks either side. I didn't want to pull out of the presentation, not so much for the fee, but for the future opportunities it might bring. It was going to be very stressful, but I calculated I could do both if I had a taxi waiting for me after the interview to get me to the other side of Edinburgh.

I prepared meticulously for both sessions, through Derrick's good offices, liaising with emergency planning officers for the police and local authority in Fife, and also speaking to a friend who was a senior health administrator. I'd spoken to one of the panel by phone before applying, as interested parties were encouraged to do, giving my brief background and checking it was worth my while applying even though I had no professional experience in the health sector. He'd encouraged me to apply, playing down that element.

The day started badly, with a delay. The woman who would be my line manager, should I be successful, informed me the HR Officer had called in sick, so she would be chairing the panel herself. The interview was a disaster – a *Bérézina*, as the French say. She persisted in repeating very specific questions on the Scottish health sector, despite me saying I couldn't give precise answers as I'd no experience in this particular field, while the man I'd spoken to by phone avoided eye contact. (Several weeks later when I still hadn't heard anything, I contacted her and she told me the post had been readvertised. I made my feelings clear).

I dashed over to Heriot Watt University, still fizzing from the grilling I'd received on areas I'd been told were not issues. I'd co-opted a couple of my children to attend the university event to assist me and luckily the session went well.

Mark McGlone was a Scouser I knew who was in a similar domestic situation to me. I had helped him move out of his house into a council flat in Bingham. He had since bought a flat in Pilton and he'd said I could have the spare room, rent free. He was a self-employed accountant and worked long hours. We bought our own food and lived fairly separate lives. I was still having trouble getting to sleep, so each night put on a CD a bridge friend, Katrina, had given me – Leonard Cohen's *Ten New Songs*, barely audible, and it did the trick.

Mark started going out with a new woman, and on New Year's Eve 2002 I was on my own in the flat while they were out at a party. I stood in the back garden in Pilton and had one of those crystalline moments of clarity I've had over the years. I'd never been one to curse the outgoing year, but each of the previous five years had been progressively worse for me. I was going to start the curve moving upwards, whatever strange direction it might take.

Chapter 17

At the start of 2003, I watched the fireworks over Edinburgh welcome in the New Year with a wee dram in my hand, and then went back into the flat and finished two or three poems I'd been struggling with for ages. I felt I could have done anything that night – like the episode of *The Phil Silvers Show* where Sergeant Bilko realises that whatever he tries that particular day will come off and he seeks desperately but, of course, unsuccessfully to capitalise on it.

Among the poems I completed were two about young Hugh Campbell, a pupil in Gabriel's primary school class who had died after falling off his bicycle on his way to school. One was written from my point of view; this one from his father's, based on a story he'd told me:

> ASTRONOMY OF THE HEART
> In memory of Hugh Campbell, for Ian
>
> After your death, the stars lost all their sheen,
> Night skies, like blind reminders of your loss –
> The sights we shared and what we might have seen –
> A universe I could not see across.
>
> And then one time, while walking on the sand,

I found a golden star and took it home,
But stars do not belong upon the land;
I brought it back, returned it to the foam.

What life was there I could not know or guess,
(It felt like such a childish thing to do),
And yet it seemed in some strange way to bless
And light my path and point the way to you.

I felt I should move out of Mark's, but I had nowhere to go. Someone in St John's Parish put me in touch with Mary, who had bought an old person's bungalow a few doors from her house in Portobello as a long-term investment for her son. She told me the rent and I had to apologise and say I couldn't afford it, as almost all my income went to my family. Very kindly, she said she would be happy for someone to be in it and just pay the utility bills. Another virtual stranger was now offering me free accommodation. I wasn't used to accepting charity. I'd always been the one trying to look after others and I found this all very humbling, in both senses of the word. The place was functional and I was very glad of it, but I couldn't put any pictures on the wall or anything of myself into it as that would have been tantamount to accepting my life having been fast-forwarded to solitary old age. Gabriel visited me there once and left the room crying.

In January I went out to visit Dave and Denise at their second home in Cyprus. They needed some stuff bringing out and it was a brief change of scene for me. Everybody there was complaining it was cold but I enjoyed walking in the hills in my shorts. While there I learned that I hadn't got another job I'd interviewed for: they said the young woman who'd got it had had more experience in the last three years, which I couldn't argue with, but what about the previous thirty? I returned to the cold and damp of Edinburgh.

On April 9th, when Baghdad fell to the coalition, I went round to Jamal's and we drank champagne. I recited *Ozymandias* while we watched on TV as Saddam Hussein's statue was toppled in Baghdad. Jamal thought he had seen one of his brothers there, but it had turned out not to be him.

As usual, I had some time with my sons in the summer at Le Vieux Chateau – precious time. I had always known that life was about making memories, not money, but I never felt this as sharply as then.

SUMMER 2003 TRANSPARENCY (SONNET)

The cattle and the donkeys munch their way
Towards us through the evening meadow.
It's still as hot as it has been all day...
In the gite's shade, I play a game with Joe
And catch a glimpse of something I once knew,
A sense of something better than I know.
Beneath Eternity's unblemished blue
The shadows frame the forest's golden glow . . .
From the old elm, by his diverted stream,
I hear a shout, wave back to Gabriel:
Were this a film, this scene would be a dream . . .
I fix the image, freeze it as a still,
Slide it into Memory's carousel
To bring warmth to a distant winter's chill.

At the end of October, for something to do with the children, I took them down to Newcastle for the weekend. We went out for the day: Helen driving the boys, me with Ma and Helen's friend Judith. For once in my life I was sitting in the back of a car. As they talked in the front, I read the *Sunday Times*. I looked for the crossword I thought I'd brought but couldn't find it. The only thing left to read was the appointments section, and there'd be nothing in that for me – Business Manager 60k+, car, etc . . .

I opened it up and saw – 'Volunteer teachers wanted for northern Iraq'. 'Who'd be crazy enough to do that?' I thought. 'Me, probably . . .' was the answer, so I applied.

I went to Wexford to visit Tony and Trish for the Opera Festival in October, something I'd been doing for the last few years. There was always such a lot going on in the coastal town at that time, including all kinds of musical, literary, theatrical and artistic events. A couple of years earlier, Tony had introduced me to Eoin Colfer, a local writer, and he had given me a lift up to Dublin and sent me one of his books for my son Gabriel, then eleven. It was *Artemis Fowl* and inscribed:

To Gabriel!
To properly enjoy this book, it must be read aloud in an Irish
 accent. Your Dad can play "Mulch" the flatulent dwarf!!

Best wishes,
Eoin Colfer

I enjoyed myself there, as usual, and kept in touch with Maureen who had placed the advertisement for the Kurdish charity. She seemed keen to recruit me and when I sounded my children out about my proposed trip to Iraq they just said, "Cool." I also discussed it with my Iraqi pals, Ghanim and Jamal. They both told me they thought the Kurds would look after me. On 13th December 2003, Saddam Hussein, who had gone into hiding, was captured in his bolthole and Kurds around the world heaved a collective sigh of relief. Some, as I found out later, woke their sleeping children to tell them they could now go 'home'.

The Campbells were going to New Zealand for a few weeks over the festive period, so I was house-minding for them, which worked out very well. I attended the traditional Hogmanay party at the home of Jim and Anne Gilchrist, just off the Prom in Portobello. Jim was a journalist at *The Scotsman* and Anne was a senior social worker. Jim played the small pipes and their three children were all very musically talented. I always appreciated their kind invite as I think they knew I had no one else with whom to see in the New Year.

INTO THE WIND
(To the Gilchrist girls – for their music, Hogmanay 2003)

At the turn of the tide, at the turn of the year,
The moon, at its first quarter, cuts a cold, glimpsed arc,
The wind would make your eyes water and freeze the tears,
Sleet strafes the sky like tracer bullets in the dark.

Nothing is moving – everything poised in the mouth
Of the frozen moment. On foot, I'm heading north
While for months the feathered traffic has all been south.
I feel the full force of the airstream from the Forth.

Still as stones upon the beach, oystercatchers stand,
Hardly flinching, in a little flock. Heads held up,
Beaks pointing forward into the flying sleet and sand,
Not sheltering behind a rock. The stirrup cup
Is not yet filled with morning's warming whisky,
But, "Into the wind!" seems to be the toast to me.

Chapter 18

In the second week in January, 2004, Mark McGlone drove me to Edinburgh Airport and I flew down to Heathrow. I spent a few days with Maureen, a feisty middle-aged woman from Sunderland, and meeting her Kurdish friends as well as Jessica, who was travelling out to Kurdistan with me. She'd turned sixty and had been a TEFL teacher in Cambodia for the last few years. We were really doing this on trust: the KCF was a tiny operation, run from Maureen's cluttered little upstairs flat in Croydon. I had gone through the motions of enquiring about personal insurance, but the companies' staff either laughed or thought they'd misheard. Even if anybody had been crazy enough to offer me cover, I couldn't have afforded the premium. I would have to rely on the charity to look after me if I got ill or injured, and to transport my body back to the UK if I died there. I was quite pragmatic about all this, making what arrangements I could to provide for my children in case something should happen to me. I'd known that I needed to take some positive – possibly outlandish – action to stop the downward spiral of my life and turn things around, and volunteering to work in Iraq was certainly a dramatic move. I had made my decision – and my will.

Maureen took us to visit a Kurdish family involved with the charity, and she divulged to us at this point that the woman's husband was a minister in the Iraqi Government. Her sister was Herohan, the wife of Jalal Talabani, founder and head of the PUK (Patriotic Union of Kurdistan), which controlled the area around Suleimaniyah. Some family members were travelling out with us. We flew from Heathrow to Amman, spending the night, although barely sleeping, in a small hotel in the Jordanian capital. There was a magnificent sunrise over the hills surrounding the city as we were driven to the airport.

"I do hope I get a window seat," said Jessica in her very well enunciated English way as we walked out to the little plane for NGO personnel.

"I think you'll find they're *all* window seats," I laughed, climbing aboard, there being just a narrow aisle with a line of seats each side.

The two South African pilots were the only crew and the drinks service was a cooler box from which you could help yourself. We flew for hours over the featureless, barren landscape of western Iraq. As we approached Baghdad, where I had not realised we would be landing, they told us it would not be like a normal landing: they would spiral in, so as to present less of a target to rockets or missiles of any kind. They clearly relished this kind of approach and I must admit I found it exciting – something to write about in my memoirs, sometime.

Having landed without incident, we had to get out of the plane and be processed in the vast terminal that for so many years had been virtually unused due to wars and Iraq's pariah status under Saddam Hussein. (One of my female companions recalled having stood in line here as a young student as Uday Hussein, one of Saddam's depraved sons, walked up and down with his tiger, lambasting them for leaving the country). I have a shaky, mauve-coloured stamp in my passport of 'BAGHDAD INTERNATIONAL AIRPORT', 'ENTRY' (and its equivalent in Arabic), '2001 JAN 12', 'IRAQ', '1434' & 'CPA' (Coalition Provisional Authority).

We returned to our tiny aircraft and were corkscrewed back into the sky, landing two hundred miles to the north at Arbil – sometimes spelt Erbil or Irbil – and also known as Hawler. There was virtually nothing there. The pilots unloaded our luggage onto the dust. A little fleet of 4x4s drove up and our small party was warmly welcomed by those sent to collect us. The airport terminal was a container in which our bags were searched. I had my photograph taken beside a fallen-down sign reading, 'Hawler International Airport', thinking 'This will be something to show people when they'll, no doubt, have a massive modern airport here in a few years.'

It was a bumpy, circuitous route to Suleimaniyah, and it was dark when we arrived. We were installed in the Ashti Hotel, a three-storey building, from where I had a view over Salim Street to the mountains.

One of the joys of being in Suleimaniyah was that the mountains were always visible, except when it was snowing. The Kurds, betrayed from ancient times to Churchill and beyond, have an often-quoted saying, "We have no friends but the mountains . . ." They have been their refuge and saviour over the centuries.

It was still the school holidays so we were taken around on various visits. One of them was to the Red Fort, the northern headquarters of the notorious Iraqi Intelligence Service where prisoners, mostly Kurdish, were held for questioning. Another was to a house where I was to deliver a present to the youngest child from Maureen, who was her sponsor. As I took my shoes off before entering through the low door, I saw a pair of artificial legs propped up against the wall. The inside was filled with children and our group, but in one gloomy corner a figure sat silently on the ground. There was an almost perceptible cloud over his head as though he sat in his own microclimate, isolated from the sun shining only a short distance away. He had lost his legs in a minefield and his brother had gone in and carried him out. His demeanour among his family had a heavy impact on me and I wrote this poem soon after:

HERO
(For Arsalan 1-6-1971 – 10-9-2004)

The pair of legs in trainers at the door
Stands on guard, as *he* must have done before
When he was a Peshmerga in the war.
Now he sits in a corner on the floor.
A portrait of the leader they adore,
Pinned proudly on one wall, all their décor;
No decorations to show for valour
In this hovel in the midst of squalor.

We come with words and dollars, nothing more,
While he asks what is left worth living for:
A question six young children must ignore
And smile, take sweets as offspring of the poor.
I'll soon get up, walk to the 4x4;
I only left my shoes outside the door.

The following year, when his wife was expecting their seventh child, he was killed in an accidental explosion while getting petrol.

We were taken out for lunch to one of the better restaurants. Kurdish food is excellent – lots of fresh fruit and vegetables and excellent lamb and fish. My mood was lifted by our female guide, who ran the sponsorship scheme, walking into the Gents' toilet by mistake and I ribbed her about this mercilessly, and was pleased to see men and women could share jokes about such things here, if not toilets . . .

◊

A few days after I arrived, my friend Jamal was due in Baghdad. I'd tried to get him on our flight but, as can be imagined, arranging for an Arab friend of an unknown volunteer to get on an NGO flight was never going to be easy. I did, however, persuade Kak Dana, who managed the Kurdistan Children's Fund, to take me down to Baghdad with them on their business trip in order to meet up with him there. The only other international NGO with staff in the area at the time was MAG (Mines Advisory Group) and en route we passed a minefield in the process of being cleared at Chamchamal, near Kirkuk, and I later wrote this poem:

CLEARING MINES IN KURDISTAN
(For those who do it)

They move along the rows as though tending
Some crop delicate as dragonfly wings,
Pricking, teasing – all that crouching, bending –
Knowing each steel seed could be the ending
Of a life, not the beginning.
                    The flags,
Lively triangles of vermilion,
Are not to scare off sparrows or pigeons,
Nor are they the accumulated bunting
From village festivals to say, "We've won!"
Forewarn a harvest stored in body bags.

The staked out plots resemble graves, a dig;
Hunched figures uncovering the remains
Of earlier civilizations, working
Painstakingly to preserve intact
Each lovingly crafted artefact.
                    Let's hope

> The Future's archaeologists might find
> Something more worthwhile than, "This land was mined?"

We stopped briefly to eat and to buy fuel sold in cans by boys at the side of the road. I needed a pee. It's very difficult to urinate when a man – even a friendly man – is standing next to you with an AK-47. We arrived safely in Baghdad, passing a burnt-out tank as a reminder of the only recently concluded open warfare of the invasion. Violence now took the form of bombings by the militant elements of the dispossessed Ba'ath Party of which Saddam Hussein had been head. Our vehicles were searched and checked with mirrors underneath. There were concrete blocks and bollards all around the hotels in an attempt to frustrate such attacks. I contacted Jamal by mobile and learned he had just arrived at his mother's house – his father had died many years before of a heart attack. When Jamal and his brother, Abdullah, arrived at the hotel, the tension in my Kurdish friends was palpable as I introduced them.

We went for a drink in the neighbouring Alhambra Hotel, where Jamal and Abdullah were searched but I wasn't. I ate at the hotel with Kak Dana and the others most nights as it was considered secure, although it has been bombed since. There were few visitors, as was generally the case, except for an occasional entrepreneur or a coterie of VIPs:

> GUNS MUST BE LEFT AT THE DESK
> (Notice on the door of a Baghdad Hotel)
>
> And yet they stand there in full uniform,
> Weighed down with weapons,
> Their young backs taut
> With the need to support
> Ammunition belts and all the other clobber,
> Aussie troops on VIP Protection,
> Boys from the Gold Coast,
> In a city poised between calm and chaos,
> What do we talk about but sport –
> Jonny Wilkinson's boot –
> And Cooper's Beer at seven per cent.

Most nights, a ghoulish-looking, louche figure played the piano to the extensive, almost-empty restaurant. During intervals I would ask him, and anyone on their own any evening – generally a foreign businessman or reporter – to join us. The pianist, who was called Samir Peter, told me stories of the old days when he played for the wealthy and the glamorous. One of the reporters I spoke to was a Yorkshireman called Sean McAllister, who was there to cover Saddam Hussein's trial for the BBC. A year or two later, when I was back in the UK, I was watching TV when a documentary called *The Liberace of Baghdad* came on. I discovered that Sean, bored due to the long delays in the case coming to court, had made a film about the pianist.

The next day, with his brother driving, Jamal showed me his home town; for years he had promised to do so "once that man has gone." It was sad how the place where he had played football as a boy was now a rubbish dump and the bookshops and the galleries were gone. Everywhere was broken. Although Baghdad was a dangerous place for everyone, the serial kidnapping of foreigners had not yet begun and at one point I got out of the car and went shopping with Jamal in a grocer's.

We met up with my friend Ghanim's brother, Paulus, who was living as a semi-fugitive, driving a dirty car so as not to attract attention and looking nondescript, as far as he could with that shock of white hair distinctive of the Chaldean Christians. He was a doctor whose life had been threatened. I asked him to administer the final dose of my rabies vaccine which I'd brought with me, though unrefrigerated, which he did in his little clinic he still visited occasionally. He invited us round to his house for a meal another night.

At Jamal's mother's we ate fish from the Tigris, bought in my honour. I had brought some fruit from a stall. The men all ate together, sitting on the floor of the best room while the women stayed in the kitchen and the children watched noisy American cartoons in the back room.

At Paulus's house, we ended up with ten of us in a small room – Jamal, Abdullah and me, together with Paulus, his wife and four daughters and one fiancé. Two of the daughters had trained in medicine and one in pharmacology; the youngest was still at school. While we were eating, a US army helicopter flew low overhead, setting off a car alarm on the road.

The engaged couple, both doctors, got married a few months later but were unable to get out of Damascus to begin a new life in the West. Paulus and his eldest daughter, also a doctor, managed to get to the UK where they became embroiled in the asylum process. Eventually Paulus was allowed to stay because of the risk to him if he was repatriated, but the authorities notified their intention of sending his daughter back on the grounds that she was too old to have been living at home as a dependent. I wrote to the Home Office, as a former officer in a British police force and a Home Office-approved police trainer, stating that I had visited their home in Baghdad and it had been clear to me that she was living there as a dependent family member. She was granted leave to remain and has been living in the UK and working as a doctor for over a decade now.

One night at our hotel there was an *ood* player performing, but unfortunately Jamal and Abdullah felt it was too late to stay. To my delight, surprise and amusement, he began playing 'Que Sera, Sera', fudging the words as he went along. It brought back memories of my Nan singing the Doris Day hit to me when I was a young boy, and I was able to write down the lyrics for the musician.

◊

We travelled back to 'Suly' and I was returned to the relative safety of the Ashti Hotel. The school holidays were over and Jessica and I began teaching at the 'Exemplary' School. It was a source of great excitement to the children, having two foreigners teaching them; it was a source of great pride for the school to have two native speakers teaching English. I liked most of the other teachers, but thought the Head a rather uninspiring man. We had to push hard to do anything innovative and he was clearly uncomfortable with us. There was a local place with a function room where I went to see live Premiership football matches projected onto a wall. I hired an *Ice Age* DVD and took some classes there to see it, on the basis of it being a fun way to improve their English. Unfortunately there were some technical difficulties – including a power cut – and the subtitles were someone's guesses: 'mammoths' were 'mammals', for example. I remember remarking to one of the staff that whoever was responsible for them had had a dictionary in one hand and a bottle of whisky in the other.

◊

Suleimaniyah was a strange place on the cusp of different cultures and times – very liberated and progressive in some ways, backward and dysfunctional in others. On several occasions we didn't know whether the school would be open on a morning, due to no one being aware whether the moon had been viewed or not to determine if a holy period had begun. Most people we met were not at all religious – the Kurds had had strong links with the Eastern bloc in previous decades – and yet they observed the fasting at Ramadan. People were generally very friendly and polite, but, as Jessica put it, AK-47s were as ubiquitous there as umbrellas were in London.

I was disappointed to discover I'd missed the BBC's Alistair Leithead, the former Radio Newcastle presenter who had called me for news items each working day at Washington Police Station. He'd been staying in the other local hotel used by Westerners.

I loved wandering around Suleimaniyah and especially the souk. It was a lively city, full of noise and traffic, and Salim Street was its main artery – filled with the battered buses where you passed your money via the other passengers to the multi-tasking driver; the manic Brazilis (the orange-and-white taxis Saddam Hussein had apparently contracted to buy from Brazil at a ratio of four-to-one for every tank he purchased); the donkeys; the handcarts; pedestrians; private cars; official saloons; 4x4s; and lurching, overloaded lorries. There were satellite TV stores, mobile phone outlets, internet cafés and a faux McDonald's called MacBatts. I remember a hard-bitten journalist who was back in Iraq doing a follow-up piece after the war, returning from an internet café where she'd gone to email her copy due to the hotel's link being down, visibly shaken, having negotiated her way through rows of screens where young boys were watching sexually violent pornography. I had a distinct sense of liberated Iraq as a child who'd been locked in a cupboard for a long time, being let out into the light and being surrounded by all sorts of things without anyone they could trust to tell them what was good for them and what was harmful.

Two of the biggest occasions in the Kurdish year fall within a few days of each other. On March 16th 1988, during the closing days of the Iran-Iraq war, a gas attack was launched upon the civilian population of the Kurdish town of Halabja in northern Iraq by the Iraqi Government. About five thousand people were killed, many of them women and children in the act of fleeing. I visited the memorial which was built there to these 'martyrs' and other victims. The day is remembered annually with blaring music and flashing images of discoloured faces.

The other day is Nawroz (New Day), celebrated on March 21st to mark the spring equinox. Convoys of packed vehicles desert the cities for picnics with roving musicians, ghetto blasters and barbecues, spreading out around lakes and along river banks and the flower-covered hillsides. They take part in prolonged, shoulder-heaving communal dances. I organised an extra event a few days later, to combine it with St Patrick's Day, and we had a music-and-dance show at a large hall which featured the best and worst of Kurdish entertainment – some good music and hopeless organisation. I had grown my hair long enough to make a ponytail and wore a green ribbon in it before visiting a local barber after the event.

The next month I was in Qala Diza in the northeast, near the Iranian border, for the thirtieth anniversary of the bombing and rocket attack by the Iraqi Air Force. The woman next to me told me she had lost her son in the raid.

I travelled there in a party with an Italian woman, Graziella Bronzini, who had raised money to help rebuild the hospital, where she was treated like a Mother Theresa figure by staff. We were staying with the family of a local KCF social worker, sleeping on the floor and sofas in communal Kurdish fashion. The social worker's father was a devout Muslim and was one of those men with whom I have formed an instant bond – like Joannis on honeymoon in Santorini – despite having no words in common. He told me, through his son, his home had been destroyed seven times and he had made new homes each time, sometimes on the same site, sometimes in another place. All his children had survived. He was old now and surrounded by grandchildren. It felt, to me, like a biblical story.

The KCF staff had received a call to say that Graziella was invited to visit 'Mam Jalal', Jalal Talabani's colloquial name, so we headed south sooner than expected. We were admitted through the security gates and greeted by the Talabanis. Graziella, wearing her Kurdish outfit, was treated as a guest of honour and we had our photographs taken and were presented with them before we left (dated 260404). We sat down to a magnificent meal with large salvers of turkey and fish. Jalal Talabani was known to be very fond of turkey and the joke was that when dining with the head of state of their northern neighbours he'd been asked which bit of turkey he'd like and he'd replied, "The southeast."

"More fish, mister?" he asked me several times.

The following April he was elected first non-Arab President of Iraq.

◊

I was invited to several meals there with Herohan and at their home in Suleimaniyah. At their country retreat, one time, she unrolled old maps of Iraq on the table in front of me which she believed proved that the oil-rich region of Kirkuk was – and always had been – Kurdish. When she asked if Jessica and I wanted to go out on the nearby lake, Jessica replied, "Ooh, yes . . ." and a short time later we were in a speedboat with Herohan and her personal bodyguard, while all the other AK-47-shouldering Peshmergas were in another, and we were roaring across the water as if we were in a scene from a James Bond film.

As well as teaching at the school, we were involved in many other activities including teaching adult classes (advertised on local radio, for which Jessica also did some work). I ran film shows of classics such as *High Noon* and *Billy Elliot*. *High Noon* was self-explanatory but *Billy Elliot* required a potted political background from me. I'd forgotten I knew a couple of actors in it from my college days, including 'Little Billy Fane' (Malcolm Collins) as the pianist, and it was bizarre to see him on screen in those surroundings.

I also organised poetry readings and one day Kawan Faraj Ali, Senior Field Officer at KCF, took me to meet the most famous living Kurdish poet, Sherko Bekas. We had a discussion about the difficulties of translating poetry – via Kawan who acted as interpreter, ironically. Sherko used an image, variations of which I've seen since, about it being like a set of lips either side of a pane of glass: they look like they're kissing, but they never meet.

During a discussion with Herohan at her TV studio, part of her media interests, she offered to publish a collection of my poetry. I had the fantastic experience of helping to design my cover with an artist/musician friend, Mohammad Diary ('Diary Floot'), and then editing the book myself and seeing five hundred printed copies appear. It featured a 'Wanted' style poster of me on the front and was called *A Fixed Expression*, from a line in my poem *A Passive Existence*. I had to leave over a hundred of them behind with the short story writer, Sherzad Hassan, for safekeeping when I eventually left.

Social life tended to involve KCF staff, students, or some of the few other ex-pats. Tom Grogan, an Irish guy working for AsiaCell, one of the main local mobile phone companies, was staying at the Ashti and he used to have a weekly drinks evening in his large room. Tom asked me to prepare some security guidelines for new arrivals, and I was glad to do so, as well as give some advice to senior management and the local architect about designing security features into their planned new HQ.

One of our main pastimes was five-a-side. I organised games involving ex-pats, waiters, students and KCF staff. Mike was one of the Canadian contingent who took part. Although his academic background was in Economics and Politics, he was teaching Modern Poetry at Suleimaniyah University. He invited me to give a session, which, of course, I agreed to and thoroughly enjoyed.

As might be expected, all manner of people are drawn to a post-war country: adventurers/thrill-seekers, entrepreneurs/opportunists, reporters/self-publicists, showmen and shysters. One guy who wandered onto the scene was Cliff, a good-looking, blue-eyed, blond-haired American in his thirties, taking photographs everywhere. If there were any insurgents in Suleimaniyah, he would certainly have attracted their attention. It transpired he was a former USAF pilot who seemed to be going through a re-evaluation of his life following the death of his sister. He had just got a job with the OSCE (Organization for Security and Co-operation in Europe) in the Republic of Georgia, monitoring activity in the Caucasus Mountains. He suggested I might like to apply and I did briefly consider it. When he left, he threw a big dinner for all his friends, including many members of the US military reserve based there.

The next day, I visited him at his hotel. I knew he had blown most of his money on the night and did not want him to take even greater risks in accepting lifts on his way back to Tbilisi. I gave him $400 and he promised to pay me back sometime. He'd invited me to visit him and I said I would.

◊

I was asked by KCF to run a summer football camp but I thought it would be too hot for me to do that and I was really missing my children. My Canadian friends were going back home via Istanbul on May 1st and I decided to travel with them. One of the Talabani family took me out to the souk to choose gifts as a thank you. I was offered the opportunity to take Mike's role at the university and I agreed to come back and do that as an extra in the autumn, as well as teaching at the school and the youth centre. Kak Dana provided transport for us to the Turkish border and from there we were collected by one of a family of taxi drivers Dave, the group leader, had used before. Dave was a very savvy guy, but also lived life close to the edge.

The Turkish customs and immigration process was lengthy, languid, and yet menacing. To an official of a state where the 'K' word was not used, the Canadians had all kinds of stuff that could, at the least, delay our entry into the country. Dozens of copies of my book, with its dedication to Herohan and acknowledgements of the Kurds' troubled history and struggles, were buried deep in my pack, but I'd given each of my friends one and Mike's was sitting on the examining table with my mug shot looking up. I surreptitiously turned it over.

I was sweating. Dave had had football shirts made from the Kurdish flag, for their five-a-side team, and had given me one. I was wearing it under my shirt, as the safest way to get it through customs. It was made of nylon, a tight fit and the sun was very hot. The customs officer was not happy with several of the items in the Canadians' luggage, querying who the individuals were in Dave's photos and asking him if he'd seen *Midnight Express*. Eventually we were allowed through and were driven in stages the distance of a few hundred kilometres to the predominantly Kurdish city, Diyarbakir, skirting the quaintly named city of Batman. According to Wikipedia, in 2008 the then-mayor began looking into the possibility of suing those involved in the production of the *Batman* films, claiming the studios had been using the name of the superhero without permission from the city, and "placing the blame for a number of unsolved murders and a high female suicide rate on the psychological impact that the films' success has had on the city's inhabitants." No lawsuit has actually been filed to date.

At Diyarbakir we booked flights to Istanbul, where we took a taxi to the Sultanahmet district. The others stayed in a hostel, but I decided to treat myself, spending a little extra for a room in a bijou little hotel around the corner called the Hotel Poem, which Dave had stayed in before. In each room was a different poem by a Turkish writer. It had free internet in the lobby. I spent three days there, enjoying the sense of safety, relaxation and not being in demand or the focus of attention.

ISTANBUL HOSTEL ROOFTOP

On the hostel's rooftop reading *Sufi* poetry,
Eating a mushroom omelette and drinking Efes beer,
Looking at the truant May sunlight playing on the sea,
Learning how to live a life that's free of guilt or fear.

138

Chapter 19

I stayed a few days with Maureen before heading north. I spent the summer with friends in England, France and Scotland. One day in August, while in Edinburgh, I got a phone call from a very English ex-neighbour called Miranda. In the course of the conversation she asked if I was still writing poetry, before telling me, in her own inimitable way, she had "a real poet coming for tea." She invited me along and I had the pleasure of meeting John Hegley and, for the first time ever, exchanging poetry books with another poet, 'real' or otherwise. He inscribed in *The Family Pack*, 'This is the book of Steve the poet and John the poet xx'.

◊

After the Festival and time with my children, I set off to make my way back to Iraq. It was not to be a direct and uneventful journey, but the most dangerous one of my life. I had decided to take Cliff up on his offer and visit him in Georgia and had arranged to link up with his mother and his Georgian girlfriend who were travelling up into the Caucasus Mountains to meet up with him. I flew from London to Istanbul, staying at the Hotel Poem. I managed to get a cheap flight to Trabzon in eastern Turkey for the next day (flights to Tbilisi for some reason were prohibitively expensive) and a shared ride to the airport. The downside was that I arrived very early for my flight at the domestic terminal and facilities were negligible. I decided to make my way through the connecting walkway to the international terminal. As I pushed my trolley down the ramp towards a bar, I heard someone call out, "Steve!" I kept on walking, registering that the bar advertised Efes beer, which I had drunk in Suly.

"Steve!"

I was conscious of someone approaching me from behind. It was Georges, a Lebanese engineer who had stayed at the Ashti. He was flying to Diyarbakir on his way back to Suly and had done the same as me in crossing from the domestic side of the airport. We had a few beers together and he agreed to take some of the DVDs I was bringing over for the film club, saving me from carrying them round for several weeks and from the risk of them being stolen. The next day, via a mixture of lifts and buses, I made my way out of Trabzon on a day trip to the ancient and spectacular monastery of Sumela.

The following morning, as I walked from my cheap hotel past the Russian Market, I asked someone about a bus to Tbilisi and he directed me to a nearby café. Here the owner gestured for me to take a seat and gave me a cup of tea. A bus would come and take me to Tbilisi. In time a young Iranian student joined me in waiting as I read *The Curious Incident of the Dog in the Night-Time*. I'm not an especially fast reader, but I had read the whole book and there was still no sign of a bus. The café owner kept fobbing me off, but eventually a long-wheelbase blue transit turned up. This immediately triggered alarm bells in my memory as the last time I remembered seeing such a vehicle I'd been in uniform and witnessed 27 men get out carrying bags and entering The Gosforth Hotel in Newcastle. It had not been a local football team's night out, but part of a protection racket. The bags, it transpired, had contained axes and at least one sawn-off shotgun . . .

The café's proprietor assured me that everything was OK and got the gorilla out of the front passenger seat for me to take his place. I had my holdall with what passed for my valuables in the footwell, having stowed Matthew's rucksack, containing all my clothes, behind the seat inside the back door. The Iranian student had walked off. One or two women and children got into the vehicle. The gorilla kept opening my door as if he'd forgotten I was there but would then give me a look which seemed to say 'But not for long . . .'

Eventually, he got in the transit and sat immediately behind me. He asked me to pass my bag back to him; I couldn't believe he was concerned that I didn't have enough legroom. When I turned to look at the other occupants, they looked down at the floor. We drove a few hundred yards and another woman and child got in. Her reaction was the same. I looked out of the window and watched women standing at doors in the evening sunlight and men going in and coming out and all became clear to me. Another gorilla was loafing in the middle of the street, basking in the heat and flexing his lazy muscles ostentatiously as the following little incident took place:

BACKSCRATCHING
(Trabzon, Turkey, 15th September 2004)

Sweating, I sit in this dodgy minibus;
Waiting to go to Tbilisi –
As I have been all day . . .
Prostitutes entice clients
From the brothel doorways . . .
A spindly seller of knick-knacks
Pushes his sad barrow by.
One of the burly pimps leans over,
Snatches a plastic backscratcher
And makes great play,
To their amusement,
Of scratching his broad back.
The 'tat' man makes submissive movements,
Curves a nervous smile, and lights
A cigarette. It's a lost cause –
The pimp, barrow boy, prostitutes and poet
All know that he can forget
About getting it back:
You scratch my back,
And I'll scratch the skin off yours . . .

The café owner was clearly running a shuttle service of Georgian prostitutes to and from Tbilisi. Another couple of women got into the back of the van, their eyes downcast. These were not shy women. If they were not making eye contact with me, it was because they knew that I was about to become a victim. I remembered references to how, in WWII RAF bomber crews, no one ever got pally with the rear gunner as they had the shortest survival times, being sitting ducks for fighter pilots' bullets. This journey was reckoned to take fourteen hours; there was no way I could keep awake – never mind alert – for all that time, and even if I could, if the gorilla had a knife or a garrotte, I would be helpless to defend myself.

A bizarre battle was breaking out in my brain between the aspiring writer saying, "There's a great story here!" and the former copper pointing out, "Maybe, but you've got to be alive to be able to write it."

The driver/keeper continued his slow pick-up routine while the gorilla kept suggesting I pass my bag back. The ex-police officer was now shouting, "Get off the fucking bus!" in my head, but I was considering what would happen if I missed my rendezvous with Cliff's mother and girlfriend in Tbilisi. Maybe I was being a bit paranoid . . .

The vehicle drove out of the Russian Market. "You've missed your chance to escape now," chided the voice of reason. My imagination was fast-forwarding to images of cheese wire being tightened in the night and mothers covering their children's eyes and ears. The minibus did a loop and then stopped for what looked like the final passenger. The gorilla tapped me on the shoulder and then pointed to the bag at my feet. I nodded, picked it up, opened my door and got out. He opened his door. I shook my head and indicated the back doors. He got out and opened them. I had choreographed it mentally a few moments before and reached in, grabbed my rucksack and was out with it on my back in a second, immediately heading up the hill. The gorilla shouted at me in consternation. "Too late," I shouted back. "I've missed my friends in Tbilisi now."

I was too emotionally drained to do anything but return to the hotel, book another night, go for a meal and a few drinks and try and get a good night's sleep. I didn't want to go to the bus station at night and didn't know if buses left then.

The next morning the young guy on the desk asked me what had happened and, when I explained, suggested I went to see the tourist police. Normally I would have dismissed this as a bad idea and just written off the $28 as a small price to pay for a close call, but, having very little money, I went to the tourist police office and spoke to them. They suggested I go and ask at the café for my money back, on the basis he'd kept me waiting all day. I walked down to the Russian Market. When I entered the café, the owner offered me a seat and then made a phone call. I told him I wasn't waiting around again – either he gave me my money back or I went to see the police. He stalled. I left. I returned to report back to the police who then drove me down there and brought him back to the station. I was in too deep to back down now. We sat around a table and a discussion took place between the police and him.

Suddenly, he stood up and stormed out. A few minutes later, he returned with the money which he handed over to a police officer who gave it to me. Throughout, he avoided eye contact with me, and I was only too aware that this whole incident was a major loss of face for him – and for the leader of a criminal gang, even a small-time one, loss of face is far worse than a loss of money.

I went to the bus station and waited for a bus to Tbilisi. If I had sweated the day before, I was now cascading. I had a long wait for a bus and he knew where I was going. I got access to the internet and checked on flights but they were hundreds of dollars. "Very bright, Stephen," the sensible internal voice said. "You've recovered $28 but in such a way that you're now considering shelling out hundreds of dollars you can't afford in order to escape the possible consequences."

When my bus pulled in, I scanned the other passengers for potential hit-men. Was that really a musical instrument in his violin case? It was paranoia at its most comically pathetic. I sat next to a young student from western Turkey who was travelling back to Tbilisi to resume his studies after the summer break. I spent the first few hours alternating between engaging in calm conversation with him and speculating on when and where they would try and get me. Probably not until we got into Georgia, I thought: the greater the distance between Trabzon and the abduction and murder, the more difficult to attribute it to the Russian Market mafia. I was writing a thriller in which I was the victim.

My profuse sweating was not alleviated by the fact that the vehicle I was travelling in was far from being an air-conditioned coach – it was a bashed-up old bus with grills on the windows which could not be opened. As almost everyone appeared to be a chain smoker, I was coming to the conclusion that if a bullet didn't kill me, then passive smoking would.

Border control between Turkey and Georgia, although less severe than that with Iraq, was even more prolonged, disorganised and frustrating. Carefully loaded luggage was required to be removed and scattered around on the ground for inspection, which turned out to be an entirely arbitrary process. It took about four hours before the bus was allowed to continue and the border crossing point was one of those where there is a perceptible difference between the country you are leaving and the one you are entering. The pigs, for one thing. They were rooting about in little roadside smallholdings and sometimes running across the road. Another difference was the remnants of industrial buildings from the years of Soviet control.

In my preoccupation with survival, I had omitted to do such simple things as change money and so, when we stopped at a café for breakfast, I was unable to buy anything, although I had brought some food with me. The people I was travelling with were quite poor, so, naturally, they offered to buy me a meal. My mood was improved by their consideration and generosity – and the good, homely, hot food.

At an earlier stop during the night, I made a telephone call on my mobile which I found still worked, thankfully, even though I had asked for its foreign connection facility to be suspended. I told my sister that if anything happened to me – or they didn't hear from me after a day or two – then the Met, or whoever, should begin their enquiries at a little teashop in the Russian Market with the police in Trabzon, but 'not to worry'! I'd also phoned and spoken to my wife and daughter in the controlled voice of a man who thinks he might not get to speak to them again.

Although my anxiety eased as the hours passed, I still felt under threat, but reasoned that if it hadn't happened by now, the most likely scenario would be that I would be attacked at Tbilisi bus station which was notorious for robberies. This would look like just another tourist crime statistic. The gorilla, or another family member, was probably flexing his muscles in anticipation. As we approached Tbilisi, I called the number I had for Cliff's girlfriend. Irma answered and said she and her sister would meet me at the Marriott. Hotel chains names are normally a turn-off for me, but now, with its associations of cups of coffee with my friend Eamonn who'd been manager at Gateshead, Sunderland and East Kilbride, Marriott was a comforting word.

A few miles before Tbilisi the bus pulled onto a piece of waste ground where a man appeared to be changing a tyre on his car.

"Does the bus usually stop here?" I asked my companion.

"Not other times. No."

I was still trying to work out whether this was a good or bad thing when the man who'd been by the car got on the bus wiping his hands on the proverbial oily cloth.

I heard him say 'taxi' and 'Tbilisi'.

A host of thoughts rushed through my head. 'It didn't look like a taxi, did it?' 'Why would anyone need a taxi to Tbilisi when the bus was going there anyway?' 'Had he really been changing a tyre?' 'Was someone else hiding nearby?' 'Once in the car would he then drive me into an ambush?'

'How much?' was the question I asked.

It was eight dollars. My student friend told me it should be half that.

"We'll take it," I said. "Come on, I'll pay for it." If it was a trap he wouldn't have set a high price – not unless he was a really good actor . . .

We got our gear out of the luggage hold as quickly as possible and in a minute or two were being driven away, waving to the good people with whom we had spent the last twenty hours. The car driver complained about the state of the roads, saying he needed a new tyre. 'This journey would probably pay for it', I thought, 'one way or another . . .'

I got him to drop us off at the side of the hotel. We carried our bags in and were greeted by the welcome sight of two similar-looking, slim, dark-haired young women. After brief introductions we left and my travelling companion went off to catch a bus to his digs while I walked with the girls to the apartment Cliff shared with some colleagues. There were a lot of security personnel nearby, and Irma told me the President had a flat in the next block along in the compound.

'Just perfect,' I thought. I wondered if the gorilla was scratching his head as I failed to walk down the bus steps at Tbilisi Bus Station. Even if they discovered I had gone to the Marriott, which was unlikely as I hadn't mentioned this to anyone but the car driver, the staff there would only be able to tell them, "Two guys left with two local girls." Nothing new in that.

And now I was safely ensconced in this luxurious apartment with 24-hour security outside. The sense of relief and exhilaration was such as people report after a near-death experience. What level of danger I *had* actually been in, I don't know and will never be able to discover, but it did appear to me from the start that at the least I was going to have some of my stuff stolen, and I couldn't see how they could do that without killing me as I could identify those responsible to the police and I suspected offences against foreign tourists would be treated harshly.

◊

Irma took me to her mother's house where I met Cliff's mother, Andrea, a lively woman in her early sixties. A day or two later, the three of us travelled north by bus and then were driven in a 4x4 up into the Caucasus Mountains. The sides of the winding tracks were marked occasionally by an axle or a steering wheel with flowers in it where a vehicle had gone over the side and its occupants been killed. At one point we had to stop as workers were making a new route through a blackened, hard-frozen avalanche, which had apparently been there since February. As we tasted some of their *chacha* (locally distilled Georgian vodka, generally made from grape pomace or residue).

After a shuddering journey of several hours, including a delay due to another enforced stop where an earth-moving vehicle had broken down, we made it to Cliff's OSCE base outside Omalo in Tusheti province just before nightfall. In the short distance from there to the Keselo Hotel our driver made a slight error of judgement and we got stuck in a large hole. With a bit of help from several burly guys, we eventually made it out and to our lodgings. Accommodation was very limited and the three of us ended up sharing a room. It was another day or two before Cliff's leave was due to start. A colleague of his had his girlfriend and her friend visiting as well. One of them was from Edinburgh and worked for Canongate Books, which had rejected, very gently, my first attempt at a novel a year before.

The hotel was a million miles from a Marriott. It was more like a hunting lodge with a picket fence added. It had one light bulb in the whole place, located in the cramped but cosy dining room. There was no electricity, so the power for this was supplied by a lorry battery in the kitchen. The water supply was from a spring which ran through the garden in a pipe the size of a hosepipe, which sat in a larger one. To brush your teeth, you lifted the hosepipe out, temporarily depriving the village of Omalo in the valley below of their water supply. When I visited Omalo, bearskins and wolfskins were drying outside the wooden homes and women were knitting woollen socks and shawls in the September sunshine.

The days were largely lived according to the length of daylight, but the time of day had no effect on drinking alcohol. Georgians were the most enthusiastic drinkers I have ever witnessed, throwing the *chacha* back in one after making the obligatory toast. I was introduced as a poet, which meant I had to do more than my fair share of toasting.

One morning I was sitting out front writing in my journal when Andrea ran towards me shouting, "Stevi, Stevi . . . Guess who's coming to visit tomorrow?"

Before I could think of a reply she yelled, "The President's wife, the President's wife!"

'Mrs Bush sipping *chacha* in the Keselo Hotel?' I mused.

"Mrs Saakashvili is coming to visit!"

There was an interesting older, English couple staying at the place who had done much to help the Tusheti region and she was apparently coming to see them. They were to go via helicopter trip to a picnic, and as we were the only other three guests I felt we would have been invited if it hadn't been for Andrea's overly exuberant and voluble reaction. The following morning we saw a helicopter land by the OSCE base below.

There was a solitary plain clothes security man by the little wooden gate in the fence.

Later, I was sitting absorbed in writing up my journal when I realised I had missed the President's wife's lowest-of-low-key entrances. I wasn't particularly disappointed, but I was pleasantly surprised a few minutes later when a woman wandered over with a young boy and said, "Hi, I'm Sandra," holding out her hand. She also introduced her son, Eduard.

◊

When Cliff's leave began he arranged for a local guy to arrive at the Keselo with a number of horses. I had been on a horse once before, many years earlier, and it had been a bit of an embarrassment, but I didn't want to miss out. Also, I was still infused with a sense of having survived a dangerous episode, which, paradoxically, makes you (even more) inclined to take risks. I got on my mount and it took off up the hillside at full tilt. Either it knew where we were going and was in a hurry to get there, or it was trying to dislodge me from the saddle on which I was bouncing up and down. I reckoned if I could hold on long enough, it would get tired and might be fooled into thinking I was a rider who knew what he was doing. Sure enough, my weight, if not my horsemanship, brought the animal to an eventual halt and I rode back down to rejoin the others.

We spent a day wending our way along mountain tracks through trees, often overlooking drops of many hundred feet. On one such path, only about ten feet across, Cliff rode past me on the outside edge, kicking my horse on the rump as he did so . . .

As we came down into a wide valley with several of the region's distinctive fortified towers, I saw a man riding his horse through the shallow river, holding his young son in front of him. A few days later I recorded this incident in a poem.

PATERNAL PARADOX

One day in the mountains I saw a man
Ride a horse across a stream
Holding his young son in front of him:
Magnificent!

The next day in the town I saw a man

Ride a bicycle along a road
Holding his young son in front of him:
Irresponsible!

It was a long day in the saddle and some of the party were certainly sore and irritable at the end of it, but it had been an exhilarating experience for me, and if I didn't feel I was a natural cowboy, I did feel I wasn't a disgrace to my East Anglian farmhand ancestors.

I felt a connection with a simpler, rustic lifestyle. The day we left, a mobile phone mast was being erected.

◊

Back in the capital, we enjoyed the benefits of electricity. We spent some time with Irma's widowed mother, family and friends. Cliff was planning a trip to use up the rest of his leave, but there were some complications and we were packed and waiting before he told us the trip was definitely on. We had wanted to go to South Ossetia, which had declared independence from Georgia in 1990 (and was subsequently supported by Russia in the South Ossetia war of 2008), but there had been armed conflict during July and August with deaths on both sides and so we settled for a less dangerous option. Just before we were due to set off (September 28th), I got an email from my doctor friend in Edinburgh, Geoff, saying Jamal had had a heart attack but was OK.

Cliff had hired a vehicle and driver to take us to a place called Kazbegi, east of South Ossetia and just south of the Russian border. We stayed in a guesthouse recommended by *The Rough Guide*. Its major selling point for us was a fireplace with an arc of permanently lit gas jets. Luisa told me the gas was piped in, virtually free, from Russia. When I asked her what she did if it got too hot, she said she opened the doors and windows. One day, we made the long climb to reach the hilltop monastery opposite and another evening, we had an amazingly good meal at a 'restaurant' outside the village. We ate inside one cabin; the food had been cooked in an adjacent one. The toilet was a wooden cubicle without plumbing; waste was expelled through a large hole in the floor directly into the fast-flowing stream underneath.

Cliff wanted to visit an OSCE base, up a nearby valley in a place called Sno. I wasn't really interested: I had been feeling out of sorts ever since I had heard about Jamal, but I went along. Luisa's son agreed to drive us out there. We travelled along the road and then off up the valley in the 4x4. When we arrived, Cliff and the others went to look at the new sauna there, but I stayed in the common room which was furnished with laptops. An Italian man kindly offered me a coffee and I thanked him and asked if I could check my emails in the meantime, explaining I'd heard just before leaving Tbilisi that a friend of mine had had a heart attack and that although I was told he was fine, I had this terrible sense of having lost a close friend. When I went into my account I saw several messages stacked up from Geoff, Helen, my sister and Matthew (my eldest), with the titles 'Jamal', 'Sad News', etc. I opened the one from Matthew, who was at Glasgow University at that time:

Hi dad sorry to have tell you this but i thought you would want to know if you haven't heard already but i read in the newspaper today - and there was a picture that's how i noticed - that your mate Derrick Scougal died on Tuesday. He was out on a jog after a police conference in Ayr when he collapsed. He was taken to hospital and was pronounced dead on arrival. A Fife police spokesman said that the cause of death would not be known until a post-mortem was carried out.

I'm really sorry Dad, i got a shock when i saw the picture in the metro. Not sure that I should have told you when you're away but it seemed best. I don't know if anyone at home knows about it if they've not seen the newspaper.

Love you Dad hope you're havin a great time and keepin safe.
Matty

I read all my messages. I was staring vacantly ahead when the Italian came back with my coffee.

"Well, how is your friend?"

"It's incredible. I still can't believe it. Jamal is OK – but another of my friends has died. Two of my best friends have had heart attacks within two days of each other . . ."

I told the others on their return and we drove to the top of the valley. I went off for a walk by myself and carried out my own ad hoc, ad-libbed little ritual – a mixture of the religious and the ridiculous and the random. I placed a keepsake Cliff had given me, a little medal, under a stone on top of a rock – a gift from a new friend to commemorate an old one. It felt as if I was burying a companion on a distant battlefield I knew I would never get to visit again. It occurred to me that anyone seeing me walking back and forward and, at one point standing still and saluting, would think I had gone crazy. I didn't find out till later Cliff had been watching me. I walked back down the valley and they collected me en route to our lodgings. That night, I was in one of my highly focussed modes. I played chess with Cliff while writing this poem:

NO PANEGYRIC
For Derrick Scougal (1958-2004)

I find out in a place called Sno
By email at a border base
In these Caucasian Mountains . . .
Of all the spots to get to know,
It seems, somehow, appropriate:
This valley's like a Highland glen,
And through it trout streams swiftly flow.
Two hawks patrol this open space,
This wild, spectacular terrain,
And, in the rugged gullies, snow –
A scene that you'd appreciate,
Were you beside me once again.

Back in Tbilisi, I went to the internet café we used and sent my friends an email dated Sunday 3rd October:

Hi
On Sunday my friend Jamal had a heart attack, but, thank God, seems to be recovering well. On Tuesday my friend Derrick Scougal, ACC Fife, collapsed and died while jogging when in Ayr for a police conference. Jamal is 46. Derrick was 45.

I'm back in Tbilisi after a second trip to the mountains, and planning to go tomorrow to Yerevan, the capital of Armenia, and stay for a few days with the aunt and uncle of an Israeli backpacker I met in Omalo. They do what they call homestays, which is just what it says — B&B in a house — for about $8 a night.
I'm well and in good form, although obviously affected by

the sudden loss of a good friend. He had sent me an email in
response to my last little bulletin on the morning he died . . .
Make the most of every day,
Cheers, Steve

Chapter 20

Maria and her friend were both students in Israel and had been camping in the grounds of the Keselo Hotel. We'd visited the local museum in one of the towers together – it was opened up just for us. They were due to stay at her aunt's around the 8th of October and since it was a small place there would not be room for us all, so I was going there before them. On my arrival, I received a message from Peter Wilson, Chief Constable of Fife, saying Derrick's widow, Susan, had asked him to try and contact me to inform me of Derrick's death because she knew I was travelling. I contacted him and emailed a copy of my poem which the vicar read at the service, which meant a lot to me.

◊

I liked Yerevan – a city of culture and collective sorrow. The first thing I was taken to see by Maria's uncle on the night of my arrival was the memorial to the Armenians massacred by the Ottoman Turks in 1915.

Arous and Otari, Maria's aunt and uncle, were generous of their time in taking me around the city. I went on a guided tour of the Yerevan Brandy Company, saw an amazing performance of Hamlet in several languages by two actors and attended a fantastic classical concert that only cost a few dollars. I was looking forward to seeing Maria and her friend and to hear of their adventures. They were due to arrive the night before I left, but were delayed by a day.

Because of long-standing antipathy between Armenia and Azerbaijan, it was not possible to move directly between the two countries, so I had to return to Georgia before travelling to Baku, the Azeri capital. When I returned to Tbilisi, I occupied myself writing and reading. I went to the launch of the paperback edition of *Bread and Ashes: A Walk Through the Mountains of Georgia* by Tony Anderson. He signed it, 'at Prospero's, Rustaveli Tbilisi 8/10/04'.

I was going to Azerbaijan to see the England football team play their national team in a World Cup qualifier. At the Georgia-Armenia border on my way to Yerevan, I had met a young ex-British army officer and we had discovered – in our brief conversation at the checkpoint as we passed in opposite directions – that we were taking the same flight to Baku. We met up at Tbilisi Airport as Irma, her mother and pals saw me off with guitar strumming, songs, gifts and kisses. At Baku we took a taxi out to a cheap but decent place to stay at an old velodrome.

I made two amazing discoveries in Baku. One was the Museum of Literature. For a small fee I got my own private guide to reveal the secrets of centuries of writing in that country. It was so exhaustive that we didn't get it finished, so she told me to come back the following day and she would complete the tour for no extra charge. As she showed me out of the building, she pointed out a door across the square where I could find an Azeri poet she recommended I meet. This was where I made the second discovery. The striking, grey-haired man I found there was Reza Sabri-Tabrizi. He had completed his PhD on William Blake at Edinburgh University in 1969 and had taught there for thirty years. Now, as well as being a university professor of English Literature in Baku, he was working in this office, promoting Azeri culture, surrounded by a bevy of some of the most beautiful young women I had ever seen. We got on well (he and I, that is), and he invited me round for dinner before the match on the Wednesday evening, as kick-off was not until 9.30 p.m. local time.

The following day was a glorious one, warm with a very friendly atmosphere in the city centre, where clusters of English football fans were enjoying sitting sipping their beers in the sunshine. There wasn't a hint of trouble that I could see. Touts were selling tickets and it was clear I could pick one up really cheaply if I waited and was prepared to be among the home supporters. Eventually I bought two. I'd had the rest of my cultural input and now I was enjoying the sporting banter. I got on well with one fan in particular, and at the end of the night I crashed out in his hotel suite rather than make my way out to the velodrome. He had a couple of bedrooms just for himself.

The day of the game was unfortunately dismal and drizzling. I went to Reza's for the meal and then took his friend's teenage son to the match, the boy's father giving us a lift there and back. The student was more interested in talking to a native English speaker than watching the game which, sadly, was not a great spectacle. England scraped a win via a Michael Owen goal. I was wearing my Newcastle top under my jacket amongst the home supporters.

◊

The next day I flew to Ankara and then on to Diyarbakir. Here I made a phone call to the taxi family who had brought us out of Iraq. The 400 dollars Cliff had repaid me was nearly gone and I haggled over whether the rate to the Iraqi border was $125 or $150. It struck me that this was bizarre, given that I was worth $20,000 dollars or so in the wrong hands. A week earlier, I'd heard of the beheading of the British hostage Kenneth Bigley in Baghdad.

When I arrived at the Iraqi border, I had $34 left. I sat at a table in the basic café there, wondering if I dare buy a cup of coffee in case Kak Dana's men failed to turn up and I was stuck there without any money. I was delighted to see two familiar faces get out of a 4x4 and I dashed after them as they walked past the building.

As they drove me back to Suly I felt a strange sense of homecoming. Ironically, it was the safest I had felt for a month. While they chatted to each other in Kurdish, I sat in the back, writing a poem trying to capture the beauty of one of the girls in Reza's office in Baku:

AZERBAIJANI BEAUTY

Azeri girl, you will wear hearts
As charms around your slender wrist,
Although your face displays no art,
Your tender lips as yet unkissed.
I wish you all Love can impart
That for myself I would have wished.

◊

I was soon back in the routine at the school and the youth centre. I began lecturing in Modern Poetry at the university and was dismayed to be reminded how low the standard was, not just of English but of literary comprehension. I'd also agreed to do an evening conversation class there. I especially enjoyed this during Ramadan when the students brought in food and we ate together after dusk. I got paid a pittance for all this – I think I got something like $16 dollars one month for about as many hours' work.

I was also teaching at a new school that had been established by the charity for returning children of the diaspora. This was one of my most challenging roles ever. These children and young people – they ranged up to 22 years of age – had been brought there by their parents from Sweden, Germany, Canada and the UK. Some of them had never been in Kurdistan before. They had been born and/or brought up in western cities such as London or Stockholm, had openly had girlfriends and boyfriends, driven cars and drunk alcohol. They did not fit in here. In my class I reckoned I had students from sixteen different countries who spoke Swedish and Kurdish . . . and I was to teach them all English. It was Babel.

Checking my emails in the office one day, I saw one entitled 'Maria'. It was from someone called Igor whose name had no connections for me. I would have deleted it as likely to be pornography – the computers were riddled with it – except that by chance we'd been speaking that day about a Spanish volunteer called Maria who my friend, Kawaj, had said might be returning. Maybe he'd given her my address . . .

Dear Steve,

It is very painful to tell you that my daughter Maria whom you've met in Georgia had an accident in the mountains of Armenia just 3rd day they moved there.
We have lost her - it happened October 12
Arous and Otari brought her and Maria was buried here in Rehovot
Arous will write you later – it's hard to her now
Did you see Maria in Georgia for some time - or was it just brief meeting?
How was she? When she came to Yerevan she told Otari that in Georgia they had three dangerous moments (one was riding in a car with drunk driver on a mountain road) — but now in Armenia she is on a native ground and feels much safer . . .

Sorry to tell you this sad news..
Sincerely yours
Maria's father — Igor

◊

During one of the holidays, one of my friends on the staff took Jessica and me on a family trip to a remote part of the country where he was from. We chanced upon a group of nomads setting up camp and it was fascinating to see the difference in lifestyle. It was clear that a few decades ago many Kurds would have lived like this.

As the weeks went by, I felt increasingly ready to return to Edinburgh and try to build a lifestyle that allowed me to spend time with my children. I'd arranged to travel out to Qala Diza on the Iraq-Iran border again with staff from the charity. In the eight years of war between the two countries from 1980-1988 – a war which had more in common with the trench warfare of WWI than modern conflicts – it is estimated that almost a million men died. I watched as staff distributed payments to widows. For hours they queued and filed past.

THE BLACK TRAIN

The black train winds behind
The first widow. She stands,
Solemn, as though prepared
To take her vows. My mind
Struggles to understand
How they have not despaired,
As this so slow process
Of widowhood takes place
And I must sit and wait
While each in their drab dress
Files through, funeral pace.
It stretches out the gate . . .
No chance of remarriage –
So many; so few men,
Who would have what to gain?
A wife who was 'damaged',
Another man's children,
Nothing but grief and pain –

So they present I.D.s,
Press left thumbs in the pad,
Leave their indigo prints
To prove that they indeed
Received their dinars, had
Fresh from the Baghdad mint,
Till next time the black train
Curls out the gate again.

I began actively looking online for jobs in Edinburgh and quite a few suitable ones came up. I was really missing my children, especially Nathaniel, the youngest, having spent so much time with him in his infancy. I'd decided to travel back to the UK for Christmas and had almost decided I wouldn't return. I left over a hundred copies of *A Fixed Expression* and some other items with the local writer, Sherzad Hassan.

Chapter 21

I applied for a post with Children in Scotland from the lobby of the Hotel Poem in Istanbul. The role was to establish and run a national Children, Fathers & Fathering Project. If nothing else, if I got the job it would help reunite one father with his five children. In Croydon's TK Maxx I bought a drastically reduced brown Italian suit for £34, having almost no money left. I travelled north in stages by bus, staying with friends en route. The interview was early in the New Year so I would know I'd failed to make the shortlist if I hadn't heard before everywhere closed for Christmas on Thursday 23rd December. Having checked online several times that day while staying with friends, Dave and Denise, I went to look one last time in the late afternoon and I still remember the elation of opening that email that said, "We are pleased to confirm your invitation to attend an interview here at the Children in Scotland offices, Princes House, 5 Shandwick Place, Edinburgh."

I spent Christmas Eve with friends Tom and Eve at Chester-Le-Street and on Christmas morning Tom drove me to my parents' bungalow. My mother was surprised but undemonstrative, as ever. My father, who was unwell, hardly lifted his head, and Helen was concerned that Maggie – who was coming down from Scotland with the children – would think she had set this up. When they all arrived, there was an initial awkwardness. If I had come back to do something to improve father-child relationships,

I had some work to do with my own. It was not the homecoming I'd hoped for, but then, how can you have a homecoming when you haven't got a home? It was an empty dream.

THE EXILED POET DREAMS OF HIS RETURN

I dream that one day that red door
Will open at my touch once more,
That loving arms will open wide,
And I'll be welcomed back inside,

And years and tears will fall away
On that imagined, longed-for, day
When I will write my final poem,
With words, like swallows, flying home.

The only presents I had to give people were copies of *A Fixed Expression*. I even sent one over to my brother with whom I had had no contact. An unexpected result of this (I presume) was that while he was speaking to my sister on the phone when she and I were at my parents', he asked if I wanted to go to the Newcastle match. She relayed the question while looking extremely perplexed. I went along to the game and we enjoyed a strange, strained, but not unpleasant fraternal afternoon.

I borrowed my father's car and drove up to Edinburgh for Hogmanay. My friends, Geoff and Jamal, turned out to be away and I had nowhere to stay. New Year's Eve is a busy time for tourists in the Scottish capital and many of the B&Bs were full, including the one on the Prom run by my Kurdish friends, Zuhair and Saddollah. It was after 9.30 p.m. before I managed to get a small room, not usually let out, in a place overlooking the sea at the east end of Joppa.

I went to a Kurdish do in the community centre in Portobello that I'd been invited to by Zuhair, earlier that evening. I took my Kurdish garb with me and one of the guys helped me with the turban and cummerbund. Afterwards I went to the Gilchrists', still in my Kurdish outfit.

◊

At my interview, I felt I did pretty well, taking a high-risk strategy and reading one of my poems. I struggled with a computer exercise because of my poor keyboard skills. Asked about young men working with children, I felt I had to raise a cautionary point, although I thought it might tell against me. Driving back down to Newcastle, I heard an interview with Kate Boydell on Radio 5 Live. She was a widow who'd set up support for those who'd lost their partners, and I decided if I got the post I'd try to involve her in the project's first conference, but I had the feeling that I'd just failed to clinch the most important interview of my life. As a day or two passed, that feeling intensified, and I was just praying for a second chance.

I got a call from Jennifer. Could I attend a second interview – at Edinburgh Airport? The director of Fathers Direct, partners with EOC Scotland in managing the project, wanted to vet me. Thank you, God. I then suffered from anxiety, realising I only had the one suit and a woman would notice that.

As I approached the escalator up to the café at the airport, I saw an Indian-looking little girl of two or three near the base. I continued watching her as the stairs rose and saw her step on. There was a woman in front of me with her teenage son.

"Excuse me," I said. "Could you look after this little girl and take her to the information desk or a police officer. I could do it, but it would be easier for you . . ."

I had a mental image of me going down the other escalator holding her hand and some relative pointing up shouting, "That's her – that man's got her!" I used this incident in my interview as an example of the problems men now had in dealing with children.

I was told they'd let me know that afternoon if I'd got the job or not. I then drove up to see Susan Scougal, Derrick's widow. We sat and chatted but the phone call never came and eventually I headed back to Edinburgh. It was the next day at Geoff's when I finally got the call, offering me the job. My delight was only slightly tempered by being told my salary would be at the bottom of the scale, considering the ad had said 'dependent on experience' and I had plenty of that. Jennifer called me back to say the next rung up would be the best they could offer. I went in and signed the contract.

Before taking up the post, I spent some time in Normandy with Ossie, checking everything was OK with the place and preparing myself for a return to full-time employment after seven years. I had arranged to stay at Zuhair's B&B on the prom until I could negotiate a mortgage to buy my own place.

◊

Walking into my office and seeing my desk with a blue, goldfish-bowl-style iMac was an extremely satisfying experience. I now had a job – the first brick in building the structure of my new life. My line manager was Eddie Folan, a likeable, down-to-earth guy from Greenock. My first challenge was to organise the inaugural annual conference to be held in the week approaching Fathers' Day, the third weekend in June. I went down to Devon to meet Kate Boydell, who I'd contacted via her website. Although initially agreeing to speak at the conference, she called me the next day saying she had changed her mind. This appeared to be a major setback on my first mission, but – although I didn't relish reporting back to Eddie that this relatively expensive venture had been in vain – I suspected it might have been for the best.

For my father's eightieth birthday, Peter had booked a box at St James' Park for Newcastle's match against Aston Villa. A few days beforehand, my father's health deteriorated dramatically and he was admitted to hospital. I travelled down with the boys and we visited him at the Freeman. We could only go into the ward in twos. A nurse said she would take Gabriel and me to his bed and then stopped to talk to another member of staff. It took me several seconds to realise that the old shell of a human being in the bed next to us was my dad. When we went back out to the waiting room, I spoke to Matthew and Joseph and warned them about what to expect. We all burst into tears but it allowed me to talk to them about death in a very intimate way.

Attending the match was a strange scenario with my father spending his birthday dying in hospital, a few miles away. Peter looked at me and nodded over towards Martha enquiringly, not recognising her – it had been so long since he'd seen her. The bizarre nature of the day was accentuated by the infamous punch-up between teammates Dyer and Bowyer, leaving Newcastle to finish the game with eight men. My father died the next day.

I bought four black suits so that the pall-bearers – Matthew, Joseph, Peter and me – were all wearing exactly the same, although Peter felt we should all wear different coloured socks, like the Barbarians rugby team. I had written my father's eulogy, which I had never thought I would be able to do because of our difficult relationship, but he had plenty of excellent qualities to celebrate: integrity, compassion, loyalty, and a strong work ethic. Although we'd only planned to carry his coffin into the church, Peter suggested we carry the coffin across the old Great North Road to the cemetery. It made me aware that one day I hoped my four sons would carry me on my last journey.

Back at work, I relished the responsibility of arranging the conference, using previous experience and developing new skills. I visited various venues in Edinburgh and settled on the Apex International Hotel in the Grassmarket. We came up with the title 'How Equal Are Fathers?: The Challenge for Public Services'. As the number of weeks to go dwindled and the number of confirmed attendees increased only slowly – despite intensive promotion – Eddie said to me, "I'm waiting for you to panic, Steve."

"I won't," I replied. "Nobody's going to die . . ."

In the end, the event was a critical, if not financial, success. The project had received media coverage and was now established. Afterwards, we all went over to the Beehive to celebrate on a sunny June evening.

◊

I bought a small, modern two-bedroomed house at the end of May, having managed to get a mortgage on the strength of my new job, even though it was just a three-year contract. Towards the end of the summer, when I had been at Children in Scotland almost six months, I was told that my probationary period was going to be extended. This completed an unwelcome hat-trick, with my experiences in teaching and the police. Eddie had brought the document for me to sign to agree to this. He was clearly very uncomfortable with the situation which had obviously been imposed from above. I told him if there was a question mark over my performance, the issues should have been raised with me long before this. At the end of our session Eddie left in agreement with me, leaving the form unsigned. Jennifer subsequently took up the task.

I was conscious I would be in a desperate situation if I lost my job; I would be unable to make the mortgage repayments on my new house. I didn't want to push them so hard that my position was made untenable. I signed the form, noting that I had not previously been made aware of these areas now considered to require further training and that I did not agree with the assessment. That was, as it turned out, the end of the matter but it did hang over for me for a while, until it was clear that nothing further would occur.

◊

In January 2006, as part of my longstanding resolve to individually take each of my children on an adventure, Gabriel and I boarded our one cent flights with Ryanair from Stansted to Sardinia. When we got off the bus from the airport in Alghero, we were met by several men trying to rent us accommodation. This was part of the experience and purpose, and we viewed two or three places with me asking Gabriel what he thought about each of the rooms and the guys trying to let them. Eventually, we went to where I'd planned, but not booked, to stay: an old convent converted into very pleasant tourist accommodation. The following day, we hired some pretty ropey bicycles and set off on a short cycling tour, staying in farmhouses and cheap hotels.

We had many adventures but the one we always talk about – the Epiphany – took place on January 6th. Although I'd managed to acquire quite a good map from a specialist map shop in Newcastle, we had come to a point where we were unsure of the way. The little dust road led up into the mountains, but we couldn't decide if it was the road that turned left into one valley or right into another. What was clear, was that if we got it wrong it would be too late in the day for us to ride back down and take the other road, as the ascent would take a couple of hours at least.

We decided to take an early lunchbreak in the warm morning sunshine. Perhaps because it was a feast day, no vehicles passed.

"We need a pick-up to come along," I said after more than an hour by the roadside. A short time later one rolled up the dusty road towards us. I waved him down. We couldn't understand each other's language. I don't speak Italian, and I'm not sure he did. After several minutes, he signalled for us to sling our bikes into the back of the pick-up and for Gabriel to crawl over the front seats into the space where his dog was. He drove sedately towards the hills in a manner which reinforced my suspicions that he'd been celebrating the holiday somewhere. This was confirmed when he made the gesture for drinking, jerking his thumb back towards his mouth. I thought he wanted me to buy him a beer at some hostelry ahead, but he turned off the road towards a pair of locked, rusting metal gates, got out and opened them. He drove into the yard. We got out and he led the way with his squat, toad-like walk towards an agricultural building with sliding metal doors. As he slid them open I was half-expecting to see naked bodies hanging from meat-hooks on the walls. There were naked bodies hanging on the walls, but I was relieved to see that 1) they were posters and 2) they were females.

He nodded towards Gabriel, whose eyes were fixed on the wall coverings, checking that he was allowed to sample the contents of a barrel, then doled us out a tumbler each of some unspecified alcohol, which I drank after watching our host down some of the same liquid. We went back into the sunlight and he shut the doors behind us, leaving the naked ladies once more in darkness.

We resumed our slow progress up through the hills in the pick-up, passing only a cluster of hunters. All the time I was registering how long this would have taken us on foot, as there was no way I could have cycled up. We reached a point near the top where the road forked and he indicated that we should lift our bikes out and take the path down to the left. I thanked him and looked at my watch. I hoped this was the right route because it was well into the afternoon by then. We mounted our bikes and freewheeled at speed down the steep side of the valley – one of the most exhilarating rides I've ever had. When we got to the bottom, I checked my watch again – it had taken a quarter of an hour to make the descent . . .

◊

One night we were late getting to our destination – a holiday chalet on a small complex that was being opened up just for us, but which was proving difficult to locate – and I affixed a couple of the many broken pieces of reflector bars from roadside barriers to the rear of our bicycles to try and make us more visible.

Another time we stayed at a farmhouse where I had some of the best food I've ever tasted. It was also a restaurant, and, hungry as we were, we could never have worked our way through the eight or so plates of food we were served. Our hosts retired early, leaving us to read and help ourselves to any drinks, some of them made from local berries.

◊

Back at work, in no time at all I was preparing for our next conference, which we held at the Marriott Hotel in Glasgow in June 2006. It went well, apart from one foreign speaker, who the Big Cheese had insisted on having, who struggled with his English, and one of our admin staff having her handbag stolen. Afterwards, I set off on a trip around Scotland, visiting a number of pre-arranged locations, most of them schools. I had collected a dozen 'tough' poems on disparate aspects of fatherhood, and read and discussed a different one at each place, asking the class to draw a picture based on it. It was a wonderful if hectic fortnight, taking

Sixth form at St Cuthbert's with me back left and Sting 2nd back row, 3rd from left

GOOD MORNING WORLD

Steve Harvey by Norman K

Top: At 'Le Vieux Chateau' with Steve Ashton; my friend Sandra's son, Leigh; & Ossie Postle

Middle: With Derrick Scougal as part of the slowest team ever to complete 'The Cheviot 2000'

Right: With my children: Martha, Joseph, Matthew, Gabriel, & Nathaniel in front

Above: Just landed at what is now Erbil International Airport, *January 12th 2004*

Below: Clearing Mines in Kurdistan: MAG at work in Chamchamal

Above: A black-and-white approach to Education in Suleimaniyah

Below left: With Jalal Talabani, future President of Iraq

Below right: With musician at wedding in Kayli, Sudan

Above: Battle of the T-shirts: with Grant at my leaving do,
Children in Scotland, 2008

Below: 'Malakal Academical'

Above: A night out in Wunrok with Pauline Cafferkey,
Audrey (of PSF), & Pauline Bethel

Below: On the Sobat River, a tributary of the Blue Nile,
en route to Baliet

Above: At The American Club, Buenos Aires, October 2010,
Eric on right, Head of St Alban's 3rd from right

Below left: With Alberto 'Bertie' Noble at Cafe Tortoni, Buenos Aires

Below right: With a Suriqui reed boat builder, Lake Titicaca

in schools of all kinds – primary and secondary; urban and rural; state and public. Locations visited included Fife, Deeside, Moray, the Mull of Kintyre, Skye, Plockton, Ayrshire and Peebles. I'd also taken part in a fathers' and children's trip to Perthshire where I gave a presentation and helped the children prepare cards for Father's Day and attended a fathers' conference at Anfield, (staying in a B&B that was Brian Epstein's childhood home). While there, I played in a football match at Melwood, Liverpool's training ground, against the likes of legends John Aldridge and Alan Kennedy, who was marking me – very successfully, as you might have guessed.

When I got back, Nicky, our new graphic designer, and I chose which drawings to use as illustrations to go with the poems in the Fathers' Footsteps calendar we were preparing.

◊

It had been a busy year. A few months earlier, I had become a grandfather for the first time when Martha gave birth to India. I took Joseph on a holiday to Madeira, walking the *levadas*. It was not as extreme an adventure as my cycling trip in Sardinia with Gabriel, but we still traversed some tricky waterfalls, including one where a German tourist had just gone over the edge, with rescuers en route. One day we covered what the guidebook suggested needed two days, but Joe was eighteen and already my height. For the second time that year, I was left trailing on an activity holiday by one of my sons.

◊

One Monday morning, my new line manager, Jonathan, gathered his staff together in the policy office. I thought, 'The charity's gone bust and we've all lost our jobs.' Instead, he told us that Nicky, our graphic designer, had been found dead. She was 32. Her death cast a long shadow over the place. On the day of her funeral, the strength, dignity and consideration shown by her poor parents – who she had just returned from visiting in the States – was inspiring.

◊

One of my best friends at Children in Scotland was Grant. He was a bearded guy in his thirties with black hair and cerebral palsy. I would hear him clumping along the corridor at six or seven minutes past nine and shout out, "Blimey! Is it that time already?"

One day he replied, "You'll not be laughing when you see me." He popped his head round the door to reveal a nasty gash clotted with blood. He had fallen in the shower.

For his birthday, a few other colleagues and I got him a T-shirt printed with his face on the front and the phrase 'I fought the floor . . .' On the back was his face with a Harry Potter style scar affixed by our new graphic designer and the words, '. . . and the floor won'.

Grant was a ballsy guy with a great, self-deprecating sense of humour. He went skiing on a special contraption guided by an experienced skier. We were talking about speed dating one day when he said, "Speeed daaaating wooould be no gooood to meeee – by the time I got my naaaame out my three minuuutes woooooould be uuup . . ."

Another pal, Craig, the young accountant, had asked me to go on his stag weekend to Hamburg, but I was reluctant because of the expense and all his other pals being, like him, in their twenties. "You've played football with them. You're not the only older guy who'd be going," he said, seeing my reluctance. "My Dad's going – but come to think of it, he's younger than you . . ."

Despite everything, I did go on the trip. As the air hostess on the early morning flight served the boisterous boys all around me wearing their 'on tour' T-shirts, she gave me extra wine after checking I was alright, not realising I was one of the party. (I did put my T-shirt on later).

◊

As 2007 drew towards an end, it was clear that my three-year contract would not be extended. Although disappointed that the work I'd done would not be continued – at least not in the way I thought it should be – I had no wish to stay at Children in Scotland any longer. It had still been, despite some difficulties, one of the happiest times of my professional life and the calendar we produced is one of the things I am most proud to have worked on. Other highlights included dinner with the author of *Madame Doubtfire*, Anne Fine, the night before our last 'fatherhood' conference (she was wonderful company); meeting, over a coffee in Glasgow, with Gary Lewis who played the father in the film *Billy Elliot*, and him agreeing to support the project and write the foreword for the calendar; organising a sell-out workshop featuring a compendium of skills from storytelling to football coaching (this last by Neil Orr, formerly of Greenock Morton,

West Ham, and Hibernian); a joint course with my colleague Catriona for fathers of children with health or learning issues (chaired by the poet Aonghas MacNeacail and featuring many quietly heroic fathers); and speaking before the Scottish Parliament Equal Opportunities Committee at Holyrood, where as part of my address I read Pat Morrissey's poem, *Father and Sons,* from the calendar.

Towards the end of my time there, while BC was giving a guided tour to Alex Salmond, then-leader of the SNP, she didn't bring him into S9 (my room), saying afterwards it was due to lack of time. I got an invite to the opening of the Scottish Parliament (where I was introduced to the Queen who was clearly bored and, looking over my shoulder and out of the window said, "Is it raining yet?") The SNP was in power for the first time and I got a chance to speak to Alex Salmond afterwards. I told him I'd heard his voice in the corridor outside my room. He replied that he'd been told that there was an old boy in there, scratching away with a quill.

In October 2007 I attended an evening at Jury's Inn where staff from the Irish NGO, GOAL, were seeking to recruit personnel to work abroad. Initially, it seemed unlikely they would have anything suitable for me as they primarily required medical staff, water engineers, livelihood officers and accountants. However, I was offered the post of Safety & Security Officer in either North or South Sudan. Sudan had been the scene of internal conflict for decades. At that time there was a fragile stability resulting from the Comprehensive Peace Agreement signed by both sides in 2005. I decided I would opt for South Sudan, which wasn't recognised as an independent country until 2009, providing they were prepared to wait until my contract expired in February.

I got a good send off from the staff of Children in Scotland, Grant designing a T-shirt with the words 'We will miss you Father Steve' and my face in place of Father Ted's. Craig presented me with a top-of-the-range rucksack, on behalf of my colleagues.

◊

I travelled over to Dublin, catching the bus from the airport to Dun Laoghaire and my homely overnight accommodation. I spent the day being briefed by Neil and Geraldine, HR Officer for South Sudan, and other members of staff. I saw John O'Shea, founder of the charity a couple of times, but although I was standing next to him and Neil while they spoke briefly, I wasn't introduced.

I caught the plane back to Scotland and collected Nathaniel from Maggie at Edinburgh Airport. We flew to Paris where he chose a hotel near the Eiffel Tower, which we went to visit, after eating at a nearby restaurant. While waiting for the lift down, I noticed a couple with their two young children next to us. The mother had a noticeable Dublin accent.

"Where are you from?" I asked.

"Ireland," she said.

"No, what part of Dublin?" I elaborated. "I just came from there today."

"Castleknock," she answered as her son tugged at her arm.

"Mammy, mammy . . . It's Anne-Marie's cousin."

He was pointing at Nathaniel. They were Maggie's sister Ellen's next-door neighbours and Nathaniel had been playing in their house a few weeks earlier.

Next day, Nathaniel and I were up early and took the metro from Volontaires opposite the hotel to connect with the RER line to Disneyland. We did fourteen rides in ten hours, which is not bad going . . .

The following day we took the train to Normandy and spent several days together at Le Vieux Chateau, before returning to Edinburgh.

Chapter 22

So, in February 2008, having stocked up with Malarone (against malaria) and Marmite (against homesickness), I set off for Africa for the first time, travelling via London to honour a commitment to speak at a conference on adoption and fostering. Because of the post-election unrest in Kenya in the New Year, I was now flying via Addis Ababa instead of Nairobi. The chance to spend a few days in the Ethiopian capital was a bonus. I was met at the airport by a GOAL driver and taken to their transit house. As it transpired, I spent about five days there due to complications over my visa, but it was no hardship: I liked Addis. The city is quite high – about 3,000 metres above sea level – which makes for a pleasant climate and an absence of mosquitoes. There was a member of the Addis staff staying there and I was joined by Cormac, the Logi(stician) from Juba on R & R. I spent an enjoyable few days visiting bars, restaurants and hotels.

All the economy seats were booked so I flew first class for the first time in my life (this just meant I sat in front of a curtain that everybody else sat behind), to Juba via Entebbe. There were still reminders of the Israeli raid in the shape of burnt-out aircraft. I had been warned about Juba Airport – it can seem like one of the portals of hell – but arriving was relatively problem-free. I was met by the Country Director (CD), a large-framed Irishman, my rucksack was taken by the driver, and we were driven to the office. They hadn't had a Safety & Security Officer before and there was no allocated work space. I was offered a place in the large office but preferred to take up residence in the small front room where the photocopier was. Everybody uses a photocopier and I would get a chance to talk to them all. I set my desk up looking out through the metal shutters, bars, and insect screen to the gates of the small compound. Another plus was the ceiling fan. It was *very* hot.

I spent my first day organising my work and living space while Aggy, the visiting IT guy, tried to fix me up with a working laptop. Some staff, including the Logi, stayed on site; others lived in a large house near the airport. The rest were based in a bungalow shaded by a tree within walking distance of the office; this was where I made my base.

The next day, Tuesday 4th March, was my first full working day with GOAL. I opened my emails and they included one from my sister beginning:

You must wonder about the lack of response but we've been busy with Ma 24/7. On Thursday Dr Morris (GP) was shocked by her deterioration . . .

I felt I had to tell the CD and he allowed me to use the satellite phone to call Helen. She told me the doctor reckoned our mother wouldn't see out the weekend. She said Ma had always said she would die on a Monday – the parish priest's day off – in order to spoil his round of golf.

"It will be Monday, then," I said.

The CD offered me the option of flying straight home, but I told him I'd already said my farewells to her and that, in any case, she was heavily sedated. Also, it might be some time before the funeral. I'd told Peter and Helen that if Ma died while I was away it might not be possible for me to attend her funeral and I had reconciled myself to this, but the image of my children sitting in the Sacred Heart Church beside her coffin and me not being there now felt wrong.

Thursday was poker night but there was a cock-up with the travel arrangements – something that was to be a regular feature of my time there – and I was left sitting in the bungalow. This was fine, however, as I spent the evening writing my mother's funeral address – a strange thing to do, perhaps, while she was still alive, but I was in the right frame of mind and realised I might not otherwise get the time to do it.

Ma died at 9.30 on the Monday morning, fulfilling two wishes: as well as frustrating Fr Joe's golfing activities, she'd beaten her husband's score by a good six months. To a cricketer's daughter, a better innings was important.

After travelling for two days, on Thursday 13th April I arrived at Newcastle Airport via Amsterdam (Schiphol, with its beautiful old-fashioned bar, was the other end of the airport spectrum from Juba). Helen collected me and said there was a funeral at the Sacred Heart that morning – the mother of my brother's old classmate, Neil Tennant. Although tired and having an upset stomach, I decided to go along. I didn't know the family well, but his parents had always acknowledged me and seemed to be good people. Neil did his mother proud with his eulogy, telling amusing anecdotes about her, including ones relating to her enjoyment of attending celebrity events with him when he became famous as half of the pop duo *Pet Shop Boys*. The most poignant story, however, was of when she was a young woman. She had been a seamstress on Tyneside who had answered the call during the war to staff the airfields down south, responsible for plotting the aircraft on the wall charts as they flew to and from their missions. One Wednesday she was tracking her airman fiancé's flight and the plane never returned. She was due to have married him on the Saturday. She was given the next day off and was back at work on the Friday.

◊

My stomach was still playing up two days later, but I didn't want Peter to have to deliver the eulogy. He carried Ma's coffin with Matthew, Joseph, and Gabriel. I managed to get through my speech, finishing with this anecdote:

Ma was always a worrier, and my lasting memory of her will be a little exchange that took place between us when I was sitting with her on a visit before going to Africa:

"Do you know what I'm worrying about now?" she asked.

"No, Ma," I had replied, "no idea," while thinking of possibilities ranging from 'missing the Rington's tea man' to 'escalating post-election violence in Kenya'.

"I'm worrying about falling down the stairs…"

"Well, Ma," I said, "that must be the definition of a worrier – someone who worries about falling down the stairs when they live in a bungalow . . ."

She burst out laughing. "That's a good 'un. We'll have to tell Ma . . ."

"Whose Ma?"

"Your Ma . . ."

"But *you're* my Ma, Ma . . ."

"Oh, I am, aren't I!"

And she burst out laughing again.

Well, Ma, your worries are over now.

Love you.

At the crematorium I saw my old college pal, Ossie. To say he was yellow would be inaccurate. His face was like a Belisha beacon. He was uncharacteristically and unhealthily thin. He told me he wasn't coming to the hotel as he didn't feel up to it. He said his doctor had told him he needed some tests doing and I told him not to delay . . .

Chapter 23

After the funeral, I went up to Edinburgh and spent some time with my children over Easter before travelling back to Africa with our Head of Security. We landed at Nairobi around dawn on Thursday 27th March. It took two hours to get to the apartment by taxi in the rush hour. There was another visa problem and I was again delayed getting to Juba. Neil went on ahead. It was frustrating but I enjoyed getting to know Nairobi (or Nairobbery as it was sometimes cynically called). To me, Nairobi was one of those magic place names from *Look and Learn* and sixties TV programmes such as *Daktari*.

I arrived in Juba the following week, ready to do some safety and security training with Neil for the staff. As I was driven along the dry, bumpy roads I looked out of the windows like someone watching the start of a film again after the reel has snapped. I saw a woman dressed in a blue-and-white striped dress with a full blue-and-white striped plastic bag on her head and wanted to take a photograph but didn't want to act or feel like a tourist. Instead, I wrote this:

WITH MATCHING ACCESSORY

Equatorial heat surrounds the air-conditioned pick-up
As we drive along the dusty tracks that, in Juba, pass for roads

. . .
I see a woman, tall and naturally elegant wearing a long dress,
Broad blue-and-white stripes, and on her head the ubiquitous
Blue-and-white-striped plastic bag, a full load,
Matching accessory in a place where nothing matches up.

When the driver dropped me off at the office the next morning, Neil signalled me over in an agitated manner. There had been an armed robbery at the site overnight. Various members of staff had had stuff stolen from them. I was stunned that this should have happened on my first night back and surprised that I hadn't been involved sooner. I took the point that by the time the CD and Neil attended from the airport house it was all over and there was nothing I could have done, but I was Safety & Security Officer for South Sudan and other members of staff, judging from their comments, were either genuinely surprised or were stirring things up. Either way, it wasn't good for the credibility of the post or myself.

I was informed that several armed men had appeared outside the gate with one of our drivers and that there had been a bit of an altercation. An experienced member of staff, on site for a visit, had gone out to investigate. He had been unable to resolve the situation and, under threat, the guards had opened the gate and the intruders had calmly relieved staff members of money and valuables.

The assumption was that it was an inside job involving the off-duty driver, but I kept an open mind on this: the obvious is not always the case. I was asked to investigate and began by interviewing all the ex-pat staff witnesses. Naturally, they were all still pretty shaken. I then interviewed the driver who said he had been accosted on his way home after work. He was outside his hut in the neighbouring area when a group of armed men asked him where he had come from and marched him and his two brothers (who were in their nightwear) back to the GOAL site. The two things that made me think he was telling the truth were the fact that his brothers had apparently been outside the gate in that state – the sort of detail that tends to show veracity – and that the intruders didn't know the location of anything on site, such as the Finance Office. I considered it to have been simply an opportunist crime committed by an armed gang roaming around looking for spoils. Others did not appear to share this view. I went with John Batey, a fellow Geordie who was a seasoned GOAL employee based in Addis, to report the crime to the local police station. This was a quaint little building, virtually in the middle of a roundabout, and when I went in a number of locals were sitting around

– so much for confidentiality. Confidence in the detection capabilities of the local constabulary was not enhanced by the visit. I found out from the NGO network that there had been a similar offence recently, lending further credence to my opinion that it was not an inside job.

◊

The following night was poker night. This week's venue was the Bedouin, an ex-pat watering hole near the River Nile. Again, there were problems with transport due to the demands on the two night-time vehicles. GOAL had a very inflexible policy that its international staff were not allowed to drive vehicles except with the express permission of the Country Director. Of course the CD could give himself blanket coverage to drive, and he had one vehicle for his own, virtually exclusive, use. Eventually one of the drivers arrived for us and we set off along the main road towards town. We passed a vehicle sitting up on a large rock about six feet off the ground, surrounded by an excited crowd. It had obviously just crashed. The road had bits of glass and metal strewn about – even more than usual – and as we turned off the road and headed towards the river it was clear we had a puncture.

While the driver and Joseph, the Kenyan electrician, jacked up the 4x4 to change the wheel, I asked the women – who were carrying handbags – to keep to the side of the vehicle away from the road and then secreted the bags inside. The guys were working in the dark because the battery had died. The road was not well lit, and I contacted the Logi to see if the other vehicle was in the vicinity to attend and park behind us to shine its headlamps on the scene. He was unable to contact them. I then got in touch with the CD, as the only other member of staff with access to a vehicle, to see if he was at the poker game or on his way there. He said he was at the airport house, having decided to have a night in. The wheel was changed and we managed to push start the vehicle eventually. By the time we got to the Bedouin, it was late and we only stayed for a couple of drinks before leaving, knowing we would probably have to shove the vehicle again.

The next morning, before the start of the staff training session, the CD called me into his office. Neil was sitting silently, arms folded, beside him at the desk.

"It's not your fault," the CD began. "We really should have given you a fuller briefing on Juba, but it really isn't as dangerous a place as you appear to imagine . . ."

I asked him to elaborate.

"Getting on the radio, calling the CD just because of a punctured tyre is an over-reaction to the situation."

"I didn't contact you as the CD," I replied. "The Logi was unable to get hold of the other driver and you were the only other person with access to a vehicle. I thought you might be in the vicinity. I wanted another vehicle behind ours with its lights on to ensure somebody didn't run into the back of us and to assist with lighting the scene for the guys changing the wheel. That's standard police practice in such a situation. I would have done that in Newcastle and I think it was the right thing to do here last night . . ."

We had to go and do the training but when there was a break, the CD came up to me and said, "Are we finished with that or do we need to discuss it further?"

I indicated that I felt the matter was not over and we went to his office.

"So what do you feel about what was said to you?"

"A bit miffed, to be honest."

"I wasn't criticising you. I began by saying it was our fault for not briefing you more thoroughly . . ."

"It was the first real decision I've had to make here, and I'm called into your office in front of the Head of Global Security . . . And it does seem to me my judgement is being criticised, and no amount of briefing would have altered the way I dealt with the incident. I stand by my actions."

"Well, I'm the one getting angry now. You weren't being admonished. And I have every right to have Neil with me when I'm speaking to you."

"I didn't say I was angry. I said I was 'a bit miffed' which is the mildest expression I know for my feelings about this."

What I did know, was that the one thing I had learnt from this incident was that it would have to be a case of last resort before I would contact the CD in such a situation again.

◊

After doing site checks on the three Juba properties with Neil, assessing security risks and potential improvements – something, ironically, planned for the day after the robbery – we flew up to Malakal, a city in the heart of the disputed region in which oil lies to the north, near Abyei. There was the traditional Saturday night party, attended by international staff from other local NGOs. We sat up on the flat roof, overlooking the market square with its mosque, drinking beer and chatting in the night air. A group of French staff from Médecins Sans Frontières told me there was a football game on the next day and I was keen to join in.

As I was leaving for the game on the Sunday morning, Neil, clearly not happy about me playing, shouted, "Don't get injured!"

"You never say that, Neil," I replied. "Don't you know sportsmen are superstitious, like actors . . . ?"

Together with Forbes, the Logi who was currently running the place, I came on at some point for the NGOs against the team of tall young locals. I was playing as striker and being marked by an athletic young man, but I managed to win most of the balls in the air. Early on, their keeper came out to the right of the posts to deal with a situation but the ball was hit across goal where I was waiting to coolly stroke it in. Unfortunately, the keeper flung himself to his right and made a fantastic save . . . Later on I was running flat out looking to my right to meet another cross, when I felt my right foot drop into a pothole and my knee joint jerk forward and back at the same time, like two halves of a ball held together by strong elastic. I limped off the pitch with Neil's parting comment reverberating in my brain, alongside the pain.

Back at GOAL, I was treated like an adolescent who'd been allowed to go to a party but told not to drink and had still come home completely intoxicated. A Kenyan member of the health team applied some medication – there was no ice – which eased the pain a little, but the next day I was taken to the UN Hospital, run by the Indian army. It was here that my idea for the novel *Malakal Academical*, which had been germinating in Nairobi, really began to sprout shoots.

Deirdre, a senior staff member, visited me the next day and brought me a DVD: *Babel*. The five other guys in my ward just watched the same half dozen Bollywood movies all day. I put *Babel* on for them one night, but lost my nerve when the attractive young Japanese girl began taking her knickers off. I was a guest there, and if the female orderly on duty came in and felt I was corrupting her patients, I felt it would be difficult to justify. This was much to the chagrin of the guys, whose interest, at least, had been aroused . . .

A few days later I flew to Nairobi for diagnosis and treatment. Naturally I felt awkward about the situation, although there was nothing I could do about it but get fit as soon as possible. My time there was brightened by several people. The cleaner was a middle-aged local woman of what Alexander McCall Smith refers to as 'traditional' build.

She was a devout Christian and did my washing for me. At the office there were two women working in the kitchen who I shared a laugh and joke with, as well as Noi, the administrator who was ever helpful. She had two blue tear-shaped marks to the side of one eye. I thought they were tattoos and very attractive, but she told me they were where she'd had moles removed and that she disliked them. She was from Laos and her likeable, roguish-humoured husband was from Croatia. There was also James, a young Irish accountant who fed me one of the best lines of my life. James, who it transpired was twenty-five, was tall and angular and reminded me of Dougal from the *Father Ted* TV series. Several times, as we crossed the busy, litter-strewn roads, vehicles sounded their horns, and every time James turned to look he seemed to have to turn his whole body to do so.

"If you don't mind me asking – you'll have gathered already, I'm a very direct guy – but have you something wrong with your neck, James?"

"I injured it one day when I was fourteen, and my mother fancied herself as a bit of a physiotherapist . . ."

"And you've never looked back since . . . ?" I said, and the two of us burst into fits of uncontrollable laughter, doubled up, clutching our sides on the pavement.

◊

I'd damaged the cruciate ligament in my good knee and, despite a lot of physio, it was still doubtful if I would get back to a level of fitness sufficient for me to return to the field. The situation was complicated by a surprising discovery: the staff at the private hospital had seemed much more concerned about my thick ankles and very low heart rate than the state of my knee. I had told them the ankles were genetic – my father had swollen ankles – and my heart rate had always been attributed to me being an active sportsman who had done lots of cardiovascular exercise over the years. Through extensive tests, which I was convinced were merely milking the insurance company, they established that I had an underactive thyroid gland. People who have the condition typically have low energy levels. When I told my friend, Geoff, a GP in Edinburgh, he wouldn't believe it until I sent him the results. The medical information was faxed to Ireland for GOAL to decide whether I was able to continue in my post. Despite the professional difficulties I had experienced in my dealings with the CD, I didn't want my African adventure to end here, like this.

I was given the all clear. The thyroid condition simply required me to take the prescribed amount of Levothyroxine daily, in tablet form. On Sunday 20th April, I flew out to Lokichoggio from Wilson Airport, where I met Giovanni, a quirky, funny Italian. 'Loki' is a bizarre place on the Kenyan side of the Sudanese border. Formerly the centre for aid distribution during the Sudan conflict, it was by this time a strange anachronism. As I wrote later, 'it was, without doubt, a surreal place. It looked as if the bar in *Star Wars* had turned all its occupants out onto the street at once. Long-limbed guys wearing Tyrolean-style trilby hats, jackets and shorts were striding out with their long sticks. Women with multi-coloured rings around their elongated necks, wooden studs below their bottom lips, and red Mohican haircuts walked by carrying all kinds of things – sometimes including a baby on their back, wrapped in cloth around its mother's body. Young boys kicked about a grapefruit-sized ball made of bits of fibre stuck together.'

I was collected by Shadrach, one of GOAL's two staff members there, who drove me to 748, a collection of mud huts or *tukuls*. I checked in, then caught the last twenty minutes of Newcastle United v Sunderland on the patio satellite TV – a double bonus, as we won. Up at 5.30, I was joined on the plane by Giovanni and Giorgio, a large, genial Sardinian who got off at Juba. Next stop was Rumbek, where the pilot informed us that there had been torrential overnight rain at Wau and the airstrip was closed until it dried out. We had a delay of a couple of hours, during which we had a picnic and I taught Giovanni and some others to play nomination whist. Giovanni had invited me to stay at the Oxfam house in Wau where he was now Acting CD, and when we eventually arrived, his colleagues were very welcoming but they had a shortage of accommodation and water. That evening we had a few beers at a nearby hotel called River Lodge.

Next morning I was up early again for a flight. I wrote in my journal, 'I sit in the early light under the Bougainvillea – I've waited years to write that line . . .'

Due to various other duties and delays, it was 8.30 before I was driven up to the airport for an 8.40 flight. The WFP office was closed and chained up. Not far away was a group of ten or twelve people with luggage. We joined them. About ten minutes later a 4x4 drove up and a guy got out who I recognised as Dominic, from the River Lodge the night before. He read five names off a list in his South African accent and four of us were there, the other being Mac, a freelance driving instructor/mechanic who Cormac had told me wasn't coming up till Thursday due to it being

Census Day. We put our bags in the 4x4 – the easiest check-in ever. We then walked across to the tiny aircraft and identified our bags to the same people who'd loaded them. I sat at the back of the ten-seater plane with my leg up, the first two taken up by the pilots.

We took off and flew over the landscape, largely featureless except for a few bushes and trees and a river snaking away to our left which the pilot appeared to be following. Further on there was a riverbed that looked like a serpentine golf course with waterlogged greens. This was what I'd imagined when Neil described my working life in GOAL's office in London, back in November. We finally touched down on the airstrip at the wonderfully named Wunrok, and I got out of the tiny craft to be met by a few curious children. The plane took off, in between flocks of goats crossing the landing strip. Still nobody appeared to meet me. I managed to get directions – a pointed finger and 'over there by the big tree' – and headed off across the flat, dry landscape carrying my heavy gear and still limping slightly. I was accompanied by Alex, a young trainee who was apparently going to be based at our compound for a while.

When we arrived, Andy, the Area Commander, said no one had told him we were coming. Lunch was served and it disappeared at an incredible rate: very much, 'first come and fuck the rest' – a very different atmosphere from the communal system in Malakal. I spent about four hours with Andy, a savvy forty-something guy from southern England who'd apparently been appointed on the back of his close connections with local and national leaders. We sat on the verandah outside my tent discussing contingency planning, security and the political situation

Pauline, the nurse, pointed out a green mamba eating something by my tent in her characteristic matter-of-fact way, and one of the guys despatched the snake with a stick. Problems accessing the internet made me late for the evening meal I'd seen being slaughtered and prepared earlier. I scraped a couple of goat bones out of the sauce in the bottom of the pan. Anyway, as usual in the heat, I wasn't very hungry but drank a full carton of 'Fruits of the Forest' while playing nomination whist with the two Paulines. (They were both Scottish: the nurse was Pauline Cafferkey, subsequently to feature in the media after catching ebola while working in Sierra Leone, the other was an accountant from Glasgow). Feeling like a character from M*A*S*H, I went for a starlit shower to rinse off the hairs after my full haircut and shave from the resident 'barber' but there were only a couple of drops of water in each of the overhead barrels.

The next day Andy and I travelled to Abyei, about fifty miles to the north, but arrived after Neil and David Shiels, my North Sudan counterpart, had left. After a briefing on local security issues, I went to a nearby 'bar' in a hut with a couple of ex-pat staff and then with the others to the UN for a few drinks. The next day we returned to the UN compound for a briefing, the main subject of which was the injury of a local in an RTA involving an INGO (International Non-Government Organisation) vehicle. 'Considering Abyei is in the front line of North-South tension, I found this surprising,' I later wrote in my journal. We travelled back through the hot, bleak landscape to Wunrok where Mac and Audrey, a young French woman working for PSF (Pharmaciens Sans Frontières) – and Alex's supervisor – had arrived.

I flew back to Juba, via Wau, with Audrey. A few days later, I heard an escalating disagreement at the gate and Cathy, Head of HR, entered my office. Clearly distressed, she said Taban, an ex-driver, had threatened her. He had been drinking and was red-eyed and angry, complaining about money he believed was owed to him. This was exactly the sort of situation in which staff got assaulted, rather than attacks by unknown assailants. I led him away from the compound, walking off the aggression until we parted some distance away with a handshake.

The CD was on annual leave and a likeable guy called Martin, with a very different managerial style, had come in as Acting Country Director. It was interesting to see the altered atmosphere and dynamic engendered by consultation.

On Thursday 29th April I received an email from my brother Peter saying Ossie had pancreatic cancer but the prognosis was hopeful.

◊

When I went on R & R, I decided to fly from Nairobi to the island of Lamu, an idyllic place without cars, reached by boat from the airstrip. With the help of some local agents, I found a house formerly owned by a poet which I had all to myself for a pittance, due to the continued shortage of tourists as a result of the post-election violence in Kenya. Each morning Sammy, the houseboy, came and made my breakfast. I sat on the flat roof in the sunshine reading short stories or wandered through the narrow, traffic-free streets.

I teamed up with Lani, a Canadian aid worker in her 20s, for a boat trip on a gloriously sunny day. We sailed with Hassan, sporting a washed-out Bob Marley T-shirt and a goatee beard, Omar with his bare chest and shock of hair, and Kemal with his even greater head of hair, ragged shorts, orange-coloured teeth and nickname of Fish Head. We glided though the mangrove swamps to Takma, going ashore with Hassan in a shallow-bottomed boat kept there. He led us up to the museum, passing some huge animal footprints. Sitting at a table outside the entrance was a majestic-looking black man of about forty with a greying beard. On the table was a marked-out board, upturned bottle-tops arranged on his side of it, downturned ones on the opposite side by an empty seat. He said his name was Issa or 'Jesus' and I said something about him being a prophet, knowing someone would turn up to play him at draughts. After he'd defeated me, he took us through the Baobab trees, past an arrowed sign saying 'town walls', to the ruins. From our vantage point on a small hill we surveyed the magnificent beach curving away beneath us. He told us, 'We had hippos over last night,' explaining the footprints we had seen on landing. We left for another beach, had a swim in the sea, which was the perfect temperature for my knee, and a meal of charcoal-grilled fish, vegetables and rice before sailing back to Lamu.

One morning, I made my way to the town square. A rough edge on my repaired sandals was scratching my ankle and I visited Issaiyah the cobbler, working outside in the shade of a building. A young Muslim woman, with only her sad brown eyes exposed, was waiting for her sandals to be mended and made space on the crude bench for me. Before long we were engaged in conversation and she told me about how both her 28-year-old sister and her baby girl had died during the birth, leaving her sister's poor husband with four young children. Our repairs were finished before our stories, so I told her I was going to the Hapa Hapa restaurant for a drink if she wanted to join me. I set off alone and was sitting drinking a hot chocolate by the entrance when a small but stout black-clad figure shuffled past. I couldn't be sure if it was her, of course, and didn't call out. A few minutes later she returned and sat at my table but wouldn't have anything to eat or drink. As she spoke, the material over her mouth moved in and out. The way it hung suggested a snub nose. We exchanged tales of heartbreak – our own and others – and when she left she took a small bracelet of wooden beads from her wrist and gave it to me. I had nothing to give her except my best wishes.

◊

I flew back to Nairobi. While I'd been away there had been a flare-up in Abyei:

'Fighting broke out in Abyei town between the Sudan People's Liberation Army (SPLA) and Sudan Armed Forces (SAF) between 13 and 20 May 2008, leaving scores of people dead and over 50,000 displaced.' (UNMIS website).

I had further medical checks on my knee. Returning to the office I saw Martin in the compound: I knew the night before had been his leaving party in Juba. I was told I wasn't to fly to Juba the next day, Saturday, as planned, but to wait for the CD's arrival on his way back from leave. On the Saturday evening, I was supposed to be meeting the CD at four. James said he'd seen him with a very pretty American lady. At 5.40 the CD phoned to say he was running late and would be back in about half an hour.

When the meeting eventually did take place, I made it clear that I would rather leave than remain if I wasn't wanted and utilised. He insisted that he wasn't trying to get rid of me and he hoped I could fly to SBN from Loki on Thursday. My instincts told me otherwise, but it was left at that.

The following evening, a group of us went to Tamambo's in Westlands for a meal and I had the duckling, which was very good, unlike the conversation. Most of it was gossip about other 'GOALIES' and not really my scene. I was unusually quiet though one or two tried to involve me. Towards the end, someone said something about 'blue-rinsers' and it triggered a memory of Spike Milligan's reaction to a group of them in the Turk's Head in Newcastle that day I'd spent with him in 1975. I began to tell the story, but before I'd finished, the CD bellowed out, "Who does he remind you of, with that playing squash with Spike Milligan and everything? John O'Shea!" (Founder and head of GOAL, apparently known for his namedropping). About a minute later he said, "But you didn't finish your story . . ."

I didn't get away that week, spending my time attending physio sessions and working online at the office. On Monday 26th May I finally got my signing-off certificate from the doctor in Nairobi and the all-clear to return to work from GOAL's medical advisor in Ireland. The bad news was that the logistics staff still hadn't got a new battery for my laptop, having forgotten about my repeated request. I finally got one at a supplier's in Westlands at 12.50 p.m. on Wednesday 28th, just before I was due to check in at one o'clock at Wilson Airport for a 2.30 flight to Loki. Laban drove as fast as he could and got me there at 1.15.

When I landed at Loki, the first person I saw was Audrey with some of her team. Shadrach was there to collect me, and on the way to 748 told me there would be no flight the next day as WFP (World Food Programme, jokingly known as 'What's For Pudding?') had no fuel. I spent the next few days exercising in the gym room, playing online bridge, writing, preparing training sessions, and walking along the dusty road with my Frisbee in hand. Loki is a dangerous place, and there had been several murders there in 2008, including the guy in charge of the WFP compound who was shot while driving into work.

◊

On the morning of Sunday June 1st, I was up at 5.30 for the charter flight to Kurmuk. I was travelling with a young Kenyan woman called Terry, another roving member of staff, and Kazim Alaro, an older man. He told me Alaro meant 'bad': he'd been a breech birth and when he'd eventually been delivered his maternal grandmother had said he should be discarded, his mother having died giving birth, but his paternal grandmother took him and brought him up. We were crammed towards the front of the cargo plane because our full load meant we were tail heavy. When we landed, I was met by Marion, the Area Co-ordinator, who held out a stiff, formal hand by way of greeting.

I liked Kurmuk and most of the staff, but professionally I found my situation very frustrating due to lack of communication, changes of plans and my laptop continuing to crash. Arrangements for me to visit our small base at Kayli had been off and on. One morning Marion told me she thought I should go and I had an hour's notice to get packed. Our 4x4 was greeted by Michael, a tall, mild-mannered Nuer from Bendui who was in charge there, helping with births at our clinic. I immediately warmed to him and the place, with its friendly faces and rocky outcrops.

There was a wedding celebration in the village that night. The bare earth of the *tukul* compound had been swept spotlessly clean. A few women and young children were singing songs and playing drums while others were carrying water containers.

The old guys in their long white robes advanced in a ritual dance, waving what looked like a hockey stick above each white-hatted head. They then stamped once in front of you in a scaled-down version of the Maori haka. Others clicked their fingers above their heads in an invitation to dance. The head of the household had taken a shine to me and offered me one of his daughters (or granddaughters) as an incentive to stay in Kayli. A very young, black woman of about fifteen (it was difficult to tell her age as most of them looked a lot younger than they were) took my hand and led me across the floor – to dance, I hoped, as I had a sudden, alarming thought that this blue-robed beauty was going to lead me to the bridal chamber and some line would have been crossed whereby ours was the next wedding. Of course nothing of the kind happened, but I admired her bravura performance in getting me up to dance and in managing to mirror some of my outrageously improvised dance steps . . .

A few days later I returned to Kurmuk where Marion was as intense as ever. The next day the vehicle travelling back to Kayli got stuck and Peter and Dan set out to try and winch them out. When they returned around eleven that night, Peter told me he and Dan had taken a wrong turning and ended up in a minefield, laughing it off, although obviously – and naturally – having been very scared. I told him I would require an incident report in the morning.

I needed to visit our compound at Yabus and took the twice-monthly charter flight which called in there with supplies on the way back to Loki, where Peter was going en route to Juba with stomach trouble, no doubt stress-related.

The captain of the cargo plane was the only crew. He manoeuvred the pick-up next to the hold where a drum of fuel was loaded onto it and then driven under the wing where they pumped it into the tank by hand. I sat in the co-pilot's seat, my thighs tight under the controls. The twenty-five-minute flight was like a video game but with real bumps at the end. John collected Kazim and myself while the rest took off for the next part of their journey: to collect Chris, the pilot of our outbound flight, whose plane had damaged its nose-cone on landing and who'd made his way to a nearby airstrip at Lokichong to be picked up.

The next day I did the site security assessments with John Mbugua, the very conscientious and likeable guy currently running the base. The following day I ran the threat and risk session with all available staff. Despite their initial reticence, it developed into a really worthwhile exercise covering their expressed concerns, with everyone contributing. I also managed to get some of them playing Frisbee and cards instead of just watching TV.

The hardtop was travelling to transfer materials to another vehicle, halfway to Kurmuk. I got on board with my gear, but when the driver stopped at the clinic, a short distance away, and checked the front suspension arm, he discovered it was buckled. We returned to the main Yabus compound and transferred the cargo, including the poor strapped-up poultry intended for soup in Kurmuk, into the pick-up. It was 10.30 before we finally got away, followed by the tractor. The pick-up's four wheel drive turned out not to be working properly and the tyres were quite worn. We slid around in the black cotton soil, at one point having to use a winch on successive trees to get ourselves out, taking about half an hour to cover a hundred yards before getting stuck again. We had only travelled about nine miles. Jaffa arrived on the tractor and told us we were to turn back: Marion had phoned and I had to contact her. Returning seemed to be the right decision, having seen how bad the conditions were, despite the fact that it hadn't rained for four or five days. I called Marion who gave me a hard time for having set off. I told her I didn't know the roads and I didn't make the decisions about which vehicles travelled where and when. The tractor pulled us out of the mud and we got back to Yabus at about 1.15 p.m. Two casualties of the abortive trip were my old Gola bag which had belonged to Great Uncle Arthur, destroyed by spilled acid from an unsecured battery in the back of the pick-up (luckily the contents were OK) and one of the chickens. The Kurmuk vehicle arrived at 6.10 p.m., having taken eight hours to travel just over fifty miles (87km) between the two sites.

I realised I would be in Yabus a few more days at least. There was a problem with the generator and we'd lost all power. Amos rigged up a solar-powered bulb in the mess and over supper launched into a comic but passionate tirade against the supply chain that had left him short of building materials for completion of his latrine construction work. Most of the timber was still stuck in Kurmuk, although some had arrived in the pick-up, along with Daniel and Mella. John, the butt of his remarks as the visible representation of the management, appointed Amos 'Chairman of the Stress Management Team', one of several nods to my threat & risk session. Although Amos's criticism might have been overly personal, at least it brought the tensions out into the open in a humorous way. With no power for the TV now, we played cards together.

The following afternoon I worked on my reports using the site laptop, my battery charger and one of three available batteries. There were still problems with the generator so I rotated the batteries, but just as I was trying to save my work to a memory stick the current went down. I replaced it and luckily found autorecovery had saved me again. I finished the document before my last battery crashed.

Just then some visitors arrived; they turned out to be from an American charity, SIM, (Service In Mission). They'd come to ask if they could keep their vehicle in our compound during the rainy season as their compound was over the river. The senior member of the group, a middle-aged lady with the unfortunate name of Phalice, said I could avail myself of their solar-powered battery charger if our electricity and IT problems persisted. There was no generator again that night.

The next day I worked on my reports until all three batteries were dead, and then – bearing laptop and charger, Thuraya satellite phone and charger, Frisbee, and the good news that Marion had approved their request – I made my way to the bridge leading to the SIM compound. Unfortunately, it was a ford and under a couple of feet of swirling brown water. I stripped down to my swimming shorts and, with great trepidation, crossed the river.

After playing Frisbee with my hosts, I had a simple lunch of spaghetti and lentils and a glass of water before re-crossing the river with my recharged batteries, hoping I hadn't acquired any nasty creatures such as the Black Fly, which caused river blindness and had secondary symptoms of swollen testes, or the Nairobi Fly which squirts its acid on your skin. One of the young American women had nasty burns from it.

When I arrived back at Kurmuk I asked how Peter was but Marion didn't know. I established a system of using my issued laptop to do my work (it only worked on battery, crashing for some bizarre reason if connected to any other power supply), using the inoperative one brought back from Yabus as a battery charger and the third battery as part of the rotation process. I'd never been technically-minded, but I was always resourceful.

Apart from internet access, other pluses included Pauline, the Glaswegian roving accountant, being there on a visit; Commandos Marinos (he told me he was given his name by a friend of his father's – a military man) giving me the 'Vaccinate all your children' T-shirt I was after; and Owa Waga, the tall, slender young local woman who looked after the mess, poking her pink tongue through the gap left by pulling out her two bottom front teeth. You would have thought that would have been a disfigurement, but it actually added a strange allure to her dusky beauty – or perhaps I'd just been in South Sudan too long . . .

After a long chat with Pauline, who told me she was considering leaving, I wrote a report on Stress Management which was fairly critical of how GOAL handled stress-related issues. The problem was no one had anyone they could really turn to for support, and my problem was that I had no one to whom I could usefully send the report.

The following day I read through some documents produced by Chris Godsby (a GOALIE with a strong health & safety background), including a report from a year ago. A couple of his recommendations made me smile – the recruitment of a Security Officer and the introduction of a duty officer system. When I'd suggested the latter, the CD's immediate reaction was, "I'm the Duty Officer System for South Sudan . . ."

◊

Socially, I visited a couple of the people I'd become friendly with locally: Johannes, an Ethiopian who worked for WFP and Farhat, a Pakistani lady with the United Nations High Commissioner for Refugees (UNHCR). With Johannes I sat and drank white wine (Awash) while chatting in his canvas-covered office: with Farhat I sat and drank tea and ate cake while talking in her air-conditioned house. I tended to use a spare bicycle for these trips, enjoying the exercise and independence it gave me. Other diversions included watching the European Football Championship, usually with some of the UN military observers who brought crates of beer with them, and Wimbledon (including the cracking, rain-delayed final between Federer and Nadal).

With Bernard, a likeable but slightly nervous Kenyan as Acting AC, the atmosphere became progressively more relaxed. One night some of us went for a few beers at a stall in a little plot down from the market known as Fallujah because of the amount of fighting there. Another night Sandra, back from her leave, suggested going to the Peace Hotel for a drink. By the time we got together, our driver had disappeared. It was still before 8 p.m. but already dark, and I asked her if it was safe to walk there. She said, 'Yes,' – she'd done it loads of times . . . We set off with torches and then I heard a sound that stopped us in our tracks. I pointed my torch towards the direction of the sound and saw a man with his AK-47 raised. I called out that we were aid workers with GOAL and he let us pass. A nervous man with a gun is never a good combination.

Before going to bed I had an outdoor shower around 1 a.m. I heard sustained distant rumbling which sounded like heavy plant being moved and I noticed a vehicle parked outside our gates with its lights on. Clearly, prying eyes were being discouraged. I discovered later that there had been a consignment of tanks moved in contravention of the peace agreement.

I woke up early the next morning. We had quad bike training, which was great fun. In the afternoon, I made another trip by 4x4 to Kayli. It was not the most comfortable place to stay with its hard spring mattress – and, on this occasion, rain on the tin roof and the wind blowing the shutters – but it was homely and welcoming, with smiles from Muna and Almeira, the domestic staff, a big grin from Michael, and the sight of the cranes flying home to roost in the trees among the hills.

I visited the clinic to decide which room to designate as a 'safe haven' in case of danger – it was more a case of 'least dangerous place' as there were windows facing the road just outside and some of the walls and lintels were badly cracked. Although it was a new building, the unstable nature of the black cotton soil from one season to the next rendered it liable to shift.

The next day, we took home a woman who had lost both her twins, having been brought to the clinic too late, according to Michael. We returned to Kurmuk with a woman who had to have her cervix seen to as she had lost six unborn babies.

The following day while working on evacuation plans, I had a visit from Wayne Sealey, the local UN Security Officer, who was from Trinidad & Tobago. He wanted to discuss the tank movements I had heard the other night. A few days later on 8th July, my 56th birthday, I attended a UN-convened security meeting with Daniel, a Kenyan-born Health Officer, now Acting AC. The meeting consisted mainly of the UN's military and security arms flapping about in frustration. There was talk of running a limited and low-key evacuation exercise, with which I would have been keen to be involved. The CD, however, responded forcefully to my report on the proposals, saying that the UN should always be a last resort as an evacuation option and that evacuation exercises caused alarm.

That evening, after Daniel and I had had a chat about security developments and worked on our responses to the CD's email, we held a security meeting to update the staff. Afterwards I held a little birthday celebration under the awning, having given Jeremiah 100 Sudanese pounds to get some beers and sodas to go with the two bottles of Ethiopian gin I'd bought. I appeared in my African garb – the black-and-white striped tasselled shirt I'd had made in Lamu and the wooden bracelet the girl had given me there, my round hat and the necklace Michael had bought for me at Maya's market near Kayli, and my Maban hunting stick from Yabus. I knew none of our African staff would be offended and they'd respond with delight to my attire. All of our local domestic staff attended, some ('Momma' and Martha) giving me a small amount of money (ten *birr*) as is their custom. I did a little jig for the ladies and they responded wholeheartedly, singing and whooping and ululating. Unfortunately, Angelina – a tall, slender, beautiful young woman wearing a dress she'd obviously brought in specially – had to leave, having just received word of her sister's sudden death.

After returning to the office for a while when the local staff had left, I had a second session with Pauline and Sandra and some of the drivers, turnboys (back-up drivers) and guards. They sang 'Happy Birthday' to me and I performed 'The Nyama Choma Blues' (*nyama choma* is Swahili for roast meat), a comical song which I'd written a short time before. I then showed them how to play the bottle game where you try and stand a bottle as far away as possible from you without any part of you touching the ground beyond the line you stand behind. I knew it wouldn't reflect well on the Safety & Security Officer if any injury was sustained, but I thought it was an acceptable risk and at the end we all had some good fun and emerged unscathed from the experience. It could be classed as a very effective stress relief exercise.

We had a few more songs and dances (I got Emmanuel to try to explain in Arabic the Geordie song, 'Cushy Butterfield' before I began), and then Pauline and I led the rest through the steps of 'Strip the Willow'. I couldn't recall having had a better – certainly not a more multicultural – birthday party.

Chapter 24

Things generally took a more serious turn when the UN leaked that the ICC (International Criminal Court) was intending to indict the Sudanese leader, Bashir, in a few days' time. This was not good news for the UN or NGOs, especially in Darfur, but also throughout Sudan.

Saturday evening came round again and another goat had just had its throat cut. It was a fine brown and white creature that had been bleating off and on all afternoon. Mustapha, the old guard, had bent over it with his knife, which looked ornamental but proved to be very practical. He'd made a slit horizontally just above one of the knee joints and put his mouth to the cut. I thought he was sucking blood out, but he was actually blowing up under the skin to help it come off more easily. It took him and his assistant half an hour to skin the animal, hanging it up by its hind legs from the tree to finish the task. Its last green meal spilled onto the concrete block, near which were thick vermilion streaks as if someone had trodden on two or three tubes of bright red paint. It took another half an hour to gut and sort out all the bits and pieces, which they did very precisely and tidily. Mustapha would eat these delicacies later, apparently. The goat's eyes looked like those you'd see in a painting of the crucifixion. The Holman Hunt picture *The Scapegoat* also came belatedly to mind. What was, an hour before, a living, breathing creature had now been reduced to a systematic assortment of its component parts: the edible, the useful, the waste and body fluids. When he brought the roasted meat around that night, Mustapha steered me towards the best cuts – those from the ribs – and the *nyama choma* that night was the best I'd ever had.

◊

We had occasional paying guests staying on site and the next morning, while I was in one of the outside showers, I heard Daniel, who was with UNICEF (The United Nations Children's Fund), discussing his evacuation to Khartoum via Damazin. Suddenly, he got a call to make a dash to the UN base. It was all very dramatic. He was keen that his colleague, Mohammed, also got on the flight but there were strict priorities in these matters.

He was back after about forty minutes. They had run over to the helicopter only to be told that they couldn't be taken as the aircraft was already carrying too much weight. He pointed to his trousers, ripped in the rush and described his 'Saigon moment', having been denied access as the chopper lifted off. There wasn't room for him but a female colleague had five cases of clothes on board, he'd complained. Only Daniel, Mohammed and Wayne of the UN contingent remained.

The next day, July 14th – Bastille Day – became historic for another reason: Al-Bashir was the first head of state to be indicted for genocide whilst in power. We sat tight, waiting to find out what might happen in terms of civil unrest, etc. We heard nothing – there wasn't even any email activity.

Two days later I was at the airstrip, due to fly out on our charter flight. The plane finally appeared overhead and landed but didn't arrive at the loading point. We drove to the end of the 'runway' and discovered it was stuck where it had tried to turn around. The surface had cut up, which didn't augur well for when the rains began in earnest. The plane was unloaded and the pilots dug out the wheels. I was informed the CD was in Khartoum with Neil and the CD there, everyone else having been evacuated. Was it true?

I stayed at 748 in Loki overnight before flying up to Wunrok on the same plane. I sat in one of the two seats behind the cockpit, making space for Mark, an African member of the Twic team. After two and a half hours of deafening flight, one of the crew told me, "We're not going to land at Wunrok." When I suggested Turalei, a nearby landing strip, he said he didn't think that possible. It looked like we would have to return to Loki.

Eventually we did land at Turalei and, although I'd tried to get a message to Andy via the air crew and Shadrach, for the second time landing in Twic County there was no one to meet me. I was conscious of the cost of the flight, the value of the cargo, and the fact that I was carrying nearly $100,000 of the charity's money in cash. At that point Andy arrived, followed closely by a couple of other vehicles. I travelled to Wunrok in the first vehicle. On the way there I noticed that the land – flat and characterised by palm trees and wading birds such as cranes, egrets and herons – was a lot greener than last time. The road had been improved and it took Theresa, the only female employed as an NGO driver I'd seen in Sudan, just half an hour to drive there. I locked the money sack in the stationery cupboard with the key Andy had given me and assisted with unloading the pick-up of its contents of toolboxes and tyres, raincoats and wellingtons, fruit juice and tins of food.

The genny was turned off so when Andy arrived, we used the time to count out the bundles of notes and the loose cash – they tallied, thankfully. I learned that there had been no internet on site for ten days. I did what work I could on the documents I could access and then at seven there was the usual frantic dash for dinner. The chicken was already gone, but I took one of the three burgers left, some mash and a little corned beef (which I've never liked) to supplement it. There was nothing else.

Afterwards I sat and chatted with Phillipe, the Livelihoods Officer, outside his tent before heading over the mud flats, on foot and in the dark, to the Mercy Corps site where they had allocated us access to their internet facility between 8 and 10 p.m. We sat outside the brick shell with its superimposed corrugated roof, watching insects around the solar-powered lights until the generator was switched on. I discovered I couldn't access the internet because I hadn't got the password.

"Don't you know it?" asked Cathy, one of their young American volunteers.

"No – I've just arrived," I reply.

No one in the room knew it. Someone said it was written on a piece of paper somewhere. Everybody else had it locked into their laptops. Cathy said her friend Elizabeth Sung had it, but she was on leave.

"Where?" I asked, struggling to control my frustration.

"Glasgow," she replied.

I wanted to laugh. I was supposed to be looking after people's security and I couldn't get any access to the outside world and the person with the information was in Scotland.

Cathy Skyped her. It seemed an incredibly long shot. To pass the time,

I mentioned my eldest son was currently on a placement with a firm of engineers in Glasgow.

"What kind of engineers?" she asked.

"Civil engineers," I told her.

She said, "Which one?" and I remembered it was called Jacobs. She said her friend Ryan had just returned to the States after an attachment of several months at that office.

Cathy got a call back from Elizabeth in a minute or two with the code and I was connected. Connections . . . There was an email from Ossie, forwarded by Peter: the doctors had discovered he had an extremely rare tumour that they didn't know how to treat. My second battery ran out – they were lasting less and less time, an hour each if I was lucky. I made my way on my own through the dark and the mud back to our compound. A minute after I was through the gates the generator went off, although it was due on until ten and it was only 9.30. David, the young English guy I'd first met in Nairobi who was now Andy's right-hand man, said it had run out of fuel. Just as well I was back on site: it would have been very difficult finding my way back without the lights to guide me. So I set off to my allocated accommodation, tent 5, which had no solar power, and went straight to bed – an enforced early night. Here, I thought, life was dictated more than anywhere else by such circumstances . . .

The next day began with a plus: bacon for breakfast, closely pursued by a minus: the generator wasn't working. I wrote up my journal on the verandah outside my tent while two Dinka women did their domestic duties inside. It had stopped raining and outside the compound the guys were unloading the fuel from the wagon that had brought it all the way up from Uganda. Two huge vultures perched awkwardly on one of the perimeter trees. I struggled through the day with failing batteries, literally and metaphorically.

It was a beautiful evening and I played Frisbee with three of the guys. I walked to Mercy Corps with Andy, the roving Logi, and upon checking my emails found Shadrach had booked me on a flight from Turalei in three days' time. It gave me a day less to get my work done but a day more in Juba to prepare for my five weeks of summer leave. Walking back across the flat darkness with its scattered huts, I noticed the frogs were especially noisy and it was so humid that it was no surprise when a storm struck overnight and several of the tents, including mine, took in water.

The next day was Sunday. I located the badminton net and set it up before teaching some of the guys to play. I learned later from James that the AC's nickname for me was 'Competitive Dad', which I had to admit was accurate. After badminton, I got my head and beard cropped by Moses, changing my appearance so dramatically that some of the staff didn't recognise me.

There was a poor little white kitten in the compound whose back legs didn't work and so it dragged itself around the site. The kitten seemed to me to be a metaphor for survival in this harsh environment. It was a wonder one of the vultures hadn't got it.

Lots of the guys were in the TV hut watching Lewis Hamilton cruise to another victory at Hockenheim. Later, I watched Duncan Bannatyne, a Scottish millionaire known for his appearances on BBC 2's *The Dragon's Den*, tackling BAT (British American Tobacco) over their merchandising of cigarettes to African kids. He tried to buttonhole Kenneth Clarke and the other fat cats coming out of the shareholders' meeting.

The *tukul* on the other side of the compound fence hosted an all-night party, so I got very little sleep and I was up just after seven as the disco out the back was about to be revived. Theresa drove me to Turalei airstrip for the half-hour flight to Wau where I caught the plane to Juba. I was met by a new driver: there seemed to have been a lot of changes in terms of drivers and guards at the office. The departure of Natasha, the universally popular American who declined the opportunity to extend her contract, had left a big hole in the place. She was the best networker I've ever met. There seemed to be a dearth of friendly faces. The CD was on the phone and closed the door. I did not feel like the prodigal son. I was pleased to see James and set up my IT ensemble beside him on the other desk in the Deputy CD's room.

At my meeting with the CD the following day, I told him I hadn't known he was in Khartoum until I learned the fact, by chance, from someone else. He checked his emails, saying he thought he'd included me in the email he'd sent. I also had meetings with Alice, who had got the job I put in for many months ago to set up an office for SCIAF (Scottish Catholic International Aid Fund) in Juba, and then Illke, the Finnish guy at the UNDSS (United Nations Department of Safety & Security), with whom I discussed security issues. He'd previously invited me to the house he shared with JFD, the legendary Frenchman, Jean-Francois Darcq, who he'd wanted me to meet. I had a very interesting evening discussing Sudan, history and literature with them both over a few drinks.

The next morning I flew to Nairobi and paid for my flight to Paris. I hadn't been able to do this online as the site would not accept my credit card due to my location.

The following day I went to a travel agent's, to search for a short safari for the days until my flight. I was told there would be a single supplement, but I said I was prepared to share. At that point, the one other customer, a middle-aged woman – to the obvious embarrassment of the woman attending to her – blurted out, "I'll share with you." She introduced herself as Janie and gave me her telephone number, saying she was taking some American clients to the Masai Mara. I booked for the same place – Ilkeliani Tented Camp – but went for an earlier flight.

The next morning I flew from Wilson Airport to Olkiombo airstrip. There was an array of vehicles and guides awaiting those arriving. I was met by Joseph, an impressive figure in his red and blue Masai tartan. En route to the camp, with a Pakistani couple and their two infants, we saw elephants, giraffes, Grant's gazelles, Thomson's gazelles, a tawny eagle in a tree and a lilac-breasted roller. We were welcomed with a glass of orange juice by Charles, in khaki, and the other staff in Masai tartan. Charles arranged for me to have a tent to myself at no extra charge. The place was empty except for a party of six Asians. After a lunch of broccoli soup, Nile perch with rice and green beans, and cornflake pudding, I lay on a lounger, listening to the river flowing and chatting to a sweets salesman from Vietnam.

After returning to my tent and writing up my journal, I played Frisbee with the waiters before going on an afternoon drive with the Pakistani family. Towards the end of this we spotted a lioness stalking, but her prey moved away and we headed back to camp. I had dinner with Janie and the Americans (or the 'Rich' party as they were known, after the surname of one of the couples, not their assumed affluence) who'd just arrived. They were from Kentucky and it transpired that they knew my brother-in-law Denis, who was a university professor there and who had been to their house before. One of them was an undertaker and knew Thomas Lynch, the much-admired Michigan mortician/poet I'd met at the Edinburgh Book Festival several years before. Janie and I chatted afterwards over a drink, and she told me her complicated family history before I turned in for the night. Masai tribesmen with spears kept guard in the grounds overnight, apparently to ward off any wild animals, although also for dramatic effect for the tourists, I suspected.

I was awake before six when my coffee pot and biscuits were delivered outside my tent. We were on safari by 6.30. The highlight was the sighting of a cheetah, nestled in the long grass, picked out from a great distance by its flicking tail by the ever-vigilant Joseph with his binoculars. He drove up for a closer look – none of the other guides having spotted it.

We also saw a jackal before breakfast, which we had out in the open by the Land Rover.

On the evening safari we were part of a group of vehicles watching a group of three lionesses and six cubs moving in on a group of wildebeest and zebras – a lot of group activity. Unfortunately, the cubs were spooking their prey, but this was tolerated by their mothers as part of their training. They were still stalking when we left at seven: it was becoming so dark it would have been impossible to witness any kill, if it had eventually happened. On the way back we saw an African hare and the strange jerboa-like creature called a springhare.

The next day was my 24th wedding anniversary and I wondered how many people who'd attended the ceremony would remember the date. Most of those who might have remembered – our parents, in particular – were dead. I said farewell to the staff, several of them 'Frisbee friends', and flew back to Nairobi, staying the night at the Hampton Court apartments.

◊

The next morning, I headed off to the office where I spent several hours and well over two hundred pounds just to change the name on one of Flybe's flight tickets for my children, from Martha Harvey, who wasn't coming now, to Joseph Harvey. Although I thought it scandalous, being in places such as Sudan sharpens your sense of priorities and it was worth it to have another of my children with me for the week in Rennes.

I caught the train from Paris to Normandy, and had a day or two to get some food in and the place ready. On the way down to Rennes Airport my old Volvo overheated and then had a puncture. I, too, was overheating by the time I'd changed the wheel at the side of the A84. The driver of a motorway maintenance vehicle guided me to his depot where I stocked up on bottles of water to cool the engine down. Luckily, I'd called the boys before they'd left to remind them to bring a mobile and I'd managed to contact them just after their arrival. I asked Joe to get a taxi and put the driver on the phone and then I handed it to the maintenance worker for him to give directions to our location, just off the autoroute.

When they arrived some time later – an expensive taxi ride of over sixty euros, but not begrudged at all – I was delighted and relieved. We limped most of the way back to the 'Chateau', topping up the radiator at shorter and shorter intervals, before imposing on Ian Hayward to take us the last part of the way.

◊

After a good week with the boys, we travelled to Edinburgh. As usual, I attended several readings at the Book Festival, one of the writers being Matthew Green, author of a book about Joseph Kony called *Wizard of the Nile*. We went for a coffee together and discussed the security situation in Sudan. I had arranged for Ossie to come up for a visit and we went to some great events together, particularly Simon Callow's bravura one-man show recreating the performance of two of Dickens' short stories in the same venue the author himself had performed one of them, 150 years earlier.

Chapter 25

During the course of my leave, I realised that I was increasingly reluctant to return to Sudan, and I had put in an application for a global post with Save the Children. On returning to the office in Juba, I was disappointed, but not surprised, to find both Toshiba laptops in Robert's drawer, the IT Officer clearly having done nothing about repairing them. Hilde, the Community Health & HIV Co-ordinator, was getting ready to leave and told me the thrust of her debrief was that she'd found herself in a position of 'responsibility without authority'. This phrase described my situation with equal accuracy.

I spent the next three weeks working on documents on the main PC, my laptop still awaiting repair. Pauline Cafferkey, feisty Fifer that she was, had gone off to work for GOAL in Darfur and I missed her no-nonsense, tell-it-how-it-is company when I went back to Wunrok. Upon my arrival there, Andy informed me of a theft from a visitor from AFC, another nearby NGO. I picked up the enquiry and it transpired that the items were taken during the course of an alfresco party. A set of keys had been stolen, including one to AFC's safe. I was sure the keys would have been discarded, but I volunteered to stay at their compound until they turned up and they took me up on the offer. The keys were subsequently found by one of the cleaners near a tent in our compound. Although I was sure I knew who'd done it, we couldn't prove it, much to the CD's anger.

As well as receiving a critical email from him, we also received one saying that WFP, with immediate effect, would no longer be using Turalei because livestock were wandering freely across the airstrip making it too dangerous – although I'd never seen an airstrip in Sudan where this didn't, or couldn't, happen. This meant travelling to Wau instead to pick up a flight to Rumbek. This poem was the result of that journey:

ON THE ROAD FROM WUNROK TO WAU

On the road from Wunrok to Wau in South Sudan,
I saw many people walking – some wanting a lift,
others knowing that their lot was to walk, whilst ours to ride by in clouds of dust.
I saw men in long tunics to the knee or so, bright green or red,
like Irish or Welsh rugby shirts, others light blue, deep purple, some trousered
in the same material, and men with spiky, spindly spears and even sharper eyes.
I saw boys fishing with poles in Monet-esque lily ponds,
carrying their catch on strings;
boys diving naked off low bridges, wrestling in muddy pools, washing;
young women, bare-breasted doing household chores outside their *tukuls*,
mothers feeding babies, children nursing younger children,
a woman carrying an oil drum on her head;
there were soldiers coming back to base with their AK 47s and firewood,
three men on a motorbike (five is the most I've seen),
no helmets or goggles but the rider always has a pair of shades;
cattle with twisted horns and hump backs, kamikaze goats and indifferent sheep;
a woman in a shawl holding a baby and begging;
a lorry full of people, stuck in mud; a sick donkey; a dead cow –

all these things I saw today, on the way from Wunrok to Wau.

Chapter 26

My ideas for my novel, *Malakal Academical*, were taking shape, and in Rumbek, while awaiting my flight, I visited a clinic which served as a rehabilitation centre for amputees in order to garner material for the novel. When I got to Malakal I was met by Elsa, the Area Co-ordinator, as well as by more IT difficulties.

On Friday 10th October, while conducting an interview in the course of investigating a case involving unauthorised access to and use of GOAL property, and the theft of an individual's footwear, I asked Evans to produce the shoes in question. Standard procedure.

"They know what the shoes look like, for God's sake!" she intervened.

I pointed out, as politely as possible, that this was accepted good practice and avoided any subsequent dispute over the identification of the property.

On Saturday afternoon I gave the Threat and Risk Analysis presentation to the only two members of staff who hadn't yet attended. One was David, the meek but very likeable Finance Officer, and the other, Elsa. He was open-eyed and attentive. She sat at her desk with her laptop open in front of her and the moment I started speaking she began tapping away at the keyboard. I had to tell her, in front of another member of staff, that her behaviour was unacceptable. She said she was listening, but I said I wouldn't continue unless she stopped working on something else.

Although she relented, with dramatic gestures, she subsequently kept looking at her mobile below desk level and took out her emery board and began filing her nails. Even when answering questions, she affected a schoolgirl voice. At the end, David thanked me and said that it had been helpful. Elsa said nothing.

Such an open display of a lack of respect could only occur because the CD had made it clear that I had no authority. I finally decided enough was enough. I sent Geraldine, the Dublin-based HR Officer for South Sudan, an email:

> *Hi Geraldine,*
> *Receiving a resignation from yet another roving staff member of GOAL South Sudan probably isn't the best start to the week, but here it is . . .*
> *I am giving a month's notice as of today.*
> *Hope all is well with you and you are happy back at GOAL H.Q.*
> *Cheers,*
> *Steve*

I always felt that I would resign with regret (it had become increasingly clear to me I wouldn't see out my twelve-month contract), but actually, it was with a great sense of relief and was confirmation, if any was needed, that I'd made the right decision.

The following day, Sunday, I travelled down to Baliet by boat. It was a languid journey, a pleasant lull between giving my notice and the responses and consequences. I spent the long day in a not particulary comfortable barge heavily laden with building materials, writing up my journal and reading *Emma's War*. We were only a few inches above the waterline, on a dangerous stretch of water where you were a sitting duck for any potshots from the banks. There were a couple of dodgy moments – once when we were nearly capsized by the wake of a fast-moving, passing UN vessel and, as it became dark, on the approach of another vessel whose crew called out to us in Arabic, causing our local pilot, Paulinio, to shout to the boy on board to answer. I began writing this poem as a sister piece to the one written about the road journey to Wau:

ON THE BOAT FROM MALAKAL TO BALIET

I'm travelling on an old boat called Lisa
Upstream from Malakal on the White Nile

Like in a remake of *The African Queen*,
A poor man's Humphrey Bogart,
All stubble and toothpick, to set the scene. . .
There's segregated bathing taking place,
With naked males and females separated
By the rusting hulls of river steamers.
We're carrying a cargo of timber, iron bars,
Bags of cement, under a cane-framed, tarp-covered canopy,
Heavy laden, a few inches above the waterline.
Paulinio, the boatman, steers near to the reeds,
Concentration displacing his wide smile.
Floating islets of wild hyacinth
With lilac-coloured flowers float past.
A fisherman uses one adapted as a raft,
While in green inlets solitary fishermen and egrets
Stand still. Black-and-white kingfishers patrol.
Small, plastic, soft drink bottles, used as floats,
Bob upside down in unattended pools.

Motor-powered canoes go sleekly past, lookout on prow,
Rainbow-coloured parasols shading reclining passengers
Alongside nursing mothers, infants, goats.
Overhead, eagles, buzzards, herons display their differing
Styles of flight – circling reconnaissance planes
Or bombers with heavy loads, while fighter pilot swifts
And swallows skim the river making kills.

This river's seen the Antonovs destroying human lives
Along these banks; we're on the Sobat now,
I'm reading *Emma's War*, where it's chronicled.
A lingering tern discerns its prey and dives.
It's getting dark, and distant lightning
Shimmers on the river. No sign, now, of fishermen
Standing on bank or boat checking their nets,
Just us, eyes strained, necks stretched, seeking Baliet. . .

Dedicated to the memory of the seven people who lost their lives in
a collision on this stretch of the Sobat River later that night, Sunday
October 12th 2008

I enjoyed my time in the Sobat, experiencing the harsh reality of fieldwork in an unforgiving physical environment as opposed to an unforgiving 'professional' one. As is usual working in such conditions, staff were generally resilient, supportive of each other, and good-humoured. I travelled back to Malakal in a speedboat with Ken, the Deputy Country Director. I'd stopped keeping my journal as my heart wasn't in it any more and I tried to conserve my emotional energy, saving it to say goodbye to the many staff I liked and would miss.

Chapter 27

I returned to Edinburgh and spent the next few months settling back into this city, which I love, getting fit again, applying for jobs and working on *Malakal Academical*. Towards the end of March, I received a Skype message from a senior member of staff at 'Save' asking me to contact a colleague: it appeared the Head of Global Safety & Security for SC UK was leaving soon and they wanted me to apply for the position. This informal approach struck me as strange, after a protracted application process during my time in Sudan for a previous, less senior post, for which I didn't make the short list for the London interviews. I applied nevertheless. Around this time a post came up as a part-time Safety & Security Training Officer with RedR, one of the foremost organisations in the field. This role seemed more suited to me at this stage in my life, and I was contacted and given 5th May as the interview date.

I travelled down to London, having prepared a short training session as required. The interview went like a dream, but then something strange happened. In the middle of answering a few routine questions from the panel of three female staff members, I suddenly sensed they were going to offer me the job: this set off a train of other thoughts and emotions, such as the fact that this post was partially sponsored by 'Save', so what would happen if I then got the interview for their other post? And did I want to spend my time telling new NGO recruits how to keep themselves and their property safe, and repeatedly delivering a very similar programme? One of the women asked me a question about a training programme to which I didn't have a direct answer, but I began giving a perfectly sound response until I suddenly heard myself saying something about it not being the role of interviewers to try and catch applicants out with trick questions.

I travelled on to Normandy to do some more writing there before the arrival of Jimmy and the rest of the arty-farty-up-yer-bum club for the annual bridgefest. It still hadn't fully sunk in that I had spiked the interview. I couldn't believe that I had done that when I was normally so controlled and competitive in interviews. I remembered thinking I wouldn't get the chance to finish *Malakal Academical* if I got the job and then my subconscious seemed to have surfaced and taken over.

This was a first for me, but several people have since told me they have done similar things in interviews. Naturally, I didn't get the job and subsequently I received the standard email from 'Save' saying they would not be progressing my application.

◊

At the 2009 book festival in Edinburgh, I attended a reading from *Black Sisters' Street* by Chika Unigwe, a Nigerian woman living in Belgium with her Belgian husband and children. It was about Africans in the sex industry in Amsterdam. We later went for something to eat in Brown's on George Street. Chika was very likeable and good company. Another event I attended featured a former child soldier from Sudan, Emmanuel Jal, who had been befriended by Emma McCune of *Emma's War* fame and written a book himself called *Warchild*.

My friends Geoff, Jamal, plus Richard and Alison (up from Sussex for a long weekend) came to support me at an event organised by Simon Munnery. I'd been introduced to him in the Pleasance Courtyard by John Hegley, who'd offered my services as a local poet to him for a series of gigs he was organising at Fingers Piano Bar on Frederick Street. When we arrived on the night, I discovered it was a real mixture of acts in the classic Fringe fashion, all arranged in a very ad hoc and madcap manner by Simon. He told me that I was to be last on, which I was quite happy about. Unfortunately, just before I was due to perform, Simon said he was giving five minutes to a guy who'd just walked in off the street. This large, strange individual then launched into a bizarre rant about Israel being responsible for the dismembered limbs of Palestinian children.

People were shouting, "Get him off . . ." and by the time he'd been removed, I'd inherited a very agitated audience for the closing slot. I'd decided not to refer to him at all, but I knew I could give up any hope of the audience tuning into my poetry any time before the fourth poem. It was the flattest performance I've ever given.

◊

Ian Campbell had organised a weekend at Falkland in Fife on the enneagram, a personality analysis system. I hadn't been there before: it is a fantastic place, home of the Stuarts, and we were staying in the building next to the Palace. It was an enjoyable and thought-provoking experience and I discovered I was a number 8 – someone who operates primarily at a gut level.

I was back in Edinburgh in time to climb Crow Hill, the hillfort beside Arthur's Seat, to watch the fireworks display over the city to mark the end of the Festival with Peter, Nathaniel and India. We nestled in the shelter of the crag with a wind-up radio and watched the display. India was three the next week and I wanted to make it a special adventure. I thought it might be her first retrievable memory.

I continued writing, applying for jobs, and going for the occasional interview. Towards the end of September, I went with Geoff to the Benedictine Monastery at Pluscarden, near Elgin, for a week. I used this as an opportunity to get some work done on *Malakal Academical* without distractions, although I did attend some of the offices of St Benedict's Rule each day (lauds, prime, terce, sext, none, vespers and compline) and all of the meals – very simple fare – were eaten in silence except for readings by one of the monks from the pulpit overhead. There was usually one religious and one secular book. The current secular work was Andrew Marr's *A History of Modern Britain*, so we were exposed to phrases unlikely to have been heard previously in such hallowed surroundings, including 'tit and bum' and 'a teddy bear with a stiffy'.

Ossie's condition was worsening and I drove down to Tyneside to see him. His siblings were taking turns to stay with him. His optimism, evident in previous visits, was missing, but the quiet good humour was still there. As I drove back over the river, Derrick's old Subaru Legacy, which Susan had given me, began to die on me and I managed to nurse it to a garage in Wideopen where the proprietor told me it was finished. It seemed appropriate . . .

I was due to drive Peter up to Edinburgh that afternoon before taking a flight together to Cork the next day, so I told him he'd have to take his vehicle up instead. He had been thinking of buying a new property in the Borders and we had arranged to view a few on our way north. At one of them, a place just south of Earlston with the wonderfully evocative name, 'Sorrowlessfield', I happened to mention we were going to Kinsale and the vendors recommended a Polish restaurant, Jola's, having just returned from a week's holiday there. They told us Sorrowlessfield came from the fact that it was virtually the only steading in the Borders to which all the menfolk returned safely after the Battle of Flodden in 1513.

The rationale behind our trip was a combination of things: Peter hadn't had a holiday for years and seemed in real need of one; I had been in touch through a computer dating website with a woman in Kinsale, Lily, who I wanted to meet; there was a jazz and blues festival on there at the time; and Peter had never visited his old classmate, Tony Robinson, in Wexford, although I'd been over several times when the Opera Festival was on, as it would be when we were there.

Lily collected us at Cork Airport and took us to the B&B I'd booked for us on a hill above Kinsale. It was a very well-kept place with friendly, helpful owners, an open fire and superb picture window overlooking the bay in the lounge-cum-dining room. That evening the three of us and Edith, a friend of Lily's, met up at a bar in town. Lily and I set off to look for Jola's to book a table for the four of us at nine, after Edith had attended her evening class. En route I spotted a sign in a bookshop window on one of the narrow streets for a poetry reading for that day. The shop was closed and I was disappointed to have missed the event until I noticed it didn't begin until eight. We returned to the bar, collected Peter and walked back to the bookshop which was now open. The reading was by a local poet called Desmond O'Grady. He was sitting there, a quirky old character with a red neckerchief (he later divulged to me that he wore it because it saved him having to change his shirt every day). The proprietor announced that Desmond would sign books beforehand because he knew some people might not be able to stay until the end. I picked up a copy of *My Limerick Town* and stood in line. I heard an American voice behind me and, as I turned to look, recognised the diminutive feisty female, but I couldn't immediately place her.

"Did we meet at this year's Edinburgh Festival?" I asked.

"No, I run a bar in Tbilisi, Georgia . . ."

"That's it – the Hangar Bar. I met you there in September 2004."

Again it was the sequence of events that led to this meeting that struck me rather than the coincidence itself: my online liaison with Lily; the viewing of Sorrowlessfield (the vendors of which, I discovered later, were friends of Ian Campbell's); the search for the Polish restaurant . . .

The reading was really good, not least because of Desmond's generosity of spirit in allowing other local poets to read first. Unfortunately, we had to leave for our meal. Jola's was a superb restaurant in a very atmospheric building and we had a great evening.

The next day, I managed to get hold of Desmond's phone number and invited him out for lunch with Peter and myself. We picked him up and took him to a nearby pub he'd suggested, The Bulman. As we sat there at the window, looking out to sea and chatting about life and literature, I suddenly realised that a poem in *A Fixed Expression* (which I had with me) was written of the view from the sea wall in front of us. It was from a family holiday with Maggie and the kids many Octobers ago. Asking his indulgence, I read it out to him:

RECOLLECTIONS OF KINSALE
(Beyond Summer Cove)

A swan, a seal, a sailing ship's
Distant, graceful shape completing,
From my west-facing vantage point,
A perfect, abstract, line of vision.
Remote – viewing a total eclipse
From outer space, a linear meeting
Of astral bodies, seeing God anoint
Your self, the scalpel's oblique incision.

Such moments in a life are rare,
Subjective, too, like points of view,
And this glorious afternoon
Beside the ever-widening sea,
Will be recalled by all as where
One of our family got wet through
Behaving like a shoreline loon,
Not for sublime geometry.

Desmond was great company and regaled us with tales of his Limerick contemporary, Richard Harris, and his own appearance in the classic 1960 Fellini film *La Dolce Vita*, set in Rome, where Desmond had taught from the late fifties to the mid-seventies. He'd been asked by Fellini to coach the 'lecturer' for the iconic film and then co-opted to play the role himself. He had been a founder member of the European Community of Writers, European editor of *The Transatlantic Review*, and organised the Spoleto International Poetry Festival. He'd also taught at Harvard, the American University in Cairo and the University of Alexandria. I was interested to learn he'd translated some Kurdish poetry, and I later bought a copy.

After a few days, we took the bus to Wexford and spent some time with Tony and his family before taking the ferry from Rosslare to Cherbourg. From there we travelled south by local train and made our way to the 'Chateau'. In due course I made my way back by ferry and flight, meeting interesting people on the way including Terry Newman, who worked with Richard Demarco, Scottish promoter of the arts.

◊

Back in Edinburgh I got a call to say that Ossie had died – on St Osmund's Day. His brother, Martin, began his eulogy by saying, "There was only one Osmund Postle – I know because I googled him . . ."

I was asked to carry a trowel up to the altar to commemorate his love of history and the time he'd spent on archaeological digs. It was a strangely moving thing to do.

◊

I received an invite from Terry to attend a Christmas drinks session at the annexe of Craigcrook Castle in Edinburgh and after the traditional two-day visit to Newcastle, I travelled up to Falkland with Peter and the boys where I had booked the house beside the palace for a week. There was heavy snow and the place looked even more magical, unnaturally dark on a sunny afternoon, being in the shadow of East Lomond, only a western turret catching the bright sunlight. We climbed the hill, went sledging and won the quiz at one of the local pubs, sending Nathaniel up to collect the prize as he'd got a couple of the clinching answers.

Chapter 28

I had been planning a trip to New Zealand for a while, in the absence of any job offers, and was due to fly there via Tahiti at the end of January 2010. Gabriel had been increasingly disenchanted with his architecture course at Edinburgh University and after he dropped out, I booked him a flight from Glasgow to Auckland to meet up with me.

I arrived in Papeete, via Los Angeles, after 33 hours travelling and watching more films than I think I saw in the whole of 2009. I contacted Walter, a dour German who had lived there for decades. He reminded me of the world-weary character played by Rod Steiger in the film, *The Pawnbroker*. His place, 'Chez Myrna', was recommended to me by my much-travelled friend, Iain Jackson. It looked like a neglected version of the scene on the cover of Jackson Browne's *Everyman*. Inside, a picture on the wall of two dolphins in joyful motion only counterpointed the cheerless nature of the accommodation, but I'd always been a no-frills traveller and it did me fine.

I explored the humid city and frequented the internet café at La Maison de la Presse, Les Trois Brasseurs restaurant and a Chinese-run café called Lucky Luke's. On Saturday 23rd January I took a four-hour trip on the catamaran, *The Escapade*, to Tetiaroa, the atoll purchased by Marlon Brando (on a 99-year lease) during the filming of *Mutiny on the Bounty* in 1965. Although still a classic, unspoiled island paradise, the ship I saw from the shell-covered beach was apparently bringing materials for a hotel project that was underway.

On the way back, the other passengers, all French, and myself were lucky enough to encounter a school of dolphins which swam under the boat and played as if the boat was another dolphin. I could hear them chirruping like Flipper in the 60's TV series of the same name.

Walter slept in a chair in the living room with the big fan on all night. He spoke no English and we communicated in gestures and French, with him asking me to repeat every sentence, no matter how clearly I tried to enunciate. Despite a photograph of a younger Walter with a blonde boy in the kitchen, he said he had no family and had not been back to Germany for many years. He told me he had been working for 'the bureau' when he was contaminated by the French atomic tests, and pointed to both arms, indicating injections and shaking his head.

On the Sunday I attended the Episcopal Church, which was hot and full of large women wearing straw hats. The ninety-minute service consisted of long, apparently ignored sermons, and hymns sung with gusto.

Exploring the town, I was given two free tickets for the opening of a documentary film festival. One of the people I offered the spare one to was a charismatic-looking Frenchman with long hair, but he needed another for his wife. The seven shorts were introduced by a swaggering, suave Frenchman and a Polynesian woman with an American accent, fixed smile, and a comically slick delivery. My favourite was *War Party*, with virtually no dialogue, but good acting and dramatic action.

The next day I took a bus to the other side of the island to stay in a place called Chez Flohatia for a couple of days. It was set on a little strip of land, one plot deep, between the road and the shore. Within a few minutes of my arrival, I was sitting at a table just feet from the sea, sipping lemonade made freshly by my genial hostess and writing my journal. I took a siesta in the late afternoon heat.

I woke before six and found Flohatia and her headmaster husband, Gerald, at the table by the shore. He had just finished eating a papaya and fetched me one. Dinner was at seven, so I took a short walk along the road and then the beach. I walked on the black volcanic sand, enjoying the evening light, the sense of freedom, the exuberance of children having fun surfing and playing, and the sensation of seawater up to my knees. Dinner was simple but superb: after grace, we ate avocado and egg slices, lamb and mashed potato, lychees and ice cream. The avocado, like the papaya, was from their own garden.

After a breakfast of papaya, baguettes and honey, I spent the next morning writing postcards and browsing through the FIFO 2010 film brochure. In the afternoon, I went for a walk up the hill across the road from the house, joining in with some children playing table tennis for a few games. Further on, the road was cracked and broken and totally overgrown in places, and the speed restriction signs were obscured by bushes.

I left the next morning. Flotahia gave me a hug and a shell necklace. Gerald gave me a lift to the town where he worked and from there I caught a bus and travelled past the Botanical Gardens and the Gauguin Museum. When I arrived at FIFO I deposited my bags in a storeroom and settled down to watch a film called *Lost in Wonderland*. It was about the cross-dressing Kiwi eccentric ex-policeman, Rob Moodie, and was wonderful. Later, I walked into the centre to check my emails at the Presse, mail my postcards, and have lunch at Lucky Luke's. I had a Chinese-style omelette with king prawns, chicken pieces, and rice, washed down with the milk of a fresh coconut.

I called in at the office of New Zealand Airlines to confirm my Auckland flight, due to leave at 1.30 a.m., was still scheduled, as Gerald had told me that a cyclone was expected to hit Tahiti in the next 48 hours. They assured me there was no change to my travel arrangements and I made my way through the sporadic rain back to FIFO, where I took in another half dozen films – all pretty good.

One of the attendants told me late night taxis in Papeete were very expensive and I discussed this with the French couple I'd met there on the first day. Jacques told me he was an air traffic controller at the airport and they lived nearby, and offered me a lift to the airport later. When they dropped me off at the airport, I was surprised to see no one else there until an attendant told me that the flight had been cancelled. I turned round to see my new French friends driving off. Realising I had no local currency left and nowhere to stay, I dropped my bags and ran after them, catching them as they drove back along the main road. Returning to the check-in, I found that the airline had arranged accommodation for me at a nearby hotel, at their expense. I left for the Intercontinental Beachcomber in a taxi provided by Air NZ, having arranged to meet up with Jacques and Brigitte at FIFO the next day.

The next morning was spent on the phone trying to ensure I could meet up with Gabriel at Auckland Airport as planned. This involved switching from Air New Zealand's Saturday afternoon flight to the Air Tahiti flight on Saturday morning. I phoned the family home, only to find he'd already left for Glasgow. I was conscious he didn't know where we were staying, so would be stranded if he arrived before me and didn't get my message. I also contacted the B&B by email to explain the delay.

When I arrived at the film festival I saw Brigitte getting out of a car. I paid for two day tickets and she invited me to dinner. After an afternoon of watching films – including *Strange Birds in Paradise: A West Papuan Story*, which I thought was the best (it looked as if it would be an ego-trip but turned out to be anything but) – we headed back to Brigitte's for a great meal of avocado starters (prepared by their friend Sylvie, who joined us), fish goujons, prawns and salad, and ice cream. Jacques provided the entertainment, playing the Breton pipes and then the guitar. As Sylvie drove me back to the hotel, I saw there was a ring around the moon and hoped this did not signify the cyclone approaching. Luckily, the worst of the weather passed us by.

Saturday was spent, largely, in the air. Although the flight was only five and a half hours, we crossed the International Date Line into Sunday, and it was 2 p.m. when I arrived in Auckland. I had no idea whether Gabriel had got my message, but as I walked into the arrivals lounge, he called out to me. His flight had arrived only five minutes ahead of mine. We took 'the chopper' – a minibus with a trailer for luggage – driven by a kindly Chinese driver to our accommodation, 811 Dominion Road. The place was run by a couple, David and Brian. One was a theatrical set designer and the house was a repository of quirky props. There were no locks on the room doors and the place had the relaxed and convivial atmosphere of an old-style café in a quaint county town. Tea and Christmas cake were served, on the house, to the small group of guests, including Judy, an elderly drama coach, and her husband Leonard who had twinkling eyes and a trim moustache.

After a substantial fried breakfast the next morning, Gabriel and I caught the bus to Auckland city centre. We called in at the Magic Bus office to sort out travel arrangements. They ran a daily service on a figure-of-eight route around the country. You could get on or off at fixed points and board again as and when it suited you. The driver also dropped off and picked up at various hostels. There was a festive spirit prevalent in the city, especially by the quays where a Scots band of bagpipes and drums played outside the Maritime Museum and a nearby street entertainer amused passers-by.

Two days later, David dropped us off at the Magic Bus office where we picked up the coach heading south. It was driven by Muz (Murray), an ex-chippy, and took us through Thames and Hobbiton to Rotorua. The weather was beautiful but the sulphurous smell from the hot springs pervaded the place. Muz was staying at the same hostel as us, Kiwipaka, and told us Alexandra, where we'd arranged to go working in a vineyard, was regularly the hottest town in the country. I'd found the place in a woofing register (Working On Organic Farms) that I'd bought in Auckland. One of the attractions – apart from the obvious – was that the owners played bridge.

The next day we were away by 7.30 a.m. to visit Waitomo Caves. The guide (a great granddaughter of the Maori chief who'd first explored the caves with a '*paheka*' or white man) asked for a volunteer to test the acoustics and as everyone else was too shy, I made them pay for their reticence with a verse of 'Cushy Butterfield'. When the lights went on you could see all the threads lowered by the glow worms to catch prey. They made a magical display. Outside there were blue skies and Gabriel went tandem skydiving while I went walking along the river above the Huka Falls.

Because we were needed to set up netting at the vineyard as soon as possible, we were just staying one night at each place, which meant Muz would be our driver until Wellington. When we arrived on Friday afternoon, Wellington was heaving with groups of young men and women dressed in the most fantastic fancy dress costumes I'd ever seen. Among the best was a group of Scrabble letters, complete with values. They were heading to the Westpac Stadium for the Rugby World Sevens. We spent the evening in bars watching the games on TV and admiring the outfits of returning revellers.

When we left on the shuttle for the ferry to the South Island just after 7 a.m., there were still people out partying. We were met at Picton Terminal by Richie, our new driver, who was young, edgy and funny. He stopped at a river for an afternoon swim and later at a lake where he dared anyone to dive in, and Gabriel did. We stayed at Paradiso Backpackers in Nelson, where we had superb blue cod and chips at the local chippy. This was next to the upmarket Sprig and Fern Tavern, but we walked along to what Richie on the bus had called 'the old man's pub', with an inclination of his head in my direction. We sat drinking jugs of beer with a fellow passenger, Glen Gulley (a guy from Oregon to whom I pointed out that his name means 'Valley Valley'), and Joe, an old local. It struck me that my photographer friend from my Iraq and Caucasus days was from Oregon and called Cliff, and I wondered if geographical names were the fashion there.

We revisited the chippy whose attractions, as well as the best fish and chips I'd ever had, included scallops and very attractive girls serving behind the counter. Gabriel spent a long time deciding his order from the new girl, who he thought was even hotter than the last. We finished the night off with a glass of cider in the Sprig and Fern.

There was a great bunch of guys on the bus the next day, including Michael and Cyrille, two Bretons on holiday from the French naval base in Tahiti, a 71-year old Irishman called Hugh who was a big Leinster rugby fan, and a group of young English guys with whom Gabriel got on well. These relationships were strengthened by a visit to Monteith's Brewery in Greymouth, which confirmed their 'Original' as one of our favourite beers.

The next morning we set off from Noah's Ark Hostel for Franz Josef, where we arrived in time for lunch. Glen and I walked up to the glacier and back, while Gabriel and the other young guys signed up for a climb on the glacier itself. On our return we soaked in the hot tub at our hostel, Chateau Franz. Glen, Gabriel and I were sharing a bunk room with some girls. During the night, I was woken by an unearthly shriek and instinctively reached out from my bottom bunk as something fell past, screaming. It was Gabriel. I'd tried to catch him, or rather break his fall. He'd been having a bad dream and had completely turned around in the upper bunk, which is fortunate because he had gashed his leg on the dangerously-placed DVD player's stanchion on the wall and it would have been his head otherwise. The whole room was instantly awake and the girls screaming too. One of them spent the rest of the night on the floor, fearful that she too might plunge from her upper bunk.

The following afternoon we parted company with our fellow travellers, and were dropped off at the 'Big Fruit' symbol in Cromwell. From here we were collected by Angela who took us to Judge Rock Vineyard in Alexandra, owned by her and her husband, Paul. Once he arrived home from work at a civil engineering company, we had dinner and tasted their second string wine, a very nice Pinot Noir called Venus. We were accommodated in a basic, one-room backhouse, with use of the kitchen and toilet facilities in the house.

◊

Early next morning we began work. Our detail was 'bud-rubbing'. As if this wasn't already a worryingly lascivious-sounding action, we were to do it with what Angela called, 'Paul's amazing tool', without a hint of double entendre. It was a kind of hoe, used to remove any young shoots from the bottom length of the vine to prevent it absorbing any of the spray, which was the next part of the viticulture cycle. Working steadily, it took us nearly three days to finish the task in time for Paul to do the spraying before we did the netting over the weekend. On the Saturday we worked from 9 a.m. until nearly seven, spreading the nets dispensed by a vertical mechanical arm attached to the tractor. We then went to the Monteith bar in town to help Garry, our heavily tattooed Ulster colleague, get through the $100 free tab he'd won the week before. Later on, we were given a lift all the way back to Hillview by the pub's proprietor, as she was obliged to do by New Zealand law to prevent drink driving. Incredible.

We spent Sunday finishing the operation, only with fewer hands to help, and the next few days were spent with the regular staff straightening things out, 'walking through' between the lines of vines, pushing the slack overhead, stretching nets manually to reach ends of runs left short, and covering gaps. I began blasting music from the large speakers outside the house to boost flagging morale. Rescuing goldfinches from the nets cheered my evenings. On our last working day, I borrowed a fellow-worker's car and fetched some cider and nibbles from Alexandra for a little celebration. There was some light rain before the sky cleared and returned to its pristine blue, to which we'd become accustomed.

The next day, Angela gave us a lift to Queenstown where she was collecting her brother from the airport for a family wedding. We checked into Bumbles, our hostel, just up from the lakeshore. Queenstown is the adrenalin capital of the country – its over-stimulated heart, its hormonal organ. It is a spectacular adolescent playground. We climbed the hill behind the town to the Skyline café where we ate our buffet meal overlooking the lake and the superb surrounding landscape with the backdrop of The Remarkables mountain range, the cable cars and the bungee jump.

I took a gondola down and arranged to meet Richie, our old bus driver, who was in town. He was in The World Bar, sipping cocktails from a teapot with three English girls. He asked Gabriel to choose the next cocktail for accepting his dare to jump into the lake the previous week. They came in a wide variety of flavours.

The next day we were up early to take a coach trip to Milford Sound, which, we were told on our short cruise, was really a fjord. Our sightseeing day was rounded off in the bus on the way back by the showing of *The Fastest Indian in the World*, a rather cheesy, feel-good film about an ageing and eccentric motorcycle enthusiast from Invercargill taking on the machines and bureaucracy of the USA played by Anthony Hopkins. The best line in it by a mile was, "Even dirty old men need love . . .'

That night our sleep was disrupted by two of the eight occupants of Block 2 returning drunk. A girl wearing only her bra and panties was lying crying on the floor. Outside a guy was arguing with his companions who were struggling to get him into the building.

The next day, by way of compensation for the disturbance, one of the staff gave us a couple of 'Fergburger' vouchers redeemable at the local burger bar. Gabriel and I discovered the Frisbee golf course in the park and spent hours playing. We were amazed to see people queuing to tee off and carrying small 'putting' discs as well.

My concession to the place's thrill-seeking ethos was a jetboat ride on the Shotover River. Gabriel and I sat right at the front of the craft, driven by Mat, a young man with just the right amount of confidence in his ability. It was good fun, with 360 degree turns and dousing splashes. The water level was really low, but Mat told us his jetboat could operate at a minimum of ten centimetres (4").

After several days of fun, freedom and Frisbee golf, we got up early to resume our travels on the Magic Bus. In the kitchen was a woman who told me she was travelling with her daughter. She complained her sleep had been disturbed by someone 'shaking the dice', a euphemism new to me (on looking it up online for this, I was amazed at the length of the list of alternative phrases for this practice, noting especially 'reading poetry': I wonder how many times statements of mine might have been misconstrued). She told me she had lost her adventurer husband several years previously, when he was presumed to have been swept overboard on a yacht one night.

Our bus was driven by a taciturn Maori named Manu who wore his long hair in a blue bandana. It felt odd stopping in Alexandra where we got a couple of pies while Manu was faxing the hostel booking requests. By lunchtime, we'd arrived at the Leviathan Hotel, Dunedin, where we were staying with some fellow passengers including Dan, a ginger Brit, and Sam, an attractive Indian girl, who we'd met in The World Bar in Queenstown. Their pal, Rob, hadn't travelled with them because he hadn't been able to find his rucksack with all his documents in it. The latest news from him was that it looked like the rucksack had been stolen and he had to try and arrange a new passport. He was due to go to Fiji the following week for his thirtieth birthday with Dan.

We went to a park over the road and spent a glorious afternoon playing Frisbee. That evening, the four of us went out for a meal. We settled on The Terrace in the Octagon – a good choice. I had a lamb shank and all the others had sizzling stone-grilled meat of sundry sorts. We ended up

– with Katerina, a Swedish blonde that Dan too-obviously fancied – in Albar on Stuart Street, a good pub where Gabriel and I had previously had a quiet lunch. Now it was packed and four musicians were knocking out some Chieftains tunes in fine style. There was Sean from Belfast playing a cittern (a stringed instrument, resembling the banjo in appearance but not in sound), an English guitarist, a guy playing the *uilleann* pipes and a female flautist. Just perfect . . .

We visited Dunedin Railway Station, which I thought was a fabulous building, and then took a bus to the Albatross Centre, although it didn't go all the way there. At Portobello, where the bus turned round, the driver advised us that the road from there on was uphill and winding, and that there wasn't much room for walkers. It was yet another hot day and it took us quite a while to walk the two and a half kilometres to the centre, frequently stepping aside to allow the eco-tourism coaches to pass. The place was too commercial for us and after a quick look around and a short walk along the headland, we set off walking back towards Portobello, hoping to hitch a lift. Forty-two vehicles passed us – mainly tourist couples in silver saloons – before a tatty-looking van with a trailer on the back pulled up. An empty beer bottle fell out when the passenger door opened. The driver said he wasn't going very far but could drop us at a better place to catch a lift. His large companion, sporting a ginger beard and earring, crawled awkwardly over the seat into the back. Gabriel joined him and the dog there. It reminded me of the lift we'd got in the pick-up in Sardinia six years earlier.

The driver introduced himself as Jeff and his passenger as Scott. We told him our names and that we were from Portobello, Edinburgh, in Scotland and travelling to visit its namesake. He insisted on driving us all the way there and they joined us for a couple of jugs of 'Steiny' in the Portobello Hotel. He said he was a 'scrappy' and just scraped a living at it but the advantages included being able to give a couple of hitchhikers a lift and have a beer with them on a hot afternoon. He stated, 'Numeracy and literacy are overrated' and I found myself unaccountably agreeing with him. He told us he'd had a difficult upbringing with lots of surrogate fathers. At fifteen his life could have gone either way, but a lodger showed him how to strip down an engine and he found his salvation working on vehicles. He said, 'Cars are my thing. I've got three tyres now for one and I'm off to look at what I hope is going to be the fourth . . .'

He declined my offer to share the seafood platter and wedges we'd ordered on his recommendation, which was a pity since the platter itself came with chips and the portions were enormous. He and Scott headed off to find the fourth tyre and I wished them well in their quest. We took a few snaps of premises bearing the Portobello name before the number 18 bus arrived, turned round, and took us back to the Edinburgh of the South.

Chapter 29

The next morning we were back on the Magic Bus. Our driver, who styled himself as 'Disco', was a small man who did things slowly and methodically. First stop was Baldwin Street, where we took the opportunity to climb what is reputedly the world's steepest residential street. We had a full English breakfast at the café overlooking the Moeraki Boulders, which look like large, pale Maltesers marooned on the beach. We stopped at Oamaru, a quaint provincial town with old colonial buildings. Disco went shopping with the $10 per head he'd collected from all those wanting to have an evening barbecue by Lake Tekapo, which was that night's base. I walked around Oamaru taking photos, aware that one of my favourite writers, Janet Frame, spent much of her childhood there (the Waimaru of her debut novel and subsequent fiction).

The next day we travelled on to Christchurch where we stayed at Stonehurst Hostel. We met up with Dan who told us Sam had moved on and Rob had managed to obtain a replacement passport and would be able to go to Fiji. After playing Frisbee in a local park, we went with Disco and a group of fellow passengers to a rugby match between the Crusaders and the Sharks of South Africa. The increasingly multicultural composition of New Zealand's population was underlined by the fact that the driver of our taxi was Al from Afghanistan. The cost of our tickets to see some of the best players in the world – including Dan Carter – was just over $20 NZ each, even with add-ons.

I spent the next day on a trip to Akaroa, leaving Gabriel to his own devices. It was a little place on the coast discovered by a Frenchman who had sailed back to his homeland and persuaded 57 compatriots and half a dozen Germans to return with him and settle there. He called in at the English colony on the North Island en route and on reaching Akaroa again, discovered the Union Jack flying there. It struck me as a metaphor for a lot of lives.

It was a beautiful place and a beautiful morning. I sat reading *The Motorcycle Diaries* at a table outside a café where I had a leisurely and excellent cooked breakfast before taking a walk up the back of Stanley and then resting on a bench overlooking the harbour. Afterwards I visited the old French cemetery, St Patrick's R.C. Church, an old engine room turned into an art gallery, and a café where I sat at a table on the lawn and ate a smoked salmon panini. On the shuttle bus, the woman sitting next to me said she was on a sentimental journey and had just visited a shop which once belonged to her family. Back in Christchurch, Gabriel and I played Frisbee in the local park with other backpackers until it was too dark.

As we got ready for the bus the next morning, Sunday 28th February 2010, we turned on the TV and saw that there had been an earthquake of 8.8 on the Richter Scale in Chile. While we were travelling, a girl approached the driver, 'Young Joe Young', a hard-nosed but likeable Aussie, saying she'd received a message on her mobile, warning of a tsunami. An electronic road sign then flashed 'Tsunami warning' and Joe received instructions to call HQ when we stopped at Cheviot. Gabriel and I were getting off there anyway to work on a local farm for a week or so. Daniel, our host, was waiting for us when we pulled into the car park of the Magpie's Rest Cafe. We transferred our bags from the bus to his black 4x4. He was in his early thirties and bouncy, with sandy hair and freckles. It took about twenty minutes to reach Mount Sandford, his 1300 acre farm. After meeting Em(maline), his wife, and having something to eat, he took us on a tour of the property in his ute (utility vehicle).

It was another glorious day and Daniel offered to take us fishing, so we set off with a couple of spinning rods and a fly fishing one. He turned right up Cat Hill Road and said, "How are you with trains?" The reason for this otherwise obscure question lay in front of us – a single-track railway bridge with a narrow path inside one railing. The main East Coast line! We decided against this option. Dan found a delightful spot, having passed on one because there was another vehicle there – New Zealanders enjoy the benefits of a small population. Daniel noticed a big trout in a pool with the help of his Polaroid sunglasses, and tried to entice it with a fly, but without success. We worked our way downstream and located another trout in another pool. I cast my golden spinner and on my second attempt hooked – and after a brief struggle, landed – a three-pound rainbow trout. We spent a pleasant hour or more on this stretch of the Hurunui River without anything further to show for it, before returning to the farm to eat our fish and get settled into our substantial and comfortable cottage.

◊

Our first working day involved clearing out a shallow part of the sheepyards so that Daniel could fill it with disinfectant for the sheep's feet. I got a crash course in tractor driving and he showed me where he wanted me to empty the dirt from the grab, over the edge into the gulley. It was quite a drop and one not to be approached without confidence in your clutch control, especially with all that weight being carried at the front. He and Em were heading off to a luncheon with her parents to mark her father's retirement, and by the time they'd returned we'd cleaned the whole area, including the run approaching it.

The next day, I drove the ute into Cheviot. Daniel had given us a list of some things he needed, including five sacks of disinfectant for the sheep's feet. The perky red-headed shop assistant carried one of the heavy sacks out to the vehicle herself. Wfhile we were there, the Magic Bus pulled up outside the café. We had a quick look but didn't recognise the driver or any of the passengers. After lunch, Daniel drove up to the high country at the back of the farm to instal an electric fence. On the way he spotted a lamb lying on the ground, a long way off, with some hawks in attendance and a black-backed gull on a fencepost on the other side of the field. He took his .22 rifle off the rack at the back of the cab, but the gull flew off before he had a chance to bag 'the dirty bastard'. When we drove up to the lamb, we saw it was still alive, kicking and shaking, its eye sockets covered in blood. He put a couple of slugs into its head and slung the twitching carcass into the back of the vehicle, the red crescent of its blood narrowly missing Gabriel. Sage, the old fox terrier bitch, licked up the blood with relish. I have to confess, my beef stroganoff was consumed almost as enthusiastically after work that evening.

We spent most of the following day 'dagging' sheep. 'Dags' are the lumps of shit which cling to the sheep's woolly backsides – hence to 'rattle yer dags' is to 'move yer arse'. My task was to follow Daniel up and down the run with an electric fence pole, using its loop to hold up the cable to prevent the shaver cutting it. When he'd finished each run he handed the shaver to me. I was the attentive nurse with the plasma loop and the cutting instrument to his surgeon; Gabriel was the porter providing the patients. The worst aspect of my role was that it was fairly static and this made me more vulnerable to the numerous flies, so Gabriel and I changed over for a spell. The sheep were surprisingly powerful and capable of crocking your knees with their sudden, crazy charges. We got a lot done and then went shooting rabbits after tea.

We finished the dagging the next day, but it did not go smoothly. The sheep were more difficult after being cooped up in the yard overnight. The shaver kept cutting out and then Daniel dropped it, damaging the $40 comb. While he was away looking to get some new ones from his uncle's farm, I made the most of the delay and the good weather by washing all our dirty clothes. When Daniel returned with the combs, we got back to the task but his bad mood was not improved by various hitches. Discovering some wethers among the sheep didn't help either, as they are too old to be classed as lambs and would have to be eaten since they had no market value.

Daniel and Em were out that night, presenting a Mount Sandford riding lesson voucher as a prize at a function, so we all had a lie-in the next morning. After breakfast we travelled with the three working dogs, Peg, Storm and Don, to Daniel's granny's farm near the coast, which overlooked a strange slab of an island. She needed her flock moving across the road and it was a difficult job even for three men and three dogs. Gabriel and I stood ready to block the traffic in both directions as Daniel and the dogs tried to steer the sheep through the two gates. A black saloon continued driving fast towards me as I stood in the middle of the road performing the number one traffic signal for the first time in years, my right arm vertical. I held my nerve but was prepared to dive to the side. At the last moment the driver braked.

"I thought you were a hitchhiker," the young woman said by way of explanation, as if hitchhikers were vermin – like possums – and to be treated as targeted roadkills.

Once the sheep had been transferred, Gabriel and I tightened up a fence while Daniel disposed of a dead sheep before we headed back to Mount Sandford and a quick lunch of crayfish and pork chop sandwiches. The good weather we'd had for so long was beginning to break, and we hurried to herd the sheep into the woolshed to keep them dry for the next day's 'crutching', a more thorough version of dagging. Unfortunately, we had not finished repairing and replacing the broken slats in the wooden floor and so Gabriel and I did this as rapidly as we could while Daniel got the sheep ready, shouting to his dogs, "Arsehole!" . . . "Dogs!" . . . "Wannago!" . . . "Left!" . . . "Behind!" . . .

Finally, as the rain came on heavier, we crammed as many in as possible. Our last task was to soak the combs and other parts of the shears and clean them for the next day. After tea, which featured the rabbit Daniel had shot, we went out in the ute looking for more. It was drizzling and only as we were about to give up did Gabriel manage to despatch an unfortunate rabbit trapped by the headlamps. It was our last night there.

The next morning, we nearly missed our bus outside the café: we were looking for the Magic Bus and the driver was looking for a man and a woman ('Gabrielle' as he pronounced it). There were a few coaches there – ours bore the name 'Nelson', due to problems with the Magic Bus liveried one we were expecting. We arrived in Kaikoura shortly before noon and it appeared to be a rather tatty tourist trap in the overcast dullness of the day. Unless you wanted to indulge in water sports or whale watching, there seemed to be very little to do. Looking around the place, I read the quirky, informative notices put up by the local historical society and took a walk through the 'Garden of Memories'. This was a small shoreline plot surrounding the monument to those who died in The Great War, transformed from scrubland and maintained by Lydia Washington, 'The Grand Old Lady', who died aged 82 in 1946.

Something else that caught my eye was a series of cards in the Encounter Gallery: they were monochrome sketches of a rather prim, unprepossessing character called Cecily. The one that most amused me depicted her standing on a small, round restaurant table to the bafflement of the couple dining there and waving a wad of banknotes in the air. The caption read, 'Money gave Cecily the sense of invincibility she only normally achieved through alcohol . . .'

Gabriel and I decided to use the hostel's sauna. Two white-skinned, bikini-clad girls adjusted their positions and towels to make room for us, but this was their only concession to our presence. One of them spoke interminably, presumably continuing a monologue which began long before we entered. It went something like this:

"Isn't it terrible how Hannah and Lucinda have fallen out? They were *such* good friends – but then I think all that group's relationships were rather *unhealthy*, don't you? And they've both ended up not speaking to *Tanya*, who's *dreadfully* upset, but then I think, well, she's only *herself* to blame – you can't just sit on the fence and expect to please everybody . . .

"And there's just so much gossip going on at Shamborough High, and I could say lots of things about the staff, but I've too much *respect* – and there's *confidentiality* to consider, of course, but I know if I tell you, you wouldn't say anything, and Madame P getting taken away in an *ambulance* because she'd had one too many at the staff Christmas party is something that none of us there has mentioned to anyone else, but the *breakdown*, kinda, that she had afterwards is why she was off school in the New Year and Henders had to cover her classes . . ."

When the two middle-aged teenagers had left, we burst out laughing.

Later, in the hot tub, we were subjected to another stream of unconsciously trivial consciousness about how Laura would find it *much* tougher when she went to *Cambridge* and how, *psychologically*, only having five-and-a-bit months left of their travels was much less daunting than six, and she would never treat her like Michelle had when she'd said she didn't want to be friends anymore . . .

I was really tempted to say something to Gabriel within their earshot about a friend of mine teaching at Shamborough High.

That evening we had steaks and a jug of Monteith cider at The Whaler before attending a blues session at The Strawberry Tree. This was a two-piece outfit from Melbourne called The Hornets. The trilby-wearing acoustic guitar player had that strange combination of characteristics: the ability to sing without faltering, yet stammering between songs, to which his electric-guitar-playing partner added some gutsy, bottleneck effects. It was a good gig in front of an appreciative and lively crowd.

Two guys Gabriel met were keen for him to stay another day so they could take him surfing, but we were committed to boarding the Magic Bus in the morning for Blenheim, where Linda was picking us up to work at her place, Pampers Escape/Falcon View.

En route to Blenheim, we visited a waterfall at Half Moon Bay, where Little Miss Shamborough scratched her knee and was attended to at the back of the bus by her chums. She should have gone to stay at Pampers Escape '. . . where it is all about you!' as it declared on its website, featuring pampered females enjoying pleasurable experiences. Customers were invited to 'indulge in our Pinot Noir and lavender bath for two.' So this was what Gabriel and I had laboured in the vineyard for under the Alexandra sun?

We stayed there for a few days. It was a very different experience from anything we'd encountered before. On our departure, Linda dropped us off by the Kuoni Lodge in Blenheim, driving off to her appointment wearing her white, matronly medical top, while we waited for the Magic Bus. We spent the two hours playing pool and eating a McDonalds. Our driver turned out to be Young Joe Young and we were soon on the ferry at Picton. It was the evening rush hour and raining quite heavily by the time we reached Wellington, where we took a shuttle to the YHA.

There was a fringe arts festival on in the city and a director and his cast were sitting in the YHA canteen chatting. After we'd eaten, we took a walk and ended up at a 'Tiddly Idol' talent contest in Molly Malone's as part of the week-long St Patrick's Day celebrations. It was an enjoyable mix of young musicians and old entertainers. One group of Irish dancers, who were called the All Greens, were heading for the World Championships in Glasgow later in the month. Their coach, Aisling, had been with *Riverdance* for five years and her partner was Tim Brown, one of the New Zealand squad for the forthcoming football World Cup.

◊

On the bus the next morning our driver was a very large Maori called Rangi. We made a stop at Mount Bruce Wildlife Centre where Gabriel had a couple of pies (one lamb, one venison) and I had a steak-and-Guinness one, followed by the best muffin I've ever had (mixed berry with cream cheese) and a hot chocolate. We were rapidly becoming pie connoisseurs. Later, we visited the Tui Brewery, an unashamedly laddish place, where I sampled the Reserve, the Wagstaff, and the Head Barman's Reserve, this last dark beer being my favourite. We arrived in Napier around 2.30 and checked into Criterion Backpackers hostel.

The next day we were dropped off at Tauranga and picked up by Lynise, a teacher, and her young daughter, Evie. She took us on a quick visit to Mount Manganui, a long strip of land beside the sea, beneath a volcanic mound reminiscent of Arthur's Seat, before driving us to her modern house, which was situated on a hill with fine views, about twenty minutes west of Tauranga.

We were kept busy the next day pruning the trees outside the house and barrowing the trimmings away, tipping them into a little gulley. After we finished, we soaked our weary bones in the hot tub with a drink in hand as the stars emerged.

The next morning I telephoned Wanderlust Hostel in Katikati, recommended by Lynise, and booked a twin room for the night with Scotty, who said we needed to be there before 5.10 p.m. as that's when he would be going out to the twilight bowls. I said it sounded fun, so he told me we could come along. I also confirmed a woofing placement near Kerkeri, up north. While Gabriel docked and sprayed the Californian thistles in the main paddock, I trimmed the hedge the length of the driveway. Lynise dropped us at the hostel before five and we accompanied Scotty to the bowls. Gabriel and I were allocated to a middle-aged couple. I played badly but we still went into the last end 10-10. With my final bowl to play we were lying one down, but I managed to take the jack and win the match.

Most of the next day was spent on buses. We travelled to Paihia in the Bay of Islands via Thames and Auckland. No food or drink – other than water – was allowed on the bus from Auckland (where our Magic Bus tickets finished), so it was a hungry journey north. We passed through Warkworth with its Percy Street – names of places with Northumbrian connections (like Cheviot) – before arriving at Paihia at 6.45. Our new host Alex, a short, active man of 52 with long, untidy, sun-bleached hair surrounding a balding crown, emerged to meet us. He drove us to his farm where we met his partner Miranda, a bouncy Dutch woman of 36. She showed us to our bedrooms – it was a little strange to be separated after so long together, but good to have a little extra space.

We were set to work replacing the fencing in the sheepyards the next morning. I removed the old fencing and extracted the nails while Gabriel dug holes for the new posts. After lunch we went into Kaikohe with Alex, who bought a green wig, and I bought a green T-shirt as it was St Patrick's Day. We then went to the auction where he bought half a dozen weaner heifers. That evening we were entered in a race on his yacht, *Mr Wolf*, and I was tasked with rolling over the yacht to redistribute the weight with a young Russian girl called Katya. It was my first – and last – time yachting. I found it an uncomfortable experience and would have preferred turning the wheel, which was done by Gabriel, who would have been more suited to rolling over the deck with Katya. We came second last but Alex got a prize at the yacht club party afterwards for the second best dressed St Patrick's crew – it was a cabbage.

I was bruised and sore the next morning as I continued removing old fencing, gates and gudgeons (the iron loops on which the gates are hung). It took us until the following afternoon to finish this, when we got a lift into Paihia and caught the 4.30 ferry to Russell, the first permanent European settlement and seaport in New Zealand. We climbed Flagstaff

Hill on a glorious evening and were back down in time to catch the end of the happy hour at the Seaport restaurant bar. I ordered a 'handle' of each of the four draught beers and we sat in the sunshine enjoying our own unreal ale festival. We strolled to the chippy and bought two portions of chips with breaded prawns and garlic butter, which we ate on a bench by the beach. We then played Frisbee there before catching the eight o'clock ferry back to Paihia, whose residents seemed to have forgotten it was Friday night.

We had the weekend off and on Saturday morning I got a really cheap deal on a car hire and drove us up to Taupo Bay where I managed to get Gabriel a few hours' surfing instruction. We made several stops, including one where we bought two kilos of passion fruit and a kilo of orange plum-shaped fruits called tamarillos. We also took a short detour for a look at the lower end of Ninety Mile Beach. We arrived back at Roseburn Farms after 8.30 and a very full day.

We set off again in the car the next day, visiting the farmers' market in Kerikeri, which was the best of its kind I'd seen, before heading west for Opononi in the heart of the Hokianga. It was another scorcher of a day. We arrived just as the speedboat which would take us out to the sand dunes opposite was coming in. Skipper Pete and his ugly mate were full of banter – "I see you're dressed for the beach," he said, looking at my long trousers.

I revealed the zips which allowed me the option of either short or long shorts and said, "Don't be presumptuous . . ." References were made to dictionaries and I replied that I saw it as my role to educate the masses on my travels.

They dropped us and two sand surfing boards at the beach where three young Maori girls were playing on the hot sand. We climbed to the top of the dune and slid down. After a few more goes, we let the girls have a try. A Maori couple then came across in a dinghy to collect the girls. The man caught a kahawai fish, gutted it, and gave it to us. Our boat eventually returned for us: maybe the delay was their way of repaying me for my cheek, but I suspect they were just having a leisurely lunch. We drove on to Omapere where we visited the lookout point over the bay's magnificently mixed scenery and treacherous currents.

From here we travelled down to the Waipoua Forest with its gigantic kauri trees. We saw Tane Mahuta, which means 'Lord of the Forest', the largest kauri known to be standing today. Its scale and its age were awesome – a much over-used word in the Antipodes. The girth of its trunk was over 45 feet and its total height 168 feet, while it is estimated to be between 1250 and 2500 years old. Its neighbour, Te Matua Ngahere, 'Father of the Forest', is not as tall but has a girth of 52 feet and is possibly even older.

On the way back we visited Ngawha Springs, where for just $6 we had access to the changing rooms and several pools of very disparate temperatures. Most of them were way too hot for us but I found 'Solomon' was just on the threshold of tolerable, although it was too much for Gabriel. The majority of people there were local Maori families, and this was clearly one of their main forms of recreation and relaxation.

Heading back, I turned on the car radio just in time to hear Chika Unigwe – who I'd met at the Edinburgh Book Festival – being introduced. Back at the farm, Alex cooked our kahawai, which we had with the vegetables Miranda had prepared.

◊

I was up early on the Monday morning to return the hire car. I gave Lily another $50 to cover the 684 km we'd done, which was still a very good deal, and she provided me with a lift back to the farm. My driver was Mabeline who was nineteen, three-quarters Maori and the other quarter Irish, with thirteen sisters and two brothers (although one had hung himself). It was eleven by the time I got back and Alex and Gabriel were on a coffee break. I rarely drink real coffee as I find it too strong, but they made theirs in a *Bialetti* 'Moka Express' and added milk boiled on the hob. It was superb. Afterwards we moved the heavy replaced timber in the yards so that the tractor forks could get under it to remove it. Once we were done, we had a cheese toastie before heading off to another part of the 200 hectare property. Alex's plan was for us to put staples into the battens, but because of the prolonged hot weather the wood was too dry. Instead, he asked us to put staples into posts where they had come out. We worked along the fenceline until the scrub became impenetrable as it dropped into a gulley.

It was three by the time we got back, and after a tea break we were on the back of the trailer again, being driven to an even more distant part of the farm where Alex wanted us to remove some old posts and fence wire. It was a messy and heavy job, made more difficult by him not having left us a large hammer or a spade. Equipped with the wire-cutters and a large stone, we tackled the task. It was about seven when we were driven back to the farmhouse on the lime hopper. My dirty clothes went straight into the wash and I went straight into the shower. I made a bacon stroganoff and Gabriel undertook a rhubarb/tamarillo crumble. Just before midnight we got a little rain and Alex hurried out to cover up the lime he'd had delivered that afternoon. I offered to help, but was relieved when he said I'd get filthy and that he could manage.

It was not as bright as normal the next morning when we went out to work on the fence again, but nevertheless I had put on my sunglasses, more out of habit than anything else. The sharp end of the wire slipped out of my glove and sprang up, hitting the centre of the lens covering my right eye. I'd little doubt I would have lost my eye if I hadn't been wearing the shades. We finished packing the posts with earth and water in the traditional way Alex had shown us. As we walked back to the farm, he strolled out and indicated for us to jump up onto the back of the trailer. It was the bumpiest ride yet as he took us to another part of the farm and another piece of dilapidated fencing that needed dismantling and replacing. This time, he showed us beforehand how to roll up the wire. We made a much more professional job of it than the last time, and stacked the rolls of wire, battens and old totara posts on the trailer – which he'd disengaged and left behind – together with the old, rusty staples. Alex would keep the posts as totara wood was highly prized for its durability, as well as for the ease with which it could be cut and worked.

It was nearly 5.30 by the time we walked the long way back. Miranda, a physiotherapist, had had a bad day, having accidentally sent a critical email to a wider list of recipients than intended, including the organisation she was impugning and the people who approved the allocation of physiotherapy and other services and resources. I asked her if she had another job in mind: she misunderstood and said, "You can water the garden, if you like . . ."

Miranda told us that she was not working the next day and would take Gabriel out on horseback to herd in the lambs together. She said that, unfortunately, I was too heavy for the third horse, and that the posture of older people made them more difficult for horses to carry, anyway. She had a project for me instead and took me over to the unoccupied farmhouse a hundred metres away, and showed me the overgrown path and garden she wanted cleared.

I got up early for Gabriel's sharp start and made the porridge. I watered the garden before the day got too hot and then groomed the third horse that no one would be riding, surprised at how much I enjoyed the experience and the sense of rapport with the animal. This was our last working day in New Zealand and I took photos of the others setting off before gathering my grubbing tools.

Gabriel really enjoyed his experience and Miranda was complimentary about his performance. After lunch it began to rain, which was welcome as Northland was suffering from a severe drought. I went with Gabriel to work in the shed, helping him weigh the lambs, marking those 38 kgs or over with blue chalk on their backs to indicate they were ready for 'the factory'. It was supposed to be a one-man job, but even with two of us it was tricky. Because they kept bashing into the gates and fences, things gradually worked loose. Suddenly, four sheep had gone through a gap (not helped by the fact that the wooden bars weren't close enough to the sliding metal entrance gate) and we realised we'd have to put the whole lot through again.

Alex returned from the livestock auction just before we put the last ones through. There was almost no chalk left (he told Gabriel later that he would have to do them all again as there would not be enough chalk on them to be visible in a week).

They were all going yachting but I didn't fancy it and decided to hitchhike out to Paihia and meet up with them afterwards. En route, I wanted to visit the place on the peninsula where I'd arranged to go woofing but had cancelled due to lack of time. There was very little traffic on the dusty, unsealed back road to Kerikeri and I'd been walking for almost an hour before a vehicle stopped. It was a pick-up driven by a large Maori called Yogi, coach of the local amateur rugby league team on his way to training. He was a very likeable guy who worked as a security officer at the district court and he dropped me off at the start of the road out to the peninsula. It was another beautiful and hot evening, the rain long gone, and two lifts in quick succession took me to the gate of The Sanctuary. Penelope was very welcoming and proffered several glasses of homemade lemonade, reminiscent of Flohatia in Tahiti. She showed me round the six-hectare property, which was in an idyllic location alongside the inlet. By the time she drove me back to the main road, the night was closing in. Eventually, when things looked pretty hopeless, a car pulled up. I got in the back, as indicated by the female driver, and sat on a hurriedly-cleared seat next to a very young girl in a child seat. Her name was Jasmine, and her parents in the front, Nicole and Anthony, were very laidback, generous and upbeat people. It was just after 8.30 when they dropped me off opposite Frank's Bar in Paihia, from where Alex collected me.

◊

We got up early in order to catch the 8 o'clock bus from Paihia to Auckland, where we arrived around noon and caught the bus back to 811, dumping our bags in our old room opposite the living room. Gabriel fancied seeing *The Hurt Locker*, which had just won seven Oscars, but it hadn't yet been released in New Zealand. I spotted an Auckland Film Festival programme on the living room table and discovered it was being shown at The Academy in forty-five minutes' time. We made it there for its first commercial showing in the country. Much of the following day was spent at the festival – another echo of Tahiti – where I saw Colin Firth in *A Single Man*, an intelligent tale of homosexual love and dashed happiness based on a Christopher Isherwood story. His character was teaching *After Many a Summer* to his class and he quoted a memorable phrase from Huxley: 'Experience is not what happens to a man – it is what he *does* with it . . .' (although I couldn't find the line in the book).

Chapter 30

My flight to Fiji was the next day and I'd not been able to book any accommodation online. I got up early and had breakfast with a quirky Kiwi couple who, when I said I was from the UK, asked, "Do you get *Coronation Street* over there?" I said goodbye to Gabriel, whose flight to Glasgow wasn't until later in the day, and David drove me to a bus stop on Mount Eden Road where I caught the airport bus. I borrowed an American girl's *Lonely Planet Fiji* in the departure lounge and Bluewater Lodge looked like a good bet. On arrival at Nadi (pronounced 'Nahn-di') an information assistant referred me to another young man, who only realised it was his twenty-third birthday when he asked me the date for a document. He contacted the hostel and reserved me a place, and for this he requested $5: everybody is entitled to their 'bowl of rice'. He took me out to the taxi and told the driver the fare would be paid by the hostel. On arrival he was paid $10 and I was shown to room 5 where a guy called Alex from Cornwall was unpacking on one of the four beds.

There was a mix of young Europeans seated around the three tables arranged end to end for dinner – Irish, German, Swiss and British. Afterwards I went over the road to the Drift In Hostel for a beer with Alex and Ferdinand, the Swiss guy. Next day, the three of us – together with Holly, the ex-debt collector from Bicester – headed off in the hire vehicle Alex had negotiated from the owner of the Drift In. We drove up to Stony Creek where we stopped for lunch. The car wasn't really suitable for the rough, rocky road and Holly was getting increasingly nervous about driving on to the village we wanted to visit, but after some discussion, among ourselves and with local residents, we pressed on and soon arrived at Nagoda without incident. One of the elders offered us 'grog', but Alex declined.

We spent most of the evening back at the Drift In (I think it's actually the Drift In Two) watching the Hong Kong Rugby Sevens. There was a chance that England and Fiji might have met in the final, but then England were beaten by Samoa and Fiji were knocked out by New Zealand in the semis.

The next morning, I played Frisbee with Ferdinand on the less-than-pristine beach before he travelled on. Alex had invited me to join him on a two-day trip to Rakiraki up the coast and I'd decided to go along with him, so the next day we were up before six to take a taxi to the main road. We eventually managed to catch a bus to Latoka. On the way we passed miles of narrow gauge lines laid to transport sugarcane in colonial times. We made it onto our next bus with seconds to spare, as it was just reversing out of the bus stand. It was the Sunbeam bus company's 8.15 express, which we were taking as far as Valeika and we slumped into the front seats with relief. It stopped twice for about ten minutes at the towns of Ba and Tavua, en route, which made me question the definition of 'express'. We arrived at our stop at 10.40, the driver announcing a twenty-minute wait for the remaining passengers.

We were approached by a taxi driver and negotiated a fare to Volivoli as an assertive young interloper trying to get our custom moved in. The accommodation was modern, clean and soulless. The camp young receptionist with the flower behind his ear gave each of us in turn the padlocks for our individual lockers and the by-rote instructions, meal-times, etc.

Once settled in to the mosquito-meshed dormitory, we walked down to the meagre beach and tiny, narrow sand spit. I noticed something at my feet and picked it up. It was light, buff-coloured, and the size of a large coin with an outline of a star on it.

"What is it?" asked Alex.

I didn't reply, engrossed in examining it. Surely it was too perfect for a fossil and too flimsy to have survived so long? Perhaps it was a decorated potato-based snack dropped in the sand by some peckish reveller last night? As I held it between thumb and forefinger it snapped and crumbled. I was bereft; Alex was highly amused. I had destroyed something ancient and delicate and beautiful. I'd hoped to find something magical like that to take back for Nathaniel. This and the thought association with my youngest, aroused a strong sense of loss. I was reminded of an incident as a schoolboy when I'd taken a baby blue tit I'd found at break into the classroom, to the amusement of my classmates, and then found it hard to contain my pain when it had died in my cupped hands.

The next morning, after waking with the daylight, I took a walk along the beach and found another stranded star and another and another. I felt like the antithesis of the man who'd been duped into buying what he believed to be a unique work of art only to discover it was one of many. I collected a few and when I showed them to the staff they told me they were called *kukusau* and are a kind of sea anemone. I enjoyed revealing my discovery to Alex just as much as he'd enjoyed my discomfort previously. He thought it hilarious.

I had been liaising on the phone with a guy called Godfrey who operated Bulavou Beach Bunglaows on the nearby island of Nananu-i-ra. He seemed to be a slippery individual and I was not convinced our conversations would come to anything until a boatman arrived to take us there. It had begun raining heavily as we made our way with our luggage to the little boat. Meli the boatman said he had to take us right round the back of the island as it was low tide.

When we met Godfrey, a strange and rather pompous man, he began by confirming the rate was $30 each for the night and then ratcheted it up to $35 on the basis that it was a holiday weekend. This was despite the fact that there appeared to be no one else there, or due to arrive. Nevertheless, it was still good value for the very large en-suite room with a king-size (or bigger) and another single bed. Alex had cast longing eyes at the expansive mattress but we had both known it was no contest: I had had a poor night's sleep the night before and was due to be travelling for 36 hours from boarding my flight at ten the next night. Plus, I was older and – as he said – wider . . .

Alex, who was in his mid-twenties, was a very good travelling companion and reminded me of my old pal, Steve Ashton, when he was that age, and of his eldest son Thomas (my godson), who was tall, skinny, quirky, witty, intelligent and talented. Verani, who'd been cleaning our room, was a very pleasant woman but was evasive when asked about the set up there. Anything other than the most mundane question and she referred me to Godfrey. He had informed us that his cook had 'gone sick' but he offered to provide us with chicken curry for lunch for $15 each. The meal itself didn't taste too bad, but the bits of chicken were as elusive as the truth in his answers.

Afterwards, Alex and I went for a walk over the hill behind the building and discovered a substantial, abandoned complex, all locked up and mothballed. The swimming pool had a couple of dead toads in it and the tennis court was totally overgrown. A woman in a nearby shack avoided any detailed explanation of how things had come to be that way, and it was only when we walked back over the hill and spoke with Warren, who ran the Safari Island Lodge there, that we learned what had happened. Warren had worked there for ten years, running his wind-surfing business when the property had originally covered sixteen acres and spanned both sides of the island from beach to beach. Then the bank had repossessed the place and only some nimble financial footwork by Godfrey, transferring ownership of the Boulavon properties into the names of other members of his family, saved them and the remaining one-acre site on which they stood.

We followed Warren's directions, walking through the narrow passageway between two fences to the other side of the island. A long jetty stretched pointlessly out to the sea, a rusting red wheelbarrow on it being even more redundant, yet evocative of the William Carlos Williams poem.

We walked around the island. I stopped to indulge in a token snorkel, but I was too far from the reef to see anything of interest.

We bought a couple of beers at Warren's and he invited us to dinner – chicken curry at $25 each – but we saw Godfrey returning by boat with Meli and we stalled on the offer. Apart from not wanting to do a quality control comparison of the same dish at different venues on the same day, we didn't want to risk aggravating what must already be a difficult relationship between neighbours on a tiny island.

Back at Boulavon, I was delegated to enter into dinner negotiations with Godfrey, as Alex planned to trim his hair, stating the seawater had made it frizzy. Our host clearly hadn't anything for starters, saying, "We'll skip the entree," in his clipped, pidgin way, which meant that $40 each for a three-course dinner had become a two-course option for the same price. It was almost 7.30 when Alex – who had performed a series of haircuts on himself in the last hour – and I went down the wooden steps from our lodging on the upper floor of the beach house to dine at Godfrey's, where he was installed regally in a cheap, plastic seat, wearing a blue-and-white T-shirt that was bulging around the midriff, and an orange sarong. Meli was squatting on the mat with a large bowl of muddy-looking fluid in front of him. Next to him was Verani, pretty in a bright, two-piece floral suit. They clapped hands three times and then

I was offered a coconut shell cup with a scoop of 'kava' in it. I sipped the earthy liquid. It tasted like water in which soil-covered potatoes had been washed. Alex told me it had to be drunk in a 'oner', which was then followed by another three slow handclaps. I noticed Verani was the only one present not to partake: I was told kava relaxes women in a way which is conducive to them indulging in sexual intercourse and men in a way which makes it less likely to occur . . .

The almost full moon silvering the beach was replaced by the golden beacon, with six hours sleep in between. Rainclouds were gathering as we were waved off by Godfrey and Verani, and the thunder and lightning began soon afterwards as Meli steered us through the lagoon, negotiable because of high tide. In keeping with previous behaviour, we discovered we were being charged for a journey that had to be made anyway, to collect staff from the bus due to arrive at our landing point, Ellington Wharf. There was a taxi there but it was booked, so we asked him to call us another to take us to the Church of the Black Christ. We sheltered from the cloudburst in a little stall, buying some bhajis which we polished off as our car arrived. By the time we reached the church twenty minutes later, the sun was out again. The church is difficult to describe except to say it has an understated spirituality.

The taxi then took us to Veileka where I withdrew $200 from a Westpac ATM to settle up with Alex, who'd been forking out to Godfrey. We were in plenty of time for the Sunbeam Express, travelling to Suva via 'The Queen's Highway', which runs around the bottom semicircle of the island, 'The King's Highway' being on the top, which I was told was the way to remember it.

At Latoka I treated Alex to lunch at the Town End Cafe, opposite the bus station. My stir-fry had a rather better meat-to-bones ratio than his curry. I gave him my left over currency from New Zealand so he could buy himself a beer in transit and he gave me a five dollar US bill for the same reason. We exchanged books – The Motorcycle Diaries for Will Self's Butt, so to speak – and film recommendations, before going our separate ways.

I caught a local bus bound for Suva where a sign by the door said:
PASSENGERS: 60
SCH.CHILDREN: 84
DRINKING LIQUOR & SMOKING PROHIBITED

A friendly Indian couple and their two children occupied the seat in front of me and the man gave me his contact details, telling me if I returned to Fiji I would be welcome any time at his home in Ba. I got off the bus by the sign for 'The Garden of the Sleeping Giant', which sounded like a fairy tale but was where the actor Raymond Burr, of *Perry Mason* and *Ironside* fame, established an orchid collection (the lease now owned by an Hawaiian-based corporation). I was sweating from the walk in the humidity by the time I arrived, and was less interested in the tour than sitting on a bench enjoying the greenness and peace of the place. After a while, I returned to reception, drank a couple of glasses of complimentary tropical fruit juice, and walked back along the drive to wait for a bus, due to pass the entrance on its way back to the main road. Locals waiting on the other side of the road told me it hadn't gone up the way yet. The mosquitoes were very active after a little rain.

Although I wasn't hitching, the driver of a hire car containing four Kiwi tourists coming out of the Garden asked if I wanted a lift and they squeezed me in, insisting on taking me all the way to my hostel, and declining my offer to buy them a drink. By the pool at Bluewater Lodge I recognise Rob, Alex's crazy Dutch drinking partner, from the photos he'd shown me. I kept him guessing for a while as to how I knew his name. He laughed and bought me a beer. I noticed he laughed a lot and also that he had a habit of smacking people on the rear, a show of affection which I was fortunately spared.

I collected the luggage they had kindly stored for me and repacked my bags for my flight. After a swim, shower, a meal of parrot fish and bananas and ice cream, and a bottle of Hawke's Bay Merlot shared with Rob, I said my goodbyes and took the taxi to the airport.

◊

My journey back to Edinburgh involved stops at LA and Heathrow, going through April Fool's Day twice as we crossed the International Date Line, watching several on-board films including *The Men's Group*, *Crazy Heart*, *The Road* and *The Men Who Stare at Goats*, all of which I enjoyed except for the last, which might have worked on the page but didn't on the screen – not for me, anyway. The highlight of the flights home occurred over Greenland. The Northern Lights looked like a shimmering magical green curtain:

AURORA BOREALIS
Sat behind plastic tombstones set
In rows, our transatlantic jet

Transports us as we view our screens,
Each one watching different scenes –
Comic, horror, martial arts,
What's top of the movie charts –
While outside, behind closed blinds
A magic lantern show: one finds
Ribbons of oscillating light
Illuminate the northern night . . .

I returned to Edinburgh on Good Friday and began applying for jobs, including one I'd been asked to put in for – again – supervising young people on volunteer programmes abroad. I didn't even make the interview stage but Gabriel, who was eligible and whom I persuaded to volunteer, got a three-month placement in Namibia. It didn't help when he told me on his return that his young supervisors were lazy and poor at their jobs. By the end of the summer, having not had any luck with finding a job in Edinburgh or a publisher for *Malakal Academical*, I decided to go on my travels again.

I planned a three-month trip backpacking around South America. I didn't know any Spanish and the only person I knew there was Maggie's Auntie Kitty, the nun in Lima. I thought of a guy who'd been at college with me for a year on a sabbatical: he had a very English name, as did the school he was from in Argentina, but I couldn't remember either. Nathaniel, who'd been to New York with his mother, told me I had to spend some time there, so I included a stopover. My friend Clive gave me John Steinbeck's *Travels with Charley* – just as the dog was the perfect travelling companion for him, so was the book for me. Steinbeck was 58 when he set off to rediscover his country, re-engaging with its ways and people. I, too, was fifty-eight as I contemplated my solo adventure, setting off to re-experience the solitary joy and vulnerability of travelling around a part of the world I didn't know, each new place an alluring stranger . . .

Chapter 31

On the morning of Monday 27th September 2010, I left my home and loaded my luggage into the cherished Mercedes of my neighbour, Bruce, who already had the engine running. At Edinburgh Airport I discovered that there were technical problems at Heathrow and my BA flight was delayed for two hours. Ironically, I was going to arrive after the later flight. Many in the long queue were trying to switch, including Kenny, who told me he ran an online gaming business – I'd put money on him getting on the other flight, I thought.

Then, who should I see switch lines at the security area and jump the queue immediately in front of me but the 'Big Cheese', my old boss from Children in Scotland? I stared at her. "Hello," I said and she looked directly at me for the first time.

"Oh, I didn't recognise you. I thought you were staring at me because I'd pushed in."

On arrival at JFK, I got the Airtrain to Jamaica and then took a subway to 103rd via 7th Avenue: I now felt I was really in 'Bagdad-on-the-Subway', as O. Henry called 'the Big Apple'. I checked the map in the train, sweating from my heavy jacket and baggage. A young African American woman asked where I was going and said she was getting off at 7th and would show me which train to get. Only as we were about to get to our stop did I see her young daughter snuggled asleep against her far side, red and blue braids in her hair. I followed them onto the platform where she told me I should get the 'B' Line to '103'; they would be getting the 'D' Line which was the express and skips '103'. She told me she was called Towanna and that until recently she'd been a city tour guide but it was difficult as a single mother and she'd taken time out to look after her six year old daughter, Tatania, who'd just changed schools. I said if she'd like to show me round, I'd meet her at 103 at eleven the next day and treat her to lunch.

At my cheap hostel, finding I was sharing room 734, I bagged the lower bunk, before going to the Metro Diner on the same block, decorated with red circles and white letters proclaiming 'FRESH' and 'DELICIOUS'. I was shown to a seat at a table near the door and listened to a public prosecutor sitting on a revolving black bar stool tell stories to the manager of cases he'd been involved in. One was about a guy who killed a chauffeur in New Jersey and then crashed the car into a tree in New York: he got three years for the murder and one for the RTA – "That's New Jersey for you . . . Too liberal and no decent prosecutors . . ."

The staff uniform was black with a white apron and a pen behind the ear. The floor was chequered linoleum – small white squares with black surrounds and smaller squares of light and dark blue at opposite corners, the benches were in red and white leatherette, and the tables had Formica tops in Italian marble style. There were stainless steel fittings, red and yellow diamond decorations on the front of the counter, dangling conical light shades and a neon 'Metro Diner' clock. Billy Joel began singing, 'Just the Way You Are' . . .

I was back there the next morning, breakfast not being included in my two-day stopover package. My roommate had turned out to be a young Hungarian girl who had slipped in and out of the room several times through the night, slim and timid as a deer.

"This is not a good invention. This is not a good invention . . ." said the distinguished-looking, white-bearded, shorts and sandals and pink-and-white, floral, short-sleeved shirt-wearing guy opposite as he spilled nuts from a little carton onto the formica top.

"They found his body in the Hudson River," said one of a pair of 'Golden Girls' to the other.

A man in a flowerpot hat and glasses with a rolled up plastic bag at his table placed his order, specifying, "Sugar-free syrup."

The Latin waitress gave White Beard his bill, and his 'Gracias,' plus a few other Spanish flourishes, was greeted with, "De nada."

"He committed suicide by jumping in the river . . . This famous chef killed himself . . ." she said to the middle-aged, taciturn waiter with the tired, bag-carrying eyes and the slicked-back black hair. He shrugged a shoulder to indicate he did not consider one less chef in the world a tragedy.

"I *won't* burn anybody," insisted the Latin waitress over her shoulder as she hurried by with a heavy glass jug of coffee.

"It's the way you're carrying it that worries me," Slick persisted.

"I'm a strong woman," she called back.

A guy opposite opened his morning paper wide and I saw the headline, *Kitchen Nightmare*, and a picture of Gordon Ramsay. 'Hotel California' was playing . . .

It was several days before I discovered that the man who'd jumped off the George Washington Bridge was not Ramsay but Joseph Cerniglia, a chef whose restaurant Ramsay had criticised in an edition of his show in 2007, saying, "Your business is about to fucking swim down the Hudson."

My two egg combo with mashed potato, four skinny, streaky strips of bacon and two pieces of seeded toast arrived – excellent value at $6.95.

Through the window, I watched people walking past the bicycles chained to the railings, putting up umbrellas and struggling with the wind. I admired the ornate and balconied windows of the building opposite, the detail compensating for the grey paint covering it. There was a sign in the window nearest the corner urging passers-by to learn English. At the base of the building, on the corner itself, was a notice recommending the 'Mediterranean Turkish Cuisine' to be found there. The white-on-green street signs said, 'W 100 St' and 'Broadway'.

"She was only eleven . . . It makes you sick. They shouldn't even bother with a trial. It shoots my pressure up another notch," broadcasted a Golden Girl. "Her mother has multiple sclerosis. You should see the picture. Beautiful . . ."

Bono was singing 'I Still Haven't Found What I'm Looking For' . . .

I spread out my map on the table. It struck me that Manhattan looked like a machine gun magazine.

The rain was now ricocheting off the streets . . .

"New York is a great rainy city," said the guy next to me in the Gents when I commented on the weather. "Pity those poor guys in LA – it's 115 there today . . ."

It was after 10.30 and I deliberated whether to return to my room and exchange my straw hat and shorts for cap and waterproof trousers, but I waited and the rain began to ease off.

It was nearly eleven when I arrived at the subway station and the little ticket area was empty except for an abandoned umbrella. I spent about twenty minutes fixing it without any sign of Towanna. Just as I was about to give up, she turned up on the other side of the grate, looking less than enthusiastic. I bought a day ticket and we travelled down to Time Square. Towanna's tepid demeanour warmed up when she met a city guide she knew there and then discovered a promotion going on for a TV programme which premiered that night. It was called *No Ordinary Family*! and was apparently about a family which acquired superhuman powers – not a show I felt drawn to watch.

The promotion stunt involved members of the public volunteering to be filmed and photographed apparently lifting the side of a large vehicle and running at super-fast speed. Towanna gave me her handbag and stepped forward. When she'd finished, I followed her. I gave her my anorak and my camera, asking her to take a picture of me in action. When I was next in line to pretend to raise the wheels off the ground, I looked around for her but couldn't see her.

"Where's the woman with my camera?" I asked a member of the crew.

"She was here a second ago . . ." she replied.

As I stepped forward, Towanna was revealed behind a large guy standing right at the front.

We explored the Square and I took photos of the electronic news banner featuring the forthcoming Ryder Cup, to fix the events in time. She took me to see Macy's, which I thought had a fabulous entrance, and the Empire State Building, which I thought was a structure of unmitigated ugliness. We met another of her former colleagues nearby and she used his radio to speak to her friend Keesha, who was at Battery Park.

Towanna chose Tad's for lunch. They did all kinds of steaks. I had a small fillet with mash, onions and gravy; she had a T-bone. She had a big appetite for a small frame. Afterwards we travelled down to see The Sphere, which stands as a temporary monument to those who'd died nearby on 9/11. We walked to the waterfront where we stood looking across the confluence of the East and Hudson Rivers to the Statue of Liberty and Ellis Island in the grey distance.

Towanna knew the city well, but had clearly not travelled much. She referred to foreign exchange centres as places where they change other money into 'regular money'. Her education had clearly been limited: whoever taught her English certainly didn't cover 'countable' and 'uncountable' nouns as she referred to 'much people'. Although we had little in common, this 34-year-old African American woman and I had spent a very pleasant afternoon together, having only met a few hours before. On the subway home, her head lay, small and sleepy, against my shoulder, as her daughter's had lain against hers the night before.

I learnt that the Mets had a game that night and travelled to Citi Field, which in 2009 replaced Shea Stadium – where the Beatles played the year it opened in 1964 – as the venue for their home baseball games. It is interesting to learn that according to their website the average width of seating has been increased by two inches, as most of the focus on site seemed to be on food and drink. I bought myself a frankfurter for $5 and then fancied a beer. The friendly, elderly vendor at the bottle stall asked the young guy in front of me for his I.D. and when my turn came, I joked about forgetting mine. His expression changed.

"No I.D., no alcohol – it's the law in New York," he informed me.

I rummaged in my jacket and located my passport. I finally got my plastic cup of Czechovar for $7.50.

The baseball itself was disappointing: a lacklustre game against the Milwaukee Brewers. The most impressive thing was the athleticism and ability of the fielders, the apogee of which was a spectacular diving catch by Milwaukee's appropriately named Prince Fielder, who covered half the distance from first base to the strike pad to make it. When I left after three of the nine innings, there was still no score.

◊

I got off at 42nd Street/Grand Central and took the subway to 103rd. As I came out of the station I gave my metro card to a guy begging for money for a metro ride but I noticed he remained outside approaching passers-by. I didn't recognise my location and I gradually realised I was on the wrong side of Central Park and it was now dark. I spoke to a couple of pedestrians and they advised me it was safe to walk along the side of 96th, one of the vehicle routes traversing the park. Although clearly not regularly used as a path, I negotiated it safely to the Metro Diner where, again, I ordered chicken soup. I was seated at a table between one with four female members of a reading group and another where a young academic was writing his study of the class system. I finished off the night with a valedictory vanilla milkshake. There was a guy asleep on the top bunk when I returned to my room.

Next morning I vacated the room and stored my rucksack and large shopping bag, although Michelle on the counter only charged me $2 for one bag. At the Metro Diner I had the number 4 again – the two egg combo. A couple was seated in the next booth.

"Butter!" said the guy to the waiter.

"There's one there," the waiter pointed out.

"One! – I've got pancakes here . . ."

Speaking to his companion he said, "I heard on the news this morning a man on the East Side was hit by an air-conditioning unit . . . It fell from the sixth floor of an apartment block . . . Killed him, of course . . . To make it worse, he'd just been evicted . . ." How that made it worse, I wasn't sure.

"Well, I suppose it saved somebody having to clear his apartment. . ." she replied.

I walked to Central Park, enjoying the sunshine, then followed the west boundary, resting on benches regularly to appreciate the fabulous piece of urban planning and forethought which was being put to a wide array of uses by citizens and visitors. There were people on rollerblades and on zimmers, pushing buggies and wheelchairs, walking dogs or carrying them, engaging in various forms of exercise and muscle flexing . . .

I reached the end, at the corner by Columbus Circle, where I bought a fun day metro card and caught a train down to Canal Street. From there, I asked directions of a cop and headed up West Broadway. On Grand Street, I chanced upon Toad Hall, a terrific character bar run by Smokey from South Carolina. I bought a bottle of Otter Creek summer beer on a $3 special and he told me there was free chicken pasta with bread and to help myself. He used to be a roadie for hip-hop bands around Europe in the eighties. I was introduced to the only other customer, Dave, who was also sitting at the bar. A guy called Boris entered with a pool cue case and went through to the table at the back where he began to play. I gave him a game and beat him. He told me his real name was Phil, but he didn't use that in the bar and that he'd been in New York for twenty years but was originally from St Petersburg.

At Smokey's suggestion, I walked along Bleecker Street, looking in the windows of bookshops, specialist coffee dealers, and outfitters (with 'Harris Tweed'). There were seductive bakeries and a butcher's shop offering 'Lady Gaga' steaks, after her recent stunt wearing an outfit made of meat. I bought a 1948 paperback Spanish/English dictionary for $1 and took the subway from Christopher Street uptown to 103rd – the right station this time. En route, we were delayed, believe it or not, by the aftermath of a battle between schoolgirls with hockey sticks. The cops retrieved a couple of the wooden weapons, one broken, and then several minutes later we moved off.

I went back to the diner for another dose of chicken soup and blarney: the place was an endless source of New York anecdotes. A large guy in front of me with eyes at different angles – but both of them staring – recounted to the man opposite him, who was only the back of a head to me, how he'd had to read one of Margaret Atwood's books for his literature class. He'd anticipated the question about what the end signified – 'not exactly Nostradamus territory' – and found her own account in an interview with the BBC, stating she was taken away by the Resistance. In class, his lecturer had given a different interpretation, stating that the authorities had seized her. She'd dismissed his version – his eyes were rolling wildly but independently now – either because she didn't friggin' believe him having found it on the BBC site or believing she had a better friggin' grip of Margaret Atwood's novel than Margaret Atwood. The back of the listening head was shaking slowly from side to side . . .

I bought a packet of Mrs Freshley's Pecan Twirls (with 0g trans fat per serving) with the last of my 'regular' coins at the corner shop and collected my bags from the Broadway Hostel. I made my way, with a few delays, by subway to JFK. After some difficulties with the electronic check-in which didn't recognise my passport or my email ticket number, I ended up via 'Resolution' being allocated a seat with extra leg room. Now *that's* what I call a good resolution.

I found my seat for the flight, facing the bulwark, and was sitting next to a young woman called Damasia Moreno. She gave me a warm but weary smile and some useful tips about tourist pitfalls in Buenos Aires. She was returning home after visiting the States with her parents for a specialist opinion on her condition. She fell asleep clutching the plastic bag containing her airline pillow and blanket, so I opened mine and covered her with my blanket.

247

Chapter 32

On arrival, I left Damasia as her worried mother watched her being helped into a wheelchair on the ramp leading into the terminal. I took my *Lonely Planet South America on a shoestring's* advice and bought a fifty peso ticket for the MTL shuttle. I lifted my rucksack into the luggage compartment of the coach due to depart in twenty minutes. A small figure smoking a stylish curved pipe loaded his case and stood waiting outside, sending aromatic smoke into the Buenos Aires air. He was a priest returning from officiating at his nephew's wedding in the States.

We were driven to a depot where we were then divided into groups on the basis of the location of our accommodation and transported by small grey minivans to our respective destinations. This was much more New Zealand than Africa, in terms of my recent experiences of the efficiency of foreign travel. A figure scavenging on the streets clad almost entirely in black and grey plastic bags, with only his skinny brown legs showing beneath, was more reminiscent of Africa.

Portal del Sur, my chosen hostel, recommended by Hannah, Geoff's daughter, had a fine old wooden door on Hipolito Yrigoyen, a narrow, busy city centre street. It was a strange, five-storey building rising like a hollow pine and representing, it struck me, a particularly high fire risk. Pablo locked my rucksack away for me in a cage in a basement that seemed familiar from a scene in *Ghostbusters*. The lift shaft housed an ancient, gently oscillating cubicle which rose slowly, taking me to the floor where Mercedes sat at the check-in desk.

My dorm wasn't ready yet, so after checking my emails on an aged PC on the top floor, I went for a walk to find some food. Heading towards the main street I passed a sign saying 'CINE' with steps leading down, above which was a Freddie Mercury headshot with a microphone, which was, I suppose, as graphic a piece of visual shorthand as you could get.

I turned the corner onto Barnard Street and looked at the menu of the restaurant there – at the top of the daily specials list was what looked like a steak for 30 pesos (for which they used the $ symbol). The waiter approached and in answer to my questions confirmed he spoke English and informed me it was a 'mustard' (peppered) steak, which sounded good until he added, "But the price is a mistake . . ."

"What should it be?"

"Thirty-four," he replied.

Damasia's words of warning on the plane, "They will always try to get five dollars more from you . . ." came back to me and I turned away . . .

At the next place, a few steps further on, the waitress came out and I said, "Do you speak English?" to which she replied, "No," and I thought, "Good", and went in . . .

A young guy in a checked trilby behind the bar did, however, and told me their specials were garlic chicken and a fish dish. He said the price would be 30 pesos, including water or a soft drink and coffee afterwards. I ordered the chicken and some still water.

There were only two couples in the place, sitting in opposite corners by the entrance.

I wrote up my journal to the accompaniment of Dido and then assorted tracks including 'That's the Way It Is' by Bruce Hornsby and the Range. After a good meal, I returned to the hostel for the free *maté* tasting session. It was a communal experience, the gourd being passed round and the liquid sipped through a metal straw without disturbing the caked leaves which gave it its distinctive flavour. An artist arrived and set up a display of his work for sale. The evening was spent passing around the *maté* and the guitar, making for a convivial session with fellow travellers from New Zealand and Brazil. I contacted a friend's cousin, Maggie, who I'd discovered lived there just before I left Edinburgh. She said she and her young daughter Rosie would call round for me the next evening.

The next day I was keen to see how the Ryder Cup was going but discovered play at the Welsh venue, Celtic Manor, had been suspended because of heavy rain. It was due to resume at 5 p.m. local time, 1 p.m.

in Argentina. I wondered where it would be on TV and remembered the American Club which Joe had discovered by chance was linked with the Royal Scots Club in Edinburgh when we'd played bridge there the week before I'd left. (He'd gone to look at the scores but they weren't there yet, so he'd picked up a club brochure and idly flicked through it.) I looked up the address on the internet – 1133 Viamonte. I asked at the desk and discovered it was only a ten-minute walk away.

I found the building and the concierge informed me the American Club was on the tenth floor. The lift delivered me to the reception area where the elderly attendant, surprisingly, didn't speak any English. He fetched a member who did and in a few minutes I was sitting in a sectioned-off part of the dining room with a cup of coffee, looking at the course on TV, although no play was taking place yet.

I examined all the trophies for golf and badminton in the book-lined room, contested for in competitions over many decades by the English, American and Strangers' Clubs. Now, only this club remained, apparently. What sounded like a reunion of some sort was going on just the other side of the partition, judging by occasional shouts of 'Speech!" and subsequent applause.

An old chap passed the open doorway on his way to the Gents, the upper half of his body at a stiff forward angle. He said something in Spanish and I replied, for what I knew would be one of hundreds of times over the next few months – that I was sorry but I didn't speak the language. He replied, in impeccable English, "I'm terribly sorry, old chap," and introduced himself as Eric. He was descended from a family who'd come over from Port Talbot in the nineteenth century to set up a steelworks there. He asked about the golf and I said I wasn't sure there would be any play as it said 'Gales'. He informed me that was Spanish for 'Wales'.

I was soon watching the rest of the day's play and Eric called in on his toilet trips to ask the score. Afterwards, he took me through to meet the rest of the group, now enjoying post-prandial drinks at the bar. When he introduced me to the Headmaster of St Alban's College, whose Old Boys' Reunion it was, I recognised the name.

"Did your school go to Newcastle on a rugby tour in the 70's?"

"Yes, in '74 – my brother led it – he's dead now," he replied.

"There was a mature student from Argentina at St Mary's. I was one of the few qualified to drive the student union's minibus. He asked me to drive some boys from his school over to the Lake District to play a rugby match while they were on tour."

"That was Bertie Noble."

"That was him – Bertie Noble!"

The Headmaster informed me Bertie was now Head of his own school. He wasn't at the reunion because he was out of the country on a school trip.

He then called over a middle-aged man, saying as he made his way over, "This is Philip, my nephew and the school's deputy head. He was on that tour."

"I must have taken you to play in a rugby game at Grasmere all those years ago . . ."

"No," he answered. "It was Keswick."

"You're right, it was."

I took some photographs to capture this bizarre but joyful occasion, and the staff brought out a chair for some to be taken of me seated in front of the group. What a strange but wonderful beginning to my South American adventure. I was the last to leave, arriving back at the hostel just before Maggie was due to call for me.

She was an hour late when she turned up with seven-year-old Rosanna. First stop was the nearby and legendary restaurant Tortoni's, but there was a long queue and we went to another place for 'empanadas', South American pasties. She ordered three types – ham and cheese, cheese and onion, and mince – and we shared a small bottle of red wine. We returned to Tortoni's. It was founded in 1858 (although it moved to its present location in 1880) and was the oldest coffee shop in the country. From there we went to Inotango to watch tango lessons. We left around 11.30 with Rosie understandably tired, and walked the short distance to my hostel through streets busy with groups of litter-sorters. Maggie told me they'd first appeared after the Devaluation of 2001, shocking everyone, but were now part of the declining economic fabric.

The next day was Saturday. It was a lovely day. Eric had invited me to attend Founder's Day at Quilmes Public School, which Maggie informed me was the most prestigious in Argentina. I found Eric where he said he'd be, serving at the drinks stall. He gave me a plastic cup of red wine and I wandered off to sit in the sun and write up my journal, pleased to have the chance to witness and record such an occasion. The girls wore blue jumpers with red logos, short red tartan kilts and red tights. The young boys wore white shorts as part of their summer outfit.

I bought tickets for a chorizo sandwich and another red wine. Eric introduced me to Malcolm, an Argentinian of Scots descent who flew to Scotland from time to time to attend Perth's bull market – pedigree stock, the buyer and the bought. Eric had clearly been involved in his own breeding programme: he pointed out his seventeen-year-old daughter and told me he had a granddaughter in the same year. I met his second wife who was busy totting up the takings and his son, Jack, who'd been helping Eric on the stall. He indulged me in a game of Frisbee, after which, and a bottle of Quilmes, the local beer, I headed off to catch the 159 back to the city centre.

◊

On Sunday morning I visited a market with Vanessa, a 29-year-old Brazilian geologist staying at the hostel. There were performances of various kinds: G, an old time tango guitarist with facial features reminiscent of W C Fields, being interviewed by a young woman with a microphone in front of a wall covered with his posters and newspaper cuttings; a puppeteer manoeuvring his drunken puppet on – and off – his little stage; a living statue all in white; a figure with an erect streaming tie and tails and a fixed expression of alarm; a passionate pair of tango dancers; and a ten-piece band, complete with battered old piano.

On Monday morning I returned to the American Club just in time to witness a missed American putt give Europe 'Game, set and match' as the commentator said in what was otherwise all in Spanish. Monty rose from his reverie and fans invaded the green as the scoreboard changed from 13½: 13½ to 14½: 13½. The Ryder Cup was ours.

Back at Portal del Sur, the evening's free event was a tango lesson which took place on the top floor and was more enjoyable than I expected, inspiring these few lines:

SUNSET OVER BUENOS AIRES

The sunlight slides over the rooftop,
Five stories high, like the shining shoe
Of a tango dancer on a polished floor –
Buenos Aires, an elegant lady who
Flashes a laddered stocking top . . .

Reclamation over the years has meant it's very difficult to get near the sea in Buenos Aires. The next day I walked east until I reached the canal, alongside which stood a line of snack bars selling hot sandwiches. From the busiest I bought a *bondiolita* (pork baguette) and a pomelo Fanta (a drink made from a citrus fruit and tasting like a mix of the juice from a mild grapefruit and a pear). I took a seat at one of the tables and perused the woofing booklet for Argentina I'd borrowed from a pair of German girls at the hostel, noting ones of interest.

That evening I set off for Maggie's flat near the zoo, using her directions. I queued in Esmerelda for the number 10 and one eventually arrived. My lack of Spanish was proving to be quite a handicap in finding my way around. A well-preserved American woman seated next to where I was standing on the crowded bus described where to get off, my stop being after hers. She worked in Buenos Aires in the cosmetic surgery business: she told me the service was good and only 25% of US prices (two Latino breasts for half an American hooter? – I'd noticed there was a Hooters restaurant by the waterside).

I walked along the Republica de la India with the smell of elephants, appropriately, in my nostrils and located Maggie's elegant flat. She'd only just arrived herself. She told me the traffic was so bad because a bus driver had been murdered the previous day and many people had driven into work when they heard, knowing that a strike was likely. It was already dark as we set off walking along the wide avenue past the polo ground and the hippodrome to El Bagual where I had a superb *lomo* steak – the best steak I've ever had.

Afterwards we flagged down a taxi which dropped Maggie and Rosanna off at home and me at Parana 340. I went down the steps and the little basement was packed out for an ensemble of excellent musicians: it was the nearest thing to being the Buena Vista Social Club of Buenos Aires. The vocalist was a famous local percussionist called Chango, and the band was a collection of his friends. He led the group with the air of a proud father, encouraging with a delighted eye, tempering with the movement of a white eyebrow or a furrowing of his brow. The exhilarating music put a lilt in my step on the way back to the hostel, despite the sight of a boy sleeping in a doorway and the scavengers in the streets.

The next morning I joined the hostel's free guided tour which followed the showing of three videos of Argentina's recent history, including the '70s, when they had five different presidents in sixteen days. We visited the Plaza de Mayo where mothers marched from 1977 onwards to protest at the disappearance of their children due to the actions of the military junta, our excellent young guides describing the significant events and supplying details about the architecture of the grand old buildings.

That evening, standing on the stairs by the hostel's entrance desk, I saw, through the glass above the front door, a face framed in a white beard. It was Bertie Noble. He took me to Tortoni's for something to eat and drink. It had been 36 years since we'd last seen each other. We reminisced, reminding each other of things long forgotten – such as the fact that he had directed St Mary's Amateur Dramatic Society's production of *Torres* with Liam Neeson in the cast when we were in the Fringe in 1974. He, like Eric, had divorced and remarried and had several children, step-children and grandchildren – as well as an OBE. We parted outside the hostel with a warm handshake: I sensed he was too British for an embrace.

The next day was my last in Buenos Aires. I spent it buying my ticket for the ferry to Uruguay, going for lunch at El Evento where I sheltered from torrential rain and settled on fried chicken and mash after a brief discussion with the lovely Leyla Melisa. I was nearing the end of Steinbeck's travelogue, so I revisited the bookshops on Corrientes and found and bought the shabby old *Adventures in Two Worlds* by A.J. Cronin (a talk on whom I'd attended at that summer's Book Festival) which I'd spotted in the meagre English language section.

The rain having eased off, I took a circuitous route back to the hostel, where I played table tennis and then attended the *maté* session, emphasising the fact that I had spent a whole week in the place. The hostel was filling up, mainly with young Argentinians for the long holiday weekend.

The next morning I was on the *Eladia Isabel*, accepting Swiss chocolate from an elderly Swiss lady and her husband at my table as we cruised down the River Plate. We overlooked a lower deck where I saw an old man combing his wife's hair. It was a rare and beautifully gentle act. A quartet of young musicians set up and began playing their violas and violins. They were joined by a cellist, a guitarist and an accordion player as a spontaneous concert took place with people clapping and dancing. A couple of singers lent their voices to the impromptu ensemble. Later, one of them came round with a hat. It was a real festival atmosphere, all the better for being spontaneous.

I left the ferry at Colonia – there was no immigration control there as that had taken place at the terminal in Buenos Aires – and set off on foot towards the oldest part of town. I followed one of my unwritten rules and passed the first place to eat that I saw: the value for money would almost certainly be lower than at the next place, where a couple of locals were eating. I had a '*chivito*', as recommended by the Swiss lady, which was a big bread bun crammed full of meat and salad ($90). I left my rucksack in the back room of a shop for a small charge, and, free from my heavy shell, I strolled around the old colonial settlement. After being a tourist for forty minutes, I retrieved my luggage and lumbered along to the bus station where I bought my ticket for Montevideo. It left at 4 p.m. and arrived on time at 6.30 p.m., despite the heavy traffic in the Uruguayan capital. Due to being misdirected, it took me an hour and a quarter to reach the Red Hostel, as I ended up walking the whole way. My accommodation had been booked for me by Mariana, a woman I'd been in touch with via an internet dating site. She arrived at eight, as arranged, and we went out for dinner at La Tribunales, a nearby restaurant. She insisted on paying for the excellent meal, after which I saw her onto her bus home.

In this hostel too there was a holiday crowd who partied long into the night. Crabby from lack of sleep, I was still having my meagre, rooftop breakfast when Jesusa, the attractive and laid-back receptionist, came up the steps to tell me Mariana had arrived. We took a bus into the old town and stumbled into the middle of a Lipton's Tea advert being filmed there, but my services as an extra were not required. After walking around admiring the architecture, we ate in the Mercado del Puerto (dating from 1868 according to my *Lonely Planet*, where it's described as 'a wrought-iron superstructure sheltering a gaggle of restaurants'). The arrays of cuts of meat – especially the '*asado de tira*' (ribs) – formed an attractive and mouth-watering display. The open, wood-fuelled ovens were a spectacular sight and there was an element of showmanship in the way the aproned staff pitched the slender logs unerringly into their maws. After visiting a Saturday market we headed back to our respective bases, meeting up again in the evening when we visited an excellent pizzeria recommended by an Italian friend of hers.

I had another night's sleep interrupted by thumping bass and passed comment to Jesusa who was on morning duty again (Jesusa, joy of Man's desire, I thought blasphemously). I caught the bus to Mariana's where the dog announced my arrival. I briefly met her father and brother who said, "Welcome to my country and to my home," before disappearing.

Mariana and I took the 10 a.m. bus to the seaside resort, Punta del Este, where she had a couple of properties. On arrival, she was upset at the sight of her tiny bungalow: she was prepared for the overgrown garden, but not the broken glass scattered around. Outside the gate there was an abandoned car. After a preliminary tidy up, she showed me to the apartment in the modern, brick-built three-storey block over the road. The beach was only a few hundred yards away and Mariana stripped to her swimsuit and strode resolutely into the Atlantic.

"I love it. I absolutely love it. The blue of the sky . . . I need my blue sea and blue sky . . ." she declared.

We returned to the house and got out her two bicycles, riding through the town in the dense holiday weekend traffic to the harbour. We arrived in time to see half a dozen huge sea lions disporting themselves by the stone jetty, as she'd predicted. We bought some king prawns from one of the fish stalls then raced back along the coast road, slaloming in and out of the mostly static traffic.

Next day we passed a seal, seal pup and eel, all lying dead on the beach.

"I could cry. I love those creatures," she said of the seals.

My next stop was Punta del Diablo. The route passed through several small towns sharing grid system layouts and a surfeit of motorbikes and dogs. Punta del Diablo itself was a place in transition – from fishing village to developing resort. It was between two stages: original charm and the rush to make it a mini Punta del Este; innocence and affluence; winter and summer. Surf's up, but it was out of season.

I met Monika, a dark-haired woman in her thirties who told me she took in visitors but not at present as her place was also in transition and being renovated. She said she had been an actress in America and her life, too, appeared to be between stages. She drove me to a hostel called Tranquilo, a card for which Fernando at the Red Hostel had given me. This was another in-between place: the lower half of the building, containing the restaurant, had been leased out to someone else; outside, a gang of guys was erecting boundary posts a metre and a half away from the building, presumably prior to another one being built on the adjoining plot which was a sloping, damp and narrow strip of land. Later, Brian, the charismatic young owner, counted notes out and asked the girl on reception to empty the already almost empty till. He was still a few dollars short of the amount he needed to settle a bill.

I settled into my empty dorm and went for a walk along the windswept beach and then back around the little place, taking Monika up on her offer and calling in for a coffee. The walls in the small, L-shaped room bore messages scrawled by previous guests. I was sitting in a visitors' book.

On my return to the hostel, I went online. At the other computer alongside mine was a young Portuguese guy called Pedro who lived in London. He didn't own or rent the place, however: he told me over an evening meal how he and two friends had broken into an old factory in the capital and set up a squat, inviting artists and musicians of various kinds to join them. They'd found compost all over the place. It transpired that it had been a vast cannabis plant, so to speak. The police had raided the place and then it had been sealed up. It had been seized as part of a court order. After Pedro and his pals had broken in they'd knocked down an internal wall and discovered another room containing a large cage. It turned out that skunk was not the only thing that had been trafficked through there . . .

Pedro told me he had claimed the room for himself and slept inside the cage where women and children had been kept captive. The place had been featured in a *Panorama* programme, he proudly informed me.

◊

The next morning I awoke to a grey beginning to the day. I trekked up the hill to the village to pick up the bus travelling north towards Brazil, having no plan except to head for Rio. After toast and coffee at Monika's, I went and stood on the corner like some ride-less sheriff in a Western waiting for the stage to come, leaving town after a brief but unsuccessful sojourn. I, too, was a man between stages. The bus I was waiting for didn't show up so I took one from another company. I asked the conductor to drop me off at the Uruguayan border post, but the bus continued past the nondescript little building and it was about a mile before I was able to get off. A mile is a long way to walk with the weight of luggage I was carrying. I was directed to the opposite side of the road where another 'R & S' bus pulled up and I clambered aboard. They dropped me off at the post where I got my passport stamped and I tramped off towards the Brazil border. After three or four miles hitchhiking without a lift or reaching any indication of having entered another country, I became worried I had somehow missed Brazilian immigration – surely it couldn't have been that insignificant, or had I taken the wrong road? I was concerned that when I came to leave Brazil in due course, some official would thumb through the pages until they reached the end without finding any sign of me having entered their country. I passed a sign saying 2062 km to Rio de Janeiro. I wondered if I was already an illegal immigrant . . .

At this point a coach approached and I waved vigorously for it to stop. It pulled in, rather uncertainly, and the conductor checked I had cash and a passport before letting me on. I had no idea where the bus was going except north, and that was enough for me. I was barely settled in my seat when the bus stopped again. It was Brazilian Immigration control and the conductor led me in. I was the only passenger who needed to go through the process, apparently. He showed me the form, filled in the method of entry section himself, and after I was legally in Brazil we reboarded the bus and I paid him the fare (just under forty *reales*) to my unknown destination. The language barrier was proving even more difficult than before, as, of course, I was now in a Portuguese-speaking country.

By this time I'd decided I would travel as far as possible, both on this bus and any other I could take on towards Rio. We passed through the marshlands until the bus reached its destination at 5 p.m. The next half an hour was a cross between a pantomime and a farce. I didn't know where I was – literally – and I couldn't find my luggage docket. The baggage man was adamant he was not going to hand over my rucksack without it, despite the fact that there was no one else left to claim it. Just as he was taking down my details from my passport, I found the little chit in one of my many cluttered pockets. He then obligingly led me to the office to enquire about an onward ticket to Rio. The situation was confused by the mixture of language difficulties and my misconception I was in Porto Alegre rather than, as it transpired, Pelotas. In the confusion I nearly jumped on a bus which was actually completing its journey, almost took a taxi to Porto Alegre city centre to find overnight accommodation when that was still a three hour drive further north, and acquired an entourage of helpful Brazilians whose level of English ranged from minuscule to nil.

Eventually I ended up returning to the Penha bus company office to make further enquiries about the morning bus to Rio. The man nonchalantly showed me on the screen that only seat number 26 was still free. I paid 260 *reales* for my ticket and he also gave me a card for a nearby motel. One of my new retinue of staff and passengers had found me a taxi driver with a few words of English and he whisked me away in a Brazilian version of a Fiat Panda after I'd taken a photograph of my befrienders to mark the successful resolution of the situation.

The picaresque quality of the day's events persisted, however, as when we managed to find the small block of rooms next to a family home, the only two faces to appear at the house window were of a boy of about six dressed in pyjamas and girl of about three or four. The boy got on a portable phone and then came outside with a key and led me over to the block and up the steps to show me one of the rooms. I returned to the taxi where my luggage remained in the boot. Although I'd paid the driver he seemed reluctant to leave, and I idly considered his motives:

It was a slow day and this was better than rejoining the long queue at the bus station

He was waiting for a bigger tip

258

He was concerned for the safety of these children if left with an eccentric Englishman

After about fifteen minutes, a man drove in and revealed motive number four, discreetly slipping the taxi driver something for bringing in a customer – it's always sweet to be paid twice for the same job. My host was called Cleber and he couldn't have been more friendly or helpful, calling on his mobile someone who spoke English to come round while he made me a coffee and provided ham and cheese for me to make myself a toastie in the sandwich-maker. A man arrived whose name was, I think, Horagio (which I take to be a Portuguese form of Horace) and who was, I believe, his brother-in-law. His English was extremely basic but I did my best to communicate, realising his reputation as the family polyglot was at stake. I was soon one of the family, too, as he told me.

Chapter 33

Next morning, Cleber drove me to the bus and I found seat 26, an aisle seat next to a young Brazilian woman and my home for the next 31 hours. In personal terms, the journey didn't get off to the best of starts: I began sneezing uncontrollably and when this eventually subsided it was replaced by a coughing fit. As I was pondering what would constitute an 'Obnoxious Travelling Companion Triathlon', I gave an involuntary belch – gold medal to Harvey and Great Britain . . .

The coach made stops at roadside restaurants at regular intervals. On entering you were given a list on which serving staff ticked the items you selected. You were charged on leaving. We called at the depot in Porto Alegre for boxes of stationery, etc, to be loaded and then it was on to Osario where a light-skinned guy boarded the bus wearing a nylon waistcoat bearing a logo with the initials ANTT and the words FISCALIZACAO and FEDERAL. He made his way along the aisle, checking tickets here and there and shining his little torch into the overhead ventilation. He asked me something and I handed over my ticket, assuming this to be what he wanted. He was about to give it back to me when something on it caught his eye and he re-scrutinised it. The cold eyes behind the light lashes didn't flicker as he handed the ticket back to me, turned and left the bus.

As we continued north, the landscape became more interesting. There were green hills on our left and for a long while we followed a lake – or an inlet – to our right.

There was a level of investment in infrastructure going on in Brazil that I hadn't witnessed in Argentina or Uruguay. Great swathes of orange soil signalled new road systems or improvements, the construction workers wearing matching orange work suits. The future was truly orange . . .

It was evening when we took a break at a restaurant at Sombrio while the coach was washed and refuelled. The restaurant being Japanese, we were each issued on entry with a plastic card with a barcode to be swiped for payment on departure. I noticed that the prices of snacks and drinks were becoming progressively higher the further north we went.

The next stage of the journey was characterised by the onset of nightfall and a mother at the front struggling to cope with a crying baby and a vomiting girl while Florianopolis flew past in a protracted flurry of waterside lights. An obliging bus station cleaner made the remainder of the journey more bearable by mopping up the pools of vomit. I managed to keep down the numerous empanadas I'd eaten, although I was concerned at the number of calories consumed, relative to those expended. Trying to vary my diet, I drank a glass of cashew juice which was a welcome new experience.

Familiar names were beginning to appear along the side of the road:
Ford
Shell
Nestle
Pilkington Glass
Honda
Hyundai
Toyota
together with Dallas Motels and Bob's Burgers. My favourite, by a Brazilian kilometre, was the Medieval Motel, which had its frontage painted as battleship-grey stones outlined in black, like the toy fort of my boyhood. The road itself was getting bigger and busier and there were overhead arrows directing drivers to the Ayrton Senna Highway.

We pulled into the bus station at Rio at 4.45 p.m. I took the *Lonely Planet's* tip, and arranged through the station taxi office for a ride. The young cab driver with the pencil-drawn beard drove as if he hoped to have a highway named after *him* one day.

I was dropped off outside my chosen accommodation, the Rio Hostel in the Santa Teresa area of the city, selected on the basis of the description of this district in the *Lonely Planet* as 'bohemian'. I struggled up the numerous steps, made even more challenging by a combination of my heavy luggage and having been sitting for nearly a day and a half. I signed in and claimed the bottom bunk by the window in the Blue Dormitory.

I went up to the bar on the roof where I was persuaded by the smiling young Brazilian barmaid to purchase a passion fruit *caipirinha*. I chatted with several of the growing number of fellow guests enjoying the relaxed atmosphere, overlooking the city of Rio – throbbing with music and coloured lights – which stretched as far as we could see below us.

The next day I headed off up the hill into the heart of Santa Teresa. Trams ran along the cobbled road, but I enjoyed the walk on a beautiful afternoon. At the top, a conductor re-engaged the tram to the line with a long pole, reminding me that that was the origin of the term 'conductor'.

There was an open-air event about to commence outside the museum. Isadora Duncan had been a guest in the building in the Twenties. I took a seat behind a white, shark-faced young guy with his handsome, attentive, oriental boyfriend.

An old woman in a mauve skirt walked into the middle of the performance area with her stick and introduced two men – one small and in his sixties, I'd guess, the other tall, heavily-built and in his thirties. They were both wearing suits, ties and spectacles and I took them to be sponsors or such, but this was all part of the desired and cleverly created effect as my preconceptions were stood on their head as the two men entered into a series of slow, graceful and impressive feats of strength and balance, made all the more dramatic because of their formal manner and attire. Their jackets were eventually removed to reveal one small sinewy body and another large, muscular one capable of supporting the other with one hand.

They were followed by a series of dance dramas, gymnastics and acrobatics of great charm and vitality – and all set against the backdrop of the Sugar Loaf Mountain. Eventually I dragged myself away to attend the football game between Fluminese and Botafogo.

Over the next few days I sampled the local gastronomic attractions, including *bolho de aipim* (breadcrumbed cassava parcels containing dried meat or cheese), *brigadeiro* (a small ball made from cocoa, butter and condensed milk and covered with chocolate sprinkles – bought from an old lady selling delicious sweets from a small stall outside her garden), and *feijao* (a dish of stewed black beans).

With Del and Linda, a couple from Glasgow, I visited the Statue of Christ the Redeemer and the Cathedral – which looked like a pitted, upturned funnel and changed colour every few seconds at night – taking photos of the 2010 Brazil World Cup team murals on urban walls on the way. We had a Danish graffiti artist staying at the hostel, and one night he returned late, agitated, claiming he and some contacts were painting in one of the *favelas* (slums) when a group of armed men had turned up; his contacts had smoothed it all out and the guns had been put away.

One of my most interesting roommates was Raphael Beinder, a charismatic 32-year-old cinematographer from Berlin. While talking about films he disclosed he'd been at the Edinburgh Film Festival in 2010 as well – promoting *Third Star* as one of the crew (he was gaffer). One day we travelled by bus together to Copacabana and played Frisbee on the beach, and then, while he went for a swim, I played keepy-ups with a few guys, including seventy-year-old Garcia. Raphael and I then walked around to Ipanema, which was full of surfers, poseurs and beach vendors.

Vendors are everywhere in Rio, selling everything. While out in a group for a meal that night I was offered tiny tins made out of bigger beer cans, poems (have to try that in the bars on the Royal Mile during the Festival) and an exquisite grasshopper made out of reeds; if there had been any chance of me being able to carry it safely around South America for two months and back home, I'd have bought it.

Another interesting character staying at the hostel was also called Rafael, although spelled differently (he told me they have a word '*xara*' – pronounced 'sharra' – used as a term of address for someone with the same name as oneself). He was a Brazilian recently arrived in Rio to work for the booming oil company, Petrobras, easily the largest corporation in the country, which had recently launched a huge recruitment drive.

I spent my last day in Rio riding on the tram all the way up to where it stopped at the far end of Santa Teresa and everyone had to jump down while the conductor lifted all the wooden bench backs over so that passengers were again facing the way they were travelling on the way back down. I paid another 60c to ride as far as the bijou cinema sitting between converging cobbled roads like a wedge of prize stilton. Outside a nearby bar, I was temporarily adopted by a 'high' and hyperactive native called Romeo who'd spent ten years of his life in the States and whose rapid-fire speech was full of political, philosophical, scientific, socio-economic and sexual references, and peppered with numberless expletives. It was a high octane spiel: a 'stream of consciousness' on 'speed' – James Joyce meets Robin Williams.

After sharing a glass of spirits he'd bummed for two instead of three *reales* at the next bar, telling them I was a long-lost American buddy – they weren't fooled and they weren't amused – I extricated myself from his brotherly embrace and left. After a kick-around in a playground with some kids and buying a slice of banana cake at the baker's, I took the tram back down the hill to the hostel. That evening I went for a meal at Minheiros, my favourite restaurant in Santa Teresa, with two new roommates – Dale, a tall, grave Canadian involved in a fishing monitoring project (local fishermen couldn't compete with the Gargantuan foreign trawlers and their sonars, hauling whole shoals out of the ocean) and Ian, a cool, tattooed, and muscular Irishman over for a friend's wedding in Salvador. At the end of the night I had a drink with the rest of the Irish revellers who'd just arrived and Ian invited me to visit the Exchequer pub, which he owned, the next time I was in Dublin (I did on a golfing trip with my sons in 2014 but he was on holiday).

◊

After a week in Rio, I embarked on another of my marathon bus journeys: it took over 24 hours to reach Foz do Iguacu where I stayed at the well-signposted Pousada El Shaddai hostel. I visited the falls (featured in the film, *The Mission*) which were impressive, but it was galling to be charged extra as a foreigner – an official policy in several South American countries at popular tourist sites. What impressed me most was the sight of the swifts flitting through the curtain of water, presumably to feed their young in nests in the rock face.

The following day I made a short bus trip to the Paraguayan border and walked across the bridge (a calculated risk as robberies occurred there) to take advantage of their tax-free prices and buy Nathaniel a national football shirt. On the bus on the way back a female official checked passengers' purchases and confiscated a DVD in a small black plastic bag from a bespectacled, bald man at the front who made only a token protest.

I got off the bus at the station and got straight back on to one to the Itaipu Dam. Although my *Lonely Planet* said it was free, I discovered the basic 'panoramic' tour was twenty *reales* and I was down to my last thirty and didn't want to change more currency as I was leaving the country the next day. The young guy on the first processing desk overheard this and stamped the Portuguese for 'Discount' for a Senior Citizen on my form, despite me telling him my age and him checking my passport. Unfortunately his generous gesture did not succeed in defeating the inflexible system as the older cashier at the next stage of the entry system charged me the full price. I couldn't say that I was overawed by what the Society of US Civil Engineers had apparently called, 'One of the Seven Wonders of the Modern World.' Not being technically-minded, or impressed by figures, the most significant aspect of the project for me was that two countries – Brazil with a current population of 198 million and Paraguay with six million – had been able to collaborate so harmoniously on such a massive venture and bring it to a successful conclusion. It was an amazing achievement, especially considering no South American country I'd visited as yet had managed to devise a plumbing system capable of coping with toilet paper.

◊

I checked out the next morning and took the bus into Argentina. It dropped the foreign nationals off at the Brazilian side of the border, giving us a voucher to use on the next bus after we'd been through passport controls. While waiting, we were approached by clipboard-carrying young interviewers about completing a questionnaire. Several of the questions were directed towards how safe we felt in Brazil and would we consider returning for the World Cup or the Olympics. I'd felt quite safe most of the time, but a lovely couple from Hong Kong staying at Rio Hostel had told me how they'd been robbed in the classic 'taxi' manner by another 'passenger' and someone had had their money stolen at knifepoint on the steps down into town. It was clear to me that the results of the survey were likely to be used to justify a clampdown on street crime in Rio, and I said as much to my fellow travellers: Macick – Mac for short – a Spanish-speaking Polish travel agent in his twenties, and a Turkish-born fiftyish female, brought up in Germany but an Argentine national. After a few minutes the next bus arrived and we assisted each other in lifting the rucksacks over the turnstile inside, clearly designed to stop people just pushing on without paying, not facilitating boarding by heavily-laden backpackers.

Mac was staying at the Garden Stone in Puerto Iguazu, which appeared to be a more attractive town than its Brazilian counterpart, and we agreed to share a taxi and then a twin room there. After settling in to our comfortable accommodation, we walked back to the bus station via the ATM. Everywhere was very quiet – we discovered it was Census Day. We took the bus to Parque Nacional Iguazu, built around the Argentinian side of the Iguazu Falls. At the gates they told us that all public places and private businesses were supposed to be closed but it had been decided to keep the park open for the sake of the foreigners. We were told that the boat trips would not be operating and the cafés, restaurants and souvenir shops would all be shut. We had a little food and water with us, however, and realised we would benefit from there being considerably fewer visitors. Another bonus that we realised from the clock in the ticket office was that we had gained an hour. Our Turkish companion was jubilant that, as an Argentinian national, she had only to pay 25 pesos as opposed to the 85 that Mac and I had to shell out each.

It was 11 a.m. and a beautiful sunny day with a clear blue sky as Mac and I set off on the Sendero Macuco Trail through the forest, seeing a couple of iguanas, a treetop colony of monkeys, and several beautiful species of butterflies along the way.

Having made good time, we just managed to catch the little train to Station 1 on our return. We walked around enjoying the various views of the numerous waterfalls and saw several bandicoots – animals the size of foxes with snouts and banded tails – foraging in the bins. Again, we returned in time to take the train – the 3.20 to Garganta del Diablo (the Devil's Mouth). En route and at the station itself we saw clouds of yellow butterflies at mud pools. It was like being in Disney's *Bambi* or *Song of the South*; I felt I should be singing 'Zip-a-Dee-Doo-Dah'. This fantastic feeling stayed with me as we walked out to the viewing platform, which gave the most dramatic aspect of the cataracts. It was one of the places – unlike other World Heritage Sites – that truly warranted adjectives such as magical, magnificent and spectacular, the spray periodically producing rainbows.

Returning on the train we saw a toucan flying alongside us. It was a beautiful bird – not the ungainly Guinness cartoon creature. As we left, we discovered that the number of visitors was two thousand, as opposed to the five thousand on a normal day. Back at the bus station in Puerto Iguazu we bumped into the Turkish/Argentinian woman again. The restaurants were beginning to open, and she joined us for a meal on the balcony of one overlooking the square. The meat – as always in Argentina – was superb. I had a *lomo* steak and sampled some of Nicky's *parrillada* or mixed grill – even the intestines were delicious.

On the bus they showed a couple of films before stopping at a bus station in the late afternoon to take on board some airline-style meals. I chatted to Marloes, a tall, young Dutch woman with a warm smile. She, like me, was finding the leg-room a problem. I told her it was a design fault and she was agreeing with me before I finished the sentence – "in some overly-tall European women." She giggled and gave that fabulous smile again.

We reached Corrientes several hours, snacks and films later at 8.30 p.m. and had a chance to stretch our legs again. I chatted with Marloes and a couple from Manchester called Helen and Sean who'd given up their jobs to trek around South America. I continued my conversation with Sean on board. He told me about a place they'd climbed in Peru called Choquequirao – like Machu Picchu, but comparatively unknown.

We arrived in Salta at nine the next morning, an hour early. I bought a ticket for Cafayate and took a seat in the bus station to wait. The Cafayate bus stopped at a solitary, spartan café where the few passengers got out and I bought a great cheese and salami baguette and a meat *empanada*. The landscape, too, was sparsely populated: sandstone bluffs, cacti, purple mountain backgrounds and blue skies – the stuff of boyhood western books and films.

On arrival in Cafayate I walked from the Flechabus depot to the vineyard, Bodega Utama, which turned out to be more of a smallholding. The place was owned by Maud (pronounced Mo), a tall Dutch woman (are they all tall?) with dyed red hair and several teeth missing from her lower mandible. There were three other woofers working there – a young Aussie couple called Paul and Myra, and a twenty-year-old American called Alisha. In addition, Maud's friend Olivia was staying. I deposited most of my stuff in the tiny twin room I was to share with Alisha. She and Myra showed me round the place and how to do the various chores such as feeding the ducks and chickens and watering the various vegetables and herbs. I showed them how to play Frisbee with a group of schoolchildren being shown around by one of Maud's sons, Sacha, who lived with his wife in another building on the site.

Yakeen and Sabina paid a visit. He was fifty and originally from Tours in France, although he'd left there thirty years before. She was twenty-eight and local. They'd met six years ago and were now married. He had the typical *savoir faire* of a man of the world; she had the look and vitality of a young woman happy with her life. They invited us up to their place, so I went to buy some beers with him and Myra in his Moke, which was almost the same age as him. On the way back, we nearly had a collision with an oncoming vehicle which had taken a bend on the wrong side of the mud road. Yakeen reacted quickly, which was just as well as there is not much protection in a Moke and one of us could easily have been thrown out.

Their place was a part-finished project further up the road overlooking

Cafayate. They planned to open it for tourists in the near future. We worked our way through the beers while Alisha and Myra tried on belly dancing costumes before beginning a lesson with Sabina. I took some coca leaves and tea for the first time before we set off to walk back beneath a starry sky.

◊

I spent a week at Utama. In that time the other woofers left, and for a while I was in the house by myself as Maud and Olivia had driven north to collect her other son and his small family. My days were spent breakfasting on polenta (a yellow cornmeal which I boiled and ate as porridge), refilling the duck pond, feeding the ducks and hens (which was quite a complicated routine as some of them – like the two roosters – had to be kept apart), watering the plants, planting marrow seeds, reading short stories by Jorge Luis Borges, walking the dog (Pepe) into town to buy unpasteurised milk poured into an old three-litre coke bottle I took with me, and playing football with a group of local youths of an evening. I wrote a poem, hoping to catch the contentment of this solitary, laid-back lifestyle.

THE HALF-OPEN GATE

Pepe lies in the sun, only the tip
of one black ear in the slow-moving shade
of the verandah where all day I sit
reading the stories of Borges; I've made
little of them – for such metaphysics
are a state of mind I can't traverse.
My life is simple now, winnowed to this –
sitting in the shade reading, writing verse,
waiting and watching the half-open gate
for a woman to walk through: it's not too late . . .

After Maud's return, I moved on, travelling back to Salta where I took an overnight bus to La Quiaca on the Bolivian border. We were seen off by a crowd of sixty or seventy parents and siblings as a group of young footballers was on board. It was an uneventful, non-stop journey and we arrived almost an hour early, just after seven. The air was cold and thin. I walked down a road called Belgrano, slowly – the altitude was nearly 3500 metres. I found the Hotel Frontera's diner, recommended in the *Lonely Planet* (there was little competition). The man indicated he wasn't yet doing food, as such, so I settled for a couple of croissants and a cup of coffee. The place was basic, with dirty tiled floors, damp, stained plasterboard ceiling panels, and patched up paintwork – a different diner altogether from the Metro in New York where I'd watched two guys examining the place, checking for any broken tile that required replacing or any break in fabric needing repair. I sat at the table by the door, looking back up Belgrano and reading *The Girl with the Dragon Tattoo*.

As I was finishing my second coffee, two women were arranging for a taxi to the border post. I asked if I could join them and they agreed. One was a middle-aged German dentist, the other a 32-year-old Korean (her ethnicity evident from her porcelain white skin – Koreans have less skin pigment than any other ethnic group). They were called Frieda and Yeung. Having lugged our luggage through the crowded customs areas, where Frieda's Spanish was very useful, we loaded it into another taxi at the far side, taking us to Villazon's railway station.

The solitary middle-aged male clerk was painfully slow in processing our tickets. It took him about ten minutes to issue mine: a single 22 *boliviano* salon ticket to Tupiza. The women were going all the way to Oruro. We stored our rucksacks in the reception area of a hostel opposite for a small fee and found the nearest internet café. The computers were even slower than the railway clerk. Outside there was a parade about to begin and the mandatory brass band played its way down the street. Groups of well-drilled little boys dressed as miners with their hammers and bits and girls in local costume with dolls in their shawls performed their routines in the heat, while women – teachers, presumably – attended to them, adjusting a strap here or tying a lace there. It went on all through the heat of the afternoon while we took lunch and photographs and a few beers.

Back at the station with our reclaimed baggage, a man in olive uniform with a pistol on his hip informed us that all rucksacks had to be loaded into the luggage carriage. The women were travelling in a higher-class compartment. Mine was oppressively hot. There were tin grills inside the windows and, along with a Swiss couple, I opened some of them. As the twice weekly Expreso del Sur pulled out of the station and gathered a little speed, the carriage began to get a little cooler. We hadn't travelled far, however, when a guard came through and closed all the windows before mopping the floor – keeping the train dust-free, it seemed, was more important than keeping the customers cool.

The journey was further marred by bad flamenco DVDs, one of Vicente

Fernandez (a famous crooner with silver hair and black eyebrows and moustache), and the Adam Sandler vehicle *Grown Ups* (yet again – it seemed to be the current travelling Hollywood film of choice in South America). Even the scenery through the closed windows was a little disappointing. At Tupiza I was last to claim my rucksack with my ticket, waiting for the others and the touts to disappear, waving the women off on the rest of their journey, and making my way into the small town.

Most of the hostels were full: a festival was being held, apparently commemorating the 200th anniversary of the Battle of Suipacha. According to *Wikipedia*, it was fought on 7 November 1810 during the Bolivian War of Independence between the Spanish colonial army and the Republican forces sent by the Primera Junta from Buenos Aires. At the time, Bolivia was known as Upper Peru (*Alto Perú*). It was the first decisive defeat of the Royalists by Republican forces. The battle took place 25 km southeast of Tupiza, near the small town of Suipacha. That evening, going for a walk after taking the last room in the Hotel Mithi at an inflated price, I witnessed a banner being hung outside a building in the Plaza Independencia celebrating the bicentennial.

I visited a little café in the square, Cramer's, and although most of the seats were already on the tables, they were happy to serve me a banana milkshake (and then a papaya fruit juice) as I joined Fernando and Oscar, a father and adult son who invited me to sit with them, watching several brass bands parade around the town.

An unexpected benefit of having a relatively upmarket room to myself, was spending a Sunday morning watching Newcastle United go fourth in the Premiership by defeating Arsenal thanks to a thumping header from Andy Carroll. Heady days indeed . . .

I'd more or less decided not to go on the four-day Salt Flats tour, but gave the woman at the office my room number (111) in case the two women looking for another passenger wanted to contact me. I was just locking up to go out at 6.15 p.m. when two English women of Indian descent rushed up pleading with me to make up the numbers for a vehicle leaving in the morning. They had to let the woman – at another hotel's tourist office – know by 6.30. After a brief chat, I went along with the synchronicity of things and agreed. They sneaked past our hotel's tourist office to that of La Torre Hotel in time to arrange things for the next day. I then went for a pizza, feeling I should have at least one in a town called Tupiza (one of the women, Andi, a doctor in London, told me there was a pizzeria there called Tu Pizza).

The next morning we nearly didn't get away as Nicki, (Andi's travelling companion and sister-in-law) felt unwell and was ill for quite a bit of the trip. Over the next few days, we took in the spectacular Laguna Colorado (4,300 metres), saw Ollague, the semi-active volcano that straddles the border with Chile, and drove through the barren landscape with nothing but patches of scrub to Chiguana and then San Juan where we bought a couple of bottles of beer in the quaint shop for our last night. At Chuvica we stayed at one of the celebrated salt hotels, virtually the whole place – walls, floors, beds, tables, stools – constructed out of blocks of salt. I managed to source a football and a Bolivia v Rest of the World football match took place on an enclosed basketball-court-cum-football-pitch in the fading light.

We returned to our evening meal at which Eli, our excellent cook, produced food on which those from other vehicles cast envious eyes, as well as a very large bottle of red wine. With the assistance of music on my companions' iPods we created a party atmosphere in the small saline dining room.

It was a dramatic experience, early next morning, to be on board one of the Land Cruisers as they raced across the salt flats known as Salar de Uyuni to see the sunrise. They are the largest salt flats in the world and because they reflect the sky, they have also been called 'the World's Largest Mirror'. Unfortunately, the sight of the vehicles turned out to be more spectacular than the dawn, which was obscured by cloud, although the rest of the sky was almost clear.

Chapter 34

Our trip having ended at The Hostal Marith, our base for lunch in Uyuni, I stayed overnight and left on a bus for Potosi at 10 a.m. the next day. There were several English youngsters on it, getting excited about a place in Sucre, the bus's final destination, which served fondue – "I'm going to have it every day," one girl declared in delight. Well, I would not be part of the fondue generation, to paraphrase Don McLean. Most of the passengers were Bolivian peasants, however, and at one pick-up point a young crew member in a boiler suit ran off, chasing something. At the next toilet stop – men on one side of the road, women on the other – the driver pointed out the three young partridges in the folds of a woman's skirt.

"Perdiz," I said knowledgeably, having heard a man use the word when getting off at the time of their pursuit.

A thunderstorm was beginning to break as I got off the bus on a street in Potosi. I took a taxi which dropped me off in a traffic-logged plaza close to La Casona Hostel where I checked in. The city, a World Heritage Site, is the world's highest at 4060 metres. It lies beneath the Cerro Rico (the Rich Mountain), having been founded in 1545 following the discovery of silver ore deposits there, and it grew into the largest and wealthiest city in Latin America. The hostel was one of many places that organised tourist visits to the mine which now operated as a co-operative venture, but still with working practices that *Lonely Planet* described as medieval. Historically, the *meta* system meant indigenous people were forced to work the mine under a form of bondage. It's been estimated that, over the centuries, eight million people died as a result of working in the mines – a kind of protracted, industrial holocaust. When I analysed my reasons for not wanting to go on the trip, they included the sense of uneasiness about visiting as a paying tourist a place other people would rather not be, but had no choice. Another reason was that I was still having a little difficulty breathing at that altitude, even without going down an unventilated, noxious pit. I limited myself to paying to watch, in-house, *The Devil's Miner*, a documentary made in 2005.

◊

On my solitary tour of the city I met a group of middle-aged men lounging in a shady area, passing around a glass of lager refilled from a large bottle. Nelson introduced me to the rest of his crew – China Man, Ugly Man, Big Man, Teacher. He was Potosi's answer to Romeo in Santa Teresa, only more influenced by English culture than American – a disaffected intellectual who anaesthetised himself with drink. He wore a baseball cap which bore the Union Jack and 'London' on the front. He told me he was a massive rock and roll fan and pulled up his shirt to reveal a tattoo of AC/DC just below his right nipple. I told him Brian Johnson, the lead singer, was from my hometown, Newcastle, and that I was once in his house. I shared some of their beer and banter before heading off.

One of the tourist visits I did decide to make was to the old mint, now a museum. It cost me twice the 'nationals' rate, but this seemed justifiable as three of us had an English-speaking guide to ourselves. The latent resentment of the exploitation by other countries of their mineral wealth was apparent. No more so than when our guide showed us the partial model of the *Atocha*. The *Nuestra Señora de Atocha* was the most famous of the ships that went down with its load of Bolivian silver off the Florida Keys in 1622, part of a fleet which was sailing to Spain. The wreck was located several decades ago and much of its cargo, valued at £450 million dollars, was recovered. The Potosi Museum's request for some of the hundred thousand coins recovered resulted in two being returned for display where they had been mined and minted.

I went to a local football game with two friendly Danish physics students called Christopher and Jacob. As in Rio, the antics of the players, referee and fans – and the surrounding views – were of more interest than the match itself. The on-field action was characterised by a high level of physical commitment at such a high altitude (surely the highest venue for a match with an admission charge in the world?), a low level of skill, prostrate players, and numerous appearances of the motorised stretcher carrier, mainly for the apparently injured play-acting. "Mucho teatro!" as the vocal fan behind us was prone to shout. Towards the end of the first half, one of the opposition players was sent off but the referee didn't notice he hadn't left the field and was about to restart the game with the linesman on that side waving his flag frantically. The national police service had to assist in his removal. One of the Potosi forwards, for his attempts to assist the recalcitrant player off, was issued with a second yellow card, but the referee didn't realise he'd already been booked so he remained on the pitch until half-time, despite the sustained gesticulation of the Cochabamba coaching staff.

At the beginning of the second half, that player didn't reappear but a substitute stood on the touchline and came on the pitch after the game restarted, without any Potosi player apparently coming off, as if some face-saving arrangement had been made. The farcical nature of proceedings was highlighted by the home supporters' brass band striking up at random points in the afternoon with what was apparently the only tune in their repertoire – 'It's a Fools' Game' – without any obvious irony.

The Potosi number 10, a substitute striker without a footballing brain (or he didn't want to damage it as he had earlier ducked a cross, letting it go for an opposition goal kick), decided the dire contest when he surprised himself, as much as everyone else present, by scoring an undeserved and ugly goal to rapturous celebrations.

From Potosi, I took the bus to Sucre. The journey was made more comfortable by a student, Miguel Morales, who allowed me to switch seats so I could stretch my legs in the centre rear seat. It was made progressively almost unbearable by the windows being closed, initially due to the dust and subsequently because of the rain and hail. It was stifling at the back of the bus and I developed a severe headache, I was sure through lack of oxygen. Once the weather cleared, I managed to prise open the nearest window and Miguel did the same on his side, letting in a little air at last. I didn't get a chance to say thanks and goodbye to Miguel as the bus decanted us into the cramped courtyard that acted as its depot, so this will have to do.

I then took a taxi with three other European passengers and ended up with an elderly Dutch couple at the San Francisco on a street named Arce.

Next morning I was regaled in my room by CNN with ninety minutes of non-stop coverage of a royal engagement – Prince William and Kate Middleton. Sucre is a city of considerable elegance and culture and I spent a couple of days playing the tourist, visiting various museums, but still finding cafés and restaurants frequented by locals in which to eat well and cheaply.

◊

I arranged a short horse-riding trek for my last afternoon there with a company called Adventurarse – obviously the owner had a limited knowledge of English. Pedro, one of the staff who spoke good English, took me in a taxi up the hill where we met up with Johnny and the horses. The taxi driver wouldn't take the 20 *bolivianos* note as there was a tiny nick out of it – a common experience on my travels, so Pedro bought something with it at a corner shop where they were less fussy. I insisted on a helmet – to hell with my image – and Johnny went off to fetch one while I slapped factor 40 on my face – might as well protect it too. My horse was Benjamin and seemed obligingly tranquil: I was wary after my Georgian horse. We headed across the road out of the suburb and up the hill through the thin trees (shades of Kirk Douglas in *Lonely Are the Brave*). Johnny, a laconic guy of around thirty who spoke little English, always rode ahead, but I was content with the quiet and the chance to enjoy the landscape on horseback. He took me through a place where they'd quarried much of the stone for Sucre, if I understood him correctly. He then showed me the remains of what was, apparently, a country club with horse-riding and clay pigeon shooting (much of this demonstrated by him in mime, telling a story which seemed to involve the twelve-year-old son of the owners falling off his horse and breaking his neck, the mother going completely mad with grief, and the father shooting his wife and himself). I would have taken a photo (I was thinking I might use this tragic story some time) but my camera was in my knapsack, so we pushed on, crossing a gas and a diesel pipe running parallel about a foot off the ground towards Sucre.

Beyond was a view down onto a strange set of edifices which I'd caught glimpses of from the nearby road while on the bus into the city. There were three towers – one in Italian style, one Chinese, and the other apparently replicating the Tower of London. I got my camera out and took some shots. Johnny suggested that many of the farms were abandoned due to a lack of irrigation, with the residents gone to the city or to Argentina.

We headed back, had a few gallops, and rejoined our outward route. As we were about to take a slight diversion, following the main track which skirted around the old country club, I asked Johnny if we could go back up that way so I could take a picture. Halfway up, we passed three young boys sitting behind a bank to our right, watching us. I heard the sound of an engine and then a tanker came over the brow of the hill towards us. I kept my horse by the high bank on the left side, the same as Johnny had done ahead of me.

Suddenly, Benjamin reared up and threw himself around violently. Now it was *Lonely Are the Brave* meets *The Horse Whisperer*. I don't claim to be a horseman, but I think many better riders than me would have struggled to hold on. The horse threw its nose so far back at one point that it struck mine. It bucked left and right, but there was nowhere to go because of the bank. The next thing I knew, something gave and I was falling, landing heavily on my left elbow, thigh and buttock. The tanker driver's brakes screeched. I lay on the dusty, stony track, taking my time to assess the damage: I'd lost my Olympus Tough camera, torn my 'cool dude' blue patterned shirt, and suspected I would have, in due course, a spectacular bruise on my buttock, which had taken most of the impact. Nothing seemed to be broken, except, possibly, the stirrup strap which Johnny had picked up. I didn't know if it had detached itself automatically under pressure like skis, but realised once it had gone I'd had no chance of staying on the horse – to use another comparison, it was like having two wheels of a car on grass.

Johnny handed me my camera as the tanker driver stood over me, looking ashen. After a minute or two, I allowed them to lift me up. I took a couple of photos to check it was working and commemorate the event. Benjamin, I was told, had run off past the tanker. The driver kindly offered me a lift back into town, but although I appreciated it, I stubbornly felt that since I'd left on a horse then I'd like to return that way, so Johnny led me on his until I was comfortable enough to ride him unaided. I felt the benefit of a good saddle. Johnny scanned the ground for Ben's hoof prints, which even a mile further on demonstrated he was still running. We reached the road without any sight of him. I caught the combi back to Simon Bolivar and walked gingerly to Adventurarse.

(I heard, in my head, Ricky Tomlinson as Jim Royle growling, "Adventure? My arse. . .") Pedro contacted Johnny and learned he still hadn't found the horse. He took me for a check-up, which confirmed no obvious problem except raised blood pressure, which could probably be attributed to the altitude and the incident and for which the doctor prescribed pills.

I took the bus for La Paz as planned that night, after it managed to get out of the bus station with the assistance of a man with a shovel, its valance catching on the uneven ground. This was the worst of my long-distance bus journeys on the trip so far. It was very hot and the attendant displayed no interest when I indicated the non-functioning ventilation system. He seemed to see his primary function as showing DVDs at full volume. Eventually I protested, pointing to the screen nearest me and asking him to turn it off. He mumbled something and gesticulated towards the back as if some passenger there was intent on viewing it on that screen. When I looked round, I could only see people sleeping – or trying to sleep.

What's the frigging point, I thought, of advertising fully-reclining seats and then showing films featuring absurd quantities of automatic weapon fire and explosions? Worse still, once the moronic flick was finished, the thing went on its default position loop for twenty or thirty circuits by which time I was ready to put the attendant's head through the screen, should he reappear.

Dawn was breaking as we reached La Paz. I checked into Cruz de Los Andes, having opted for a room to myself in a hostel with good reviews on the internet. At that stage in the trip, I felt the need of a little more comfort and privacy. This was just as well, as I had diarrhoea over the next few days, and was frightened to fart, never mind eat. When I did eat, it was generally at a recommended restaurant called 100% Natural. The rest of my time was spent drinking coca or herbal tea and playing online bridge by the window in the reception area. According to the *Lonely Planet*, the local wisdom in relation to avoiding *soroche* (altitude sickness) is '*camina lentito, come poquito . . . y duerme solito*' ('walk slowly, eat only a little bit . . . and sleep by your poor little self').

When I admired the earrings of Corina, the sweet student who was a part-time receptionist at the hotel, thinking I might buy some similar as a present for my daughter Martha, she told me her father had made them – he was a silversmith and she offered to take me to see him. We travelled by 'micro' up to El Alto, the poor, sprawling suburb above the city and arrived at her humble home. I met her mother, a traditional, triangular trader and her quiet, craftsman father. I'd emailed to Corina the logo of my creative writing enterprise in Normandy, designed over ten years ago by Harry McGroarty – now, sadly, dead – as I was trying to think of something individual her father might be able to make for me that I wouldn't be able to afford back home. I ordered several items as presents and handed over two hundred *bolivianos* as an advance.

As I began to feel better, I explored other parts of La Paz, particularly around Calle Jaen, the old colonial area with its narrow streets of craft shops. I also visited Iglesia de San Francisco and took a walk past San Pedro prison, probably the most notorious gaol in South America, its infamy deriving from the endemic corruption which allowed wealthy prisoners lavish lifestyles, unchecked cocaine production, and an unusual visiting policy which included not only wives and children – who could come and go freely and actually take up residence – but tourists. I made no attempt to gain access for reasons similar to those previously given re: *favelas* and the Potosi mine, and more. Brad Pitt's production company was currently engaged in making a film version of Rusty Young's novel, *Marching Powder*, based on the experiences of Thomas McFadden, a British inmate between 1996 and 2000 (at the last time of checking it was still classed as 'in development').

◊

Corina had asked her lecturer if I could accompany her class on a day trip to Lake Titicaca and he'd agreed. This involved getting up just after 5 a.m., taking a taxi back up to El Alto with Corina, who'd come down to meet me, staying inside on the cold, dark, misty morning until the bus arrived, and waiting for – and picking up at various points – numerous late students. The day had brightened up by the time we reached the lake where two boats took us out to Suriqui Island. This had the reputation of being the last island where the traditional boats were still made out of *totora* reeds. Corina was disappointed to discover that the minuscule museum containing some of these boats was closed, but a man approached who claimed to make them. The two of us followed him to his basic home-cum-workshop which was surrounded by cut reeds. He showed us boats in four different sizes – roughly 3", 1', 3' and 8'. We bought a couple of the smallest ones before catching up with the others who were arranging to give an alfresco performance at the local school. This was a protracted, lively, traditional affair. Following this, we had a picnic lunch on the adjoining playing field. I played Frisbee with Corina's friend Jules and several of the schoolboys, in their green and white tracksuits. When it was time to go, my favourite black Frisbee was missing. Corina appeared and sensed I was prepared to adopt confrontational measures to ensure its return, as I was sure one of the boys had secreted it. The black disc dropped to the ground as I approached a distant group of three walking away from me. I vented my spleen in horrible Spanglish but Corina gripped my elbow lightly and led me away.

The boatmaker, Mariano Arratia Bautista, had turned up, as had many other islanders, to witness the students' performance and the lecturer had expressed an interest in witnessing his craft. But only the two of us went back to his place. I'd already decided to buy the second largest boat for Corina. We were the last ones back to the boats waiting at the jetty, Corina carrying her present in her arms. It took us an hour to reach Pariti Island, fringed by reeds. The students held a musical celebration outside the little, locked church for the benefit of the group and three local onlookers. After several speeches, we walked to the museum. It contained artefacts discovered during a dig which took place from 2003 to 2005. Most of them were fragments of pots, suggesting the site was used for offering sacrifices, and many of the earthenware faces had Amazonian shapes and features, perhaps indicating people travelled from far away.

Back on the boat, the musicians climbed onto the roof and played all the way back to the mainland, despite the lake getting choppier. I felt sure someone would fall into the water, but only a wide-brimmed hat ended up overboard.

◊

The next day, my last in La Paz, Corina brought in the jewellery, and I was delighted with it all. Her father had made a great job of the signet ring, especially, with the silver quill in the apple on a black background. It was strange wearing a ring on my ring finger for the first time in several years. Corina gave me a couple of cards with really touching messages.

I took the front seat on the bus to Copacabana on Lake Titicaca, but was asked to give it up for a Bolivian couple and their infant, so I sat behind with the hippy child who'd had a protracted parting scene with her Bolivian boyfriend. She introduced herself as Sheba. An interesting eighteen-year-old from South Africa, she had been travelling on and off for three years around Africa and South America. She made and sold jewellery and had made most of the strange clothes she was wearing. We had a long chat as the bus travelled the same route from the day before for the first part of the journey.

We all had to get off the bus and take a small motor boat across a narrow stretch of the lake, the bus itself being ferried over on a flat transporter with another vehicle. It was an efficient procedure and we were soon back on the bus. On arrival, after being taken to have a look at another place by one of several people there to meet the bus, peddling accommodation, I walked to Utamu to honour the booking Corina had made for me. I was disconcerted, however, to realise I was being charged twice the agreed rate and resolved this with the guy on reception.

The sun had set by the time I wandered down to the lake shore. It was a spectacular location. There were few people about and I was approached by staff from several restaurants promoting their cuisine. I eventually decided on a kiosk on the sand (Kiosko La Playa No 4), attracted by the matronly owner's smile and the price of 18 *bolivianos* for grilled trout and chips. The place, like all the others in the row, consisted of a metal cabin with an adjoining skeletal metal framework with plastic awnings, which a young man began dismantling before I'd finished my delicious fish.

I got up, packed away my journal and books in my knapsack, settled with the senora, walked a short distance along the shore and then turned up into the town. A pack of dogs barked threateningly at me, one approaching me aggressively, but I faced them down, keeping my hands safely in my pockets as I walked on. Suddenly I realised that something was missing. I withdrew my left hand from my pocket and the ring was gone and there was nothing in the pocket. My first day wearing it and I'd lost it. Did the senora slip it off my finger when I handed over payment? If I'd dropped it on the road I would have heard it, wouldn't I? Maybe it had fallen off on the shore? I turned round and retraced my steps, scouring the ground for any glint of silver, maintaining the controlled approach of a police officer searching a scene, despite my disappointment, which was mostly in relation to how upset Corina would be if she knew.

As I approached the dangerous dogs' territory, I continued to focus my attention a few feet in front of me, ignoring their presence. Something was gripping my calf and I turned to see it was the vicious beast. A woman walking behind shouted at it and the cur let go. I continued with my search and discovered the kiosk was still open and a young woman was sitting in my seat. She and the senora showed what appeared to be genuine concern for my loss but there was no sign of the ring. There was only one hope left and I opened up my knapsack and rummaged in the bottom. I felt its chunkiness and took it out. The young woman, who turned out to be a Muscovite called Maria, suggested I wear it on my middle finger, which I did. I rolled up my trouser leg and asked her to inspect the calf. She said she couldn't see any break in the skin. Maria and I took a walk around the town, where a concert was going on in a large hall, before we went our separate ways. Back at Utuma, I flicked through some magazines on the coffee table, including a Dutch one called *Che*, apparently aimed at young men, its only English content being an advert placed by the Organ Donor Foundation featuring a bikini-clad girl with the words, 'Becoming a donor is probably your only chance to get inside her.'

During the night I awoke with a feeling of tightness in my right calf. My matter-of-fact attitude of the evening before ratcheted up to a sense of controlled horror as I considered the possibility of my having contracted rabies. I applied the rationale I'd used in Sudan Safety and Security Sessions – what was the risk of the event occurring and what were the consequences? My job was to minimise both. Well, the risk of rabies I calculated was very low: the dog was a street dog and could have the disease, but the marks on my trousers and calf suggested he'd grabbed me with the front of his jaws and my trousers were a thick, cotton pair of Marks & Spencer chinos. I sprinkled water on the indented section of the material to replicate the dog's saliva and see how long it took to seep through – a couple of seconds. My skin was probably only in contact with the material for the few moments of the dog bite. The problem was with the answer to the other question – the consequences were horrendous: a terrible, writhing death, weeks or months later.

This was the clincher for me – the thought of lying in a hospital bed, back in Edinburgh, foaming at the mouth, before dying in the most grotesque manner, with my children in attendance, horrified me. I spent several hours considering my options, getting my medical insurance and other documents together, checking the bus timetable and researching medical sections in the *Lonely Planet*. I knew that, to be effective, an emergency rabies injection needed to be given within 24 hours. The only two cities likely to have the vaccine that I could reach within that time frame were La Paz and Cuzco. The advantage of going on to Cuzco was that it was in Peru – a more modern country and I would be closer to Lima, from where I was due to fly home in two weeks' time. After a few hours' troubled sleep I was up, showered, and downstairs before 7 a.m. I spoke to Gaulberto, the guy who'd shown me to my room and had some grasp of English. When I told him I'd been bitten by a dog he said, "Wow!" He suggested I get my breakfast straight away and he'd take me to the doctor's. Although the breakfast was very good, it was difficult to enjoy it in the circumstances.

Gaulberto drove me to the doctor's at about 7.45 a.m., around twelve hours after the curious incident. It was a small building in a terrace on a narrow road. He rang the bell, but there was no response. Some moments later, a voice called out from an upstairs window, invisible because of the ledge beneath, and after a short conversation and a few minutes the door opened. I went through to the small room that served as the surgery. The doctor examined the two small red marks on my calf, no doubt left by the canine's canines. He declared, as translated by Gaulberto, that the skin was not broken and that therefore I did not need a rabies vaccine. I mentioned I'd had medication to control a surge in my blood pressure, and when he checked it, it was higher again. Hardly surprising that my blood pressure peaked after being thrown by a horse and bitten by a dog (note to myself – avoid animals during the rest of the trip). He gave me more tablets to bring it down, and charged me a hundred *bolivianos* for the session.

The doctor told me to rest up for the day, so I spent it reading, watching sport on TV and worrying. It probably didn't help that at this point in the Robbins novel I was reading, *Fierce Invalids Home from Hot Climates*, Switters, the central figure, was under the restricting influence of an Amazonian taboo and unable to walk. Berbatov and Nadal on the TV, however, were rampant, the former scoring five times in Manchester United's 7-1 disposal of Blackburn Rovers and the latter despatching a despondent Murray at the O2 Arena in London in their semi-final. As the day wore on, I became more agitated.

In the evening I went for a walk around the town but was still feeling extremely low. I visited the church where preparatory activities were commencing for what threatened to be a very long service. At one point I looked up at the ornate *reredos* and it seemed to give off an extra surge of golden light. This somehow, inexplicably, gave me the energy to get up and go back to the hotel to ask for a second medical opinion. I finally managed to get hold of Geoff on the phone and he agreed I really needed the serum to be sure I was safe, despite my previous injections.

A taxi arrived to take me to the hospital which was, in fact, a tiny clinic with two or three people on duty. Unfortunately, nobody there spoke much English, but I managed to communicate my concerns. The doctor examined the calf and also declared that he could see no sign of a break in the skin. He said that they had no vaccine, but I could not ascertain for sure if he was saying that was because they had no rabies in Copacabana. Even if it was the case that there had been no previous instances of it, I couldn't take too much comfort from this because a dog could have recently brought the disease into the place at any time. I told the doctor I intended to take the bus to Cuzco the following morning and he concurred with this course of action.

Next morning, Sunday 28th November, I checked out of Utama and walked to the tiny, open but empty, bus agency office. Outside, two young white women were already waiting. I introduced myself to my two future fellow passengers, Allena from Germany and Karen from Austria, apologising for not being my usual sociable self and explaining I was en route to find a hospital in Cuzco to try to get a rabies vaccination. Allena told me she was an intern at a hospital there. My bad luck/good luck pendulum seemed to be swinging back again. This was not seriously affected by the returning agent who said I had arranged the other day to go on Monday, so I couldn't go today. I told her I'd paid extra for a flexible ticket, I needed a rabies injection and I was getting on the bus. That was the end of the matter. As I sat on the bus I saw what I was sure was the first woman driver I'd seen in Bolivia, and struggled to recall seeing any in South America, certainly driving for a living, as she was. Our own driver was a forthright guy, direct but helpful, guiding us through customs at the Bolivia/Peru border, currency exchange (no doubt with some financial benefit to himself from the recommended vendor) and changing buses at Pune.

On arrival at Cuzco in the evening, I took a taxi straight to Clinica Pardo. As I tried to explain my problem to the receptionist, she invited a middle-aged doctor who appeared to be about to leave to act as translator. Dr Pidero spoke excellent English and told me immediately that I was outside the 24-hour window for the rabies immune globulin injection, and he recommended a course of three or five vaccinations, depending on his examination.

In the consulting room, he looked at my calf, noted some 'disturbance of the skin', and said he thought I needed all five. He issued me with a prescription for the first one which I was to take to the pharmacy and he departed. It cost me 180 *soles* ($67) and I took it to the nurse giving me the injection, who asked me for 3 *soles* afterwards. I asked, mischievously, if I could have a '*factura*' (bill, although I meant receipt) for this payment, knowing the answer.

I took a taxi to the Incama Hotel, which I'd chosen on the basis of its reviews on hostelworld.com, and booked into room 305 for 45 *soles* a night. Once I'd dumped my bags, I contacted my insurance company to inform them of the situation.

After a good night's sleep, I spent most of the morning liaising with the insurance company and their medical advisor. In the afternoon, I went for a wander around the impressive city, visiting an eating establishment which was apparently frequented by the city's more affluent citizens. I ordered alpaca which was lean and stringy, and a bit like rabbit.

◊

I felt well enough the next day to risk a tourist trip to the Sacred Valley. Our guide was Marco Antonio, a smart young smoothie, and the other passengers were mainly families and couples, whose interest in what he had to tell them seemed quite limited. At one of the stops, Pisac, I chatted to Alfredo, a heavily-built guy of Mexican descent living in California, on the way up to the ruins. Having enjoyed the views from the top, I was making my way down when I saw a small cluster of people around a short drop and Alfredo lying there, having fallen and injured his knee. We managed to get him to his feet but couldn't help him out of the area. We had to leave him for the ambulance which we passed on the way back down in the coach.

The highlight of the trip was the visit to Ollantaytambo, an imposing settlement with buildings and terraces of superb stonework in a dramatic location.

At Chinchero, we visited the Inca palace that the invading Spaniards had converted into a church. Photography was forbidden inside, according to Marco, because unscrupulous visitors took photographs of paintings which were then used to make copies which, with the connivance of bribed security staff, were used to replace the originals. We visited the local weaving co-operative, where the traditionally-dressed young women went through their routine, showing how they used natural dyes and demonstrating the difference between alpaca, baby alpaca, 'maybe' alpaca and wool.

Next morning I took a taxi to Clinica Pardo for my second of three or five injections, depending on further enquiries by the insurance company's medical advisor. Dr Pinedo was at the San Jose Hospital, so I was driven there in an ambulance, despite my offer to take a taxi. The person who I was told would meet me failed to appear, but eventually a young nurse arrived to tell me they hadn't yet received authorisation from my insurance company for my treatment as there was a snowstorm in my country. I went up to the fourth floor and found Allena doing the rounds in a group of interns with a senior doctor, all in white coats. I told her I was going for a coffee in the café on the second floor and a few minutes later she joined me for a chat.

284

I eventually got my vaccination and Dr Pinedo told me that medically there was no problem with me going on the four-day Choquequirao trek I wanted to take – it was simply a question of my level of fitness. After a meal at a local café, I did the rounds of the tour agencies trying to sort out a deal. I returned to the hotel where there was an email from the insurance company's senior medical officer, telling me they now felt I should have the full course of five injections, taking into account that the last of my previous series in 2004 was the one I had carried with me to Iraq: it had been exposed to high temperatures before being administered, possibly compromising its effectiveness. At his invitation, I phoned him to discuss it. I considered abandoning my Choquequirao plan, on the basis that if I got injured and couldn't get back I'd miss my next, time-critical jab, but he was adamant that there was no need.

I returned to the square to try to finalise my hike, but there was much to-ing and fro-ing. It was very difficult to know who you were dealing with as a lot of these people were trip pimps for several agencies. There was a protracted argument when I returned after realising I'd been ripped off over the rate of exchange. At one point, the guy who seemed to be the boss asked for my receipt back and was about to return my cash, but it was too late for me to arrange anything else, so a compromise was reached. My young guide, Julio, had stood mutely by during the disagreement. I learned there would just be him and me on the trek, the two other guys due to go having pulled out. That suited me fine, as, if there was any medical problem I'd not be messing up anyone else's trip.

◊

I was standing outside the door of the hotel by 5.20 the next morning, not knowing whether Julio would turn up or not. The arrangements had been rushed and vague, but I was just going for it, and felt as long as my guide turned up things would work out OK. I understood we had to catch a bus at 6 a.m. After about twenty minutes, a car pulled up and Julio got out. I jumped in, and we were instantly off towards the bus station, some distance away. We caught the bus to Ramales with little time to spare. I sat at the back and placed my knapsack, plastic bag with food and drink, battered straw hat and brolly on the rear shelf. Although it was a bumpy ride, we both nodded off from time to time. Suddenly we'd arrived at the drop-off point and I gathered my gear together and struggled off the bus behind Julio. There were a few cars there, apparently offering rides. We took one to San Pedro de Cachora and when we arrived, I realised I'd left my umbrella on the bus. I quite liked the idea of the brolly I'd picked up in a subway station in New York continuing its journey on a rural bus in Peru, but I would have preferred it to have happened after the trek, the one time I might actually need it on my travels through seven countries.

Julio, who was a young man of 27 with a strong, Amerindian face, installed me in a rustic café where we were to have lunch while he went off on an errand. We were supposed to have a horseman and packhorse to carry the tent and other equipment as well as my knapsack. He returned saying, "No horse," and then, "No problem."

After a good meal of delicious soup followed by chicken and rice, we set off on foot, me with his mountaineer's stick he'd given me to replace my brolly. Julio was carrying more than twice the weight I was, but then I was carrying over twice his years. It took us from noon until 5.15 to walk the nineteen kilometres through spectacular scenery with snow-capped peaks to the tiny campsite at Chiquisca. It was a humble affair just above the Rio Apurimac. Julio erected the tent with practised ease, but then modern tents are a doddle compared to the one Steve Ashton and I had with us in the Himalayas in 1975 – I was to be reminded of that trip often on this trek. I was too tired to do much other than sup my soup and eat some spaghetti and tomato sauce while watching returning young men hobble ominously past, before I slithered into my sleeping bag.

After a bad night's sleep on the hard, sloping ground and a breakfast of pancakes, porridge and hot chocolate, we set off just after 6.30, already some time behind a grumbling Frenchman in his fifties called Henri. It was an hour's knee-trembling descent to the bridge (Briar Rosalita, according to Julio) and from the other side it was uphill all the way. My breathing got heavier as the track wound higher and the sun got hotter. I had to stop every hundred metres, then every fifty, then sometimes thirty. Julio was very patient, but I sensed his concern as the trek would only get tougher as the altitude and temperature increased over the course of the day. In the middle of the saga of arranging this trip, I'd enjoyed a creamy chicken cottage pie and a bottle of Samuel Smith's organic cider at Paddy Flaherty's on the corner of the Plaza de Armas in Cuzco, which claims to be the highest Irish bar in the world. The fantasy/intention of repeating this order sustained me at difficult times over the next few days.

The little hostel at Santa Rosa, if more limited in the range of beverages on offer, was, nevertheless, a godsend: I bought a bottle of Powerade, a bottle of liquid of a radioactive green colour, but I emptied it in two thirsty swigs. It was very satisfying, despite not being refrigerated due to the absence of electricity. I also bought a two-and-a-half litre bottle of water, although the trip pimps had told me food and drinks would be provided. It wouldn't fit into my knapsack, so I had to carry it in a plastic bag. Julio took over this task as I struggled up the hillside and eventually he set off ahead, the bottle almost empty. We had overtaken the Frenchman by this time, just after the 27 km marker.

It was after 2 p.m. when Julio returned to tell me it was only ten minutes to the campsite at Marampata. He offered to carry my knapsack, but I had enough male pride remaining to gratefully decline and suggest he might want to help Henri with his rucksack, an idea that, understandably, did not appear to appeal to him. I gave him my camera to take a photo of me by the Marampata sign and then walked on into what was a smallholding in a hamlet of two or three dwellings, taking a seat at the thatch-covered lean-to which housed a table. I didn't eat much, feeling a little sick from the heat, altitude and exertion. Our ravenous French friend arrived and finished off my meal. It had taken me nearly seven and a half hours to walk just nine kilometres and him over eight, but with a much heavier pack. I retired to my tent in exhausted triumph.

After nearly three hours of lying there, unable to sleep, just trying to let my body recover, tent flaps snapping in the breeze and chickens pecking at its perimeter, I emerged. I played Frisbee with Julio, took a few photos and bought another bottle of Powerade – it is one of the laws of nature that the higher you climb, the more expensive that everything is. The three of us discussed trying to take a looping route from Choquequirao, which Julio thought might be viable instead of taking the same path back as was the standard practice.

I was awoken by the sensation of cold, wet feet – how could that be, in my socks, in a sleeping bag, in a tent? It was raining steadily, but not heavily, and rain was coming in just about everywhere. My trousers, lying beside the tent wall were soaking. I gathered up my things and hurried over to the mud hut. Julio, nobly, gave me his sleeping bag and got some blankets from the senora, and went to sleep on the other side of the wall. The ground was hard and uneven but dry. I spent the night trying to find a part of my body that was not sore to lie on.

After a breakfast of omelette, hot chocolate and herbal tea, we set off by six and covered the four kilometres to Choquequirao quickly, Julio hurrying on ahead and Henri behind me. I was stopped on the track by an official who asked if I had a permit. I told him that there was no one at the booth I'd passed earlier. He asked if I had a guide and when I said he'd gone on ahead, he radioed to someone, presumably in the modest modern building I could see far below, before taking my 37 *soles* entrance fee. I reached the site, which was still far from fully excavated but currently deserted. Henri arrived, close behind me, and we had the entire place to ourselves. He told me he had visited Machu Picchu many times during his years in Peru, but that the setting of this place, with its magnificent panoramic views of the surrounding snow-capped mountains, was even more spectacular. I asked him how many people would have been there at that time and he replied, "Deux mille." The two of us explored the place as if we were its discoverers. I looked at a peak from the priest's house and thought of Keats' poem, *On First Looking Into Chapman's Homer*, and its last lines about Cortez catching his first sight of the Pacific and his men staring at each other, 'Silent, upon a peak in Darien'.

I read in a paper recently about a planned cable car to Choquequirao and the current entry in Wikipedia states that it 'will reduce a two-day hike to a 15-minute cable car ride' and that it's claimed that in the first year of operation, it will carry 200,000 tourists, 'which will generate an income of US $4 million'.

Chapter 35

We found a path with a sign saying '*Pikiwasi*', which, I discovered during the course of writing these memoirs, refers to the Administrative Housing: the path turned out to be blocked by fallen branches – nobody had been through there for months. Spectacular and spiritual as it all was, as I suspected, the getting there was a greater thrill than the experience itself – so often the case in life. I cleared a route through with Julio's stick and we made our way down to the building we'd seen. The official we found there told us our guide had gone looking for us. Julio soon returned and told me he'd managed to hire a horseman to take the tent and Henri's rucksack on ahead. I put on plenty of sun block and insect repellent as I was wearing shorts, due to my trousers still being wet. The insects were vicious (I'd omitted to put repellent on the underside of my forearms the previous day and watched, in a few seconds, a row of bites spring up like red press studs. Julio had offered to carry my knapsack, but I'd told him I was fine). Having spent most of the previous day climbing, we were now heading down towards the river and I took to trotting down the zig-zag slopes as this was actually easier on my old, injured knees than walking slowly. On crossing the bridge, we were disappointed to discover the building at Playas Ignatius was boarded up.

After a short break, we travelled a little further, climbing again until we reached the Hacienda Ignatius. It, too, was deserted but there was a new building beside it with a green corrugated metal roof and a family living there. At the green house I had an Inca Cola – not nearly as good as the Powerade, which I'd expected to have conferred superhuman powers on me by now, but still very welcome. Julio made some soup: I only felt up to fluids. We learned that the horseman, or muleteer, had left our bags there, not believing we'd reach the village Julio had told him was our destination.

So we were soon back on the track, but with my companions heavily encumbered once more. I strode out ahead, driven to get back to a bathroom and the other comforts of civilization. It was a long, hot trek along the trail but I stopped only rarely. Towards the end of the day, when I was waiting for the others to catch up, we saw a 4x4 parked up on the far side of a river from a house we'd just passed. I suggested to Julio, who had been delayed supporting Henri, that he ask the driver if he could take us into the village or perhaps further. He returned to tell Henri and myself he wanted eighty *soles* to drive us to Hualpa; I was happy with that but the other two thought it too much. We pressed on and got lost in thickets as darkness closed in. Julio had never travelled this route before. My bare legs were quite badly scratched and bitten. By chance, we met a couple of boys on bicycles who pointed us in the right direction.

Exhausted, we reached a large, modern *hacienda* with a big 'Bienvenidos' sign outside large metal gates and security lights. It transpired that the place was run by an Italian and his adult daughter. He wouldn't sell us any water as we weren't clients, but he would give us accommodation, an evening meal, and breakfast for 100 *soles* each. This was exorbitant by our standards. Julio left his gear and went on ahead to see if there were any other options of accommodation or transport. It started to drizzle and I sheltered under the entrance canopy while a disgruntled Henri prowled about cursing Italians. Julio returned. We were out of luck. I was prepared to pay the hundred *soles* as we seemed to have exhausted all options as well as ourselves. Julio said he would run back and get the 4x4. I suspected that he would find the rate inflated, but he set off running into the rain and the dark.

Half an hour later we saw approaching lights shining into the bend, and the 4x4 appeared. We piled our gear in. The middle-aged couple drove us through the drizzle and mist towards Hualpa. It was no wonder Julio hadn't found anything – there was nothing to find. The windscreen kept misting up and we nearly left the track a couple of times. It was 8.30 by the time we arrived at the village and it was raining heavily. Torrents of brown water were running down the steep streets. Although it was a Saturday night, the place was deserted and the doors closed for the night. There was a simple sign for lodgings down a side road. Julio and the woman pounded on the door but it was only after about ten minutes that they got an answer and we were waved at to take out our packs and make a dash for it through the downpour. We were glad of the bare, cold, but basically dry building. We sat on the rough, wooden benches on the earth floor in the dismal downstairs room and were supplied with some hot water and two tea bags. Julio ran off into the torrent in search of food. About thirty minutes later he returned with two wrapped dinners. I was still feeling ill and after eating the fried egg off the top of mine and a few chips, I gave the rest to Julio, who scoffed it down. He then hurried out again, while I made a dash for the outside toilet.

Our room was upstairs. It had four beds and a leaking ceiling. The beds were of various shapes and sizes and with mattresses of different levels of discomfort. The matronly owner, on one of her many journeys through on her way to and from her own adjoining room, placed a plastic bowl on the floorboards under the ceiling's damp circle to catch the drips. She was anxious because Julio hadn't returned and she wanted to lock up again. I waited up for him to let him in without disrupting the whole household, but he didn't reappear.

Henri gave me a call at 5 a.m. but as Julio wasn't back I refused to emerge from the warmth of the covers. A short time later he turned up in a 'taxi'. I got up, dressed and made another dash to the toilet. There were two other guys in the estate car and Julio sat in the boot as we picked up another passenger. As with the previous night's journey, the front seat passenger spent most of it in a vain attempt to keep the windscreen clear. Although we were supposed to be trying to catch a bus from Ramales to Cuzco at six, the driver stopped several times in the miserable early morning mizzle to chat to the occupants of passing vehicles on the muddy, mountain track. It became obvious we would not make it, so I accepted the fact and relaxed. It was 6.30 by the time we arrived. We were told that there would be a bus around seven, but I managed to get one of the Lima-Cuzco coaches to stop and the attendant allowed us to climb aboard, despite the obvious reservations of the driver. We settled into the comfortable, warm seats, congratulating ourselves on our good fortune, but before long the bus stopped and the driver came upstairs and told us we had to get off. I was tired, unwell, and frustrated but Julio said something about it going to be a problem for them at the checkpoint. I gathered my gear and made my way truculently off the cosy, air-conditioned coach. We followed Julio as he strode ahead along the main road through the town until he reached a place where he secured three seats in a shared people carrier preparing to depart for Cuzco. It dropped us near our accommodation and I was back in the hostel for 10.20 a.m. and went straight to my bed.

When I woke up, I took a taxi to the clinic, got my rabies injection, and then another taxi to Paddy Flaherty's, where I met up, as arranged, with two young Aussie guys staying at the hostel and we had a few ciders. They didn't make it to breakfast the next morning, but surfaced some time later and I went with them to Jack's Cafe, a legendary eating place amongst tourists. I had a cooked breakfast which served as my lunch. In the late afternoon I left for the bus station and boarded my coach to Lima. Around 6 p.m. we were given a small, tepid airline meal; we got nothing else to eat for another fourteen hours, and there was no supply of drinking water on board. My emergency rations were exhausted before I reached Lima, where I took a taxi to Hostel Tradiciones, which proved to be every bit as good for a weary traveller as its visitors' reviews promised. It was a family home in the relatively affluent suburb of Miraflores. The owner, Angelo, was an urbane, extremely helpful man, fluent in English, who pointed me in the direction of interesting places to visit and good places to eat.

I spent the next day with Maggie's Auntie Kitty, a nun in her seventies who had spent almost fifty years of her life in Chile and then Peru, serving the poor. I was only too pleased to be able to take her Christmas cards, and those of two other sisters in the order, to post once back in the UK.

My straw hat had disintegrated to such an extent that even I couldn't wear it and so, reluctantly, I consigned it to the waste basket though I would rather have cast it, in a last, dramatic act, into the Pacific.

◊

It was a sharp start the next morning to catch my flight to Miami. From my window seat I looked down on the coastline and then the stunning view of Key West in its shallow, shimmering, turquoise waters. In Miami Airport, awaiting my onward flight to Heathrow, I indulged myself with a nostalgic visit to the Dunkin' Donuts outlet. While sitting eating outside Border Books, I saw something on the bookstand I'd long dreamed of – a book with my name on the cover. Displayed between George W. Bush's *Decision Points* and Keith Richards' *Life*, was an autobiography entitled *Straight Talk*. Unfortunately, the book didn't bear my photograph but that of the black American comedian also called Steve Harvey.

I had a strong sense that I was on the final leg of what might prove to be the last big trip of my life, but then I'd thought my travelling days were over when I was in my forties, married with five children. Circumstances had dictated otherwise, and maybe another challenge or adventure might still entice me from the shire of retirement.

Anyway, having since written these memoirs for my grandchildren, who knows, perhaps one day I might see on a bookstand somewhere a copy with my name *and* photograph on it . . .

"I want to be thoroughly used up when I die, for the harder I work, the more I live.

I rejoice in life for its own sake. Life is no 'brief candle' to me. It is a sort of splendid torch which I have a hold of for the moment, and I want to make it burn as brightly as possible before handing it over to future generations."

George Bernard Shaw

*

Remembering Derrick, Ossie and the other torch bearers who have gone before . . .

Acknowledgements

Vicki Hendry for comments on the beginning of an early draft before I'd seriously considered publication.

My old friend and travelling companion, Steve Ashton, for suggesting amendments.

Norman Kirtlan, my former police colleague, for his 'Good Morning World' cartoon.

Trevor Pake, for help with some of the images.

Rosie Virgo of John Blake Publishing for permission to use the quote and school photo from *Sting and I* by Jim Berryman, my former classmate and house football team captain.

Sean Sutton and MAG for use of the photo of mine-clearing in Chamchamal, Iraq.

Katy MacDougall, former colleague at Children in Scotland, for use of the photo of Grant and myself.

Pauline Bethel & Pauline Cafferkey, former colleagues in Sudan, for reading through that section for me and for use of the photograph in Wunrok.

Julio Pena Ramos, my guide on the Choquequirao trek.

Henri Blasselle, who was my sole companion on Choquequirao and took the photo on the back cover

Clare, for going against her better judgement and publishing the memoirs of an unknown poet and Ellen for proofreading and putting up with my last-minute tinkering.

Graeme Clarke for creating the cover and organising the photographs.

Anne for her support in getting this book over the line.

And all those people I've met on my adventures who've shared difficult paths and dangerous places…